PRAISE FOR
**MARKETING
PLAN
HANDBOOK**

OFFICIALLY
DISCARDED

I'm in love with this book—and I hadn't expected to be. Most marketing books give you a list of cookie-cutter tactics you don't have time or budget for along with some examples from famous brands that don't apply to anyone else's reality. This handbook is completely different. It's specifically for an entrepreneur or small business owner who needs to figure out a marketing plan that fits their special vision, wished-for lifestyle, and customers like a glove. Even if you're thinking of hiring a marketer or agency to help your business, read this book FIRST. You'll need it to give them the perfect directions for your unique business.

> —Anne Holland
> Founder,
> Marketing Sherpa

This book gives the small business owner all of the strategies, tools, and techniques to create a winning marketing plan. Bob takes the mystery out of marketing with all of the steps laid out to ensure success. Follow Bob's field-proven advice, and your vision for the business will materialize before you!

> —Bob Martel
> Marketing Consultant
> Author, *How to Create All of the
> Business You Can Handle*

D0050443

The Marketing Plan Handbook is Bob Bly's gift to anyone who sells and markets products or services—or wants to. That's because he lays out a specific step-by-step process for success, which is clear, logical, and achievable. This is no abstract, theoretical musing, but a practical manual by a man who's been on the shortlist of marketing greats for 30 years. More, he pulls back the curtain and fearlessly shows you how he applies his own advice. If there is a better one-volume resource on contemporary marketing, I can't think of it.

> —Robert Lerose
> Lerose Copywriting

It never ceases to amaze me that every time Bob writes a book I learn something. But then again, every time I have a conversation with Bob I learn something. I think it's because Bob has the uncanny ability to take huge concepts and break them down in to practical, actionable steps. And he does it again in *The Marketing Plan Handbook*. It's a no-brainer that applying the wisdom is this book will add incremental dollars to your business's bottom line.

> —MaryEllen Tribby
> Publisher/CEO Early To Rise
> Founder Working Moms Only.com

You've got to love the two questions Bob opens with, "Who wants to be successful" (all the hands go up) and "Who knows the meaning of success?" (all the hands go back down). How true. It's just amazing how many of us will slave the hours away without knowing exactly what target we're trying to hit. And yes, that's even true of seasoned marketers. Bob's book does a brilliant job of helping you change all that. And maybe not just in business, but in that whole "what's my goal in life?" kind of way too. This is really great stuff!

> —John Forde
> Publisher,
> The Copywriter's Roundtable

I've read a lot of marketing books and have never seen one like this. Instead of the usual A-to-Z nuts-'n'-bolts marketing advice, veteran marketer Bob Bly starts off by forcing the reader to confront lifestyle choices, put them in writing, and model a business accordingly. Having stumbled through nine jobs in my first 12 years in the work force—blindly grabbing whatever came along and trying to make the most of a situation—Bly's provocative approach could well have changed my life and very likely made me rich (or at least personally fulfilled). *The Marketing Plan Handbook* is also loaded with rules, secrets, case histories, forms, charts, and worksheets on every facet of marketing and direct marketing. Here is the heady stuff we all love—creative, offers, testing, media selection, product development, customer acquisition, and winning Internet strategies. At the same time, Bly never lets you lose sight of the essentials—continual accountability, analyzing (and besting) the competition, and the all-important arithmetic of return on investment. I only wish I had had Bob Bly's *Marketing Plan Handbook* 50 years ago when I got out of the Army or 25 years ago when I was launching the newsletter, WHO'S MAILING WHAT! Damn!

—Denny Hatch
Founder,
Who's Mailing What!

On page 2 of his book, Bob Bly asks, "How many of you want to be successful?" Now, at first glance, that might seem like a loaded question. After all, who wouldn't want to be successful? The problem is, most of us aren't—or at least not as successful as we hoped to be. But read on ... Bob concisely lays out in front of you the secrets to his success. And the very tools he uses to make hundreds of his clients more money than they ever dreamed possible. Don't stop. Start reading this book now—before your competition does!

—Steve Wexler
President,
The Steve Wexler Creative Group

The Marketing Plan Handbook is perfect for anyone who has a vague idea for a business but isn't sure what to do next. The book is a road map to success—each individual reader's success—with checklists and worksheets to take you from "I have this idea" to "Here's what I need to do to make it happen." Follow this map, apply your imagination and it will lead you directly to your own definition of success.

—Ilise Benun
Founder, Marketing-Mentor.com, Co-producer of the Creative Freelancer Conference, and author of several books, including *The Art of Self Promotion* and *The Designer's Guide to Marketing & Pricing*

MARKETING PLAN HANDBOOK

Develop
Big Picture
Marketing Plans
for Pennies
on the Dollar

ROBERT W. BLY

Entrepreneur®
Press

Publisher: Jere L. Calmes
Cover Design: Kaochoy Saeteurn
Production and Composition: CWL Publishing Enterprises, Inc., Madison, WI

This publication is designed to provide accurate and authoritative
information in regard to the subject matter covered. It is sold with the
understanding that the publisher is not engaged in rendering legal,
accounting or other professional services. If legal advice or other expert
assistance is required, the services of a competent professional person
should be sought.

ISBN   13: 978-1-59918-362-6
       10: 1-59918-362-5

Library of Congress Cataloging-in-Publication available.

Printed in Canada
13 12 11 10 09   10 9 8 7 6 5 4 3 2 1

This book is for

Bob Cohen and Milly Bly

CONTENTS

PREFACE XV

Chapter 1

HARNESS THE POWER OF VISION.. 1

Design Your Business to Deliver the Lifestyle You Seek 3

SIDEBAR Write Conversational Copy for the Best Marketing Results....... 9

Go Confidently in the Direction of Your Dreams............................11

Begin With the End in Mind 12

Paint a Picture of the Possible...13

ACTION Write Your Vision Statement......................................15

SIDEBAR Crafting Your Unique Selling Proposition (USP) 18

Let Your Vision Protect You From Making Bad Decisions 21

Chapter 2

DECIDE WHAT BUSINESS YOU'RE IN 23

SIDEBAR Crafting Your Elevator Pitch.................................... 26

Creating a Business to Fulfill Your Vision.................................. 27

What Is a Niche?.. 28

SIDEBAR Micro-Niche Your Way to Success 32

Why Is This a Good Niche for Us?... 34

ACTION Describe Your Niche...40

SIDEBAR Are You Too Old to Start a Business? 41

Chapter 3

GET TO KNOW EVERYTHING ABOUT YOUR IDEAL CUSTOMER........ 43

Qualifying Prospects 44

Create a Customer Database 46

Know Your Customers' "Core Buying Complex" 50

What Do I Want to Know About My Ideal Client? 52

SIDEBAR What *The Apprentice* Can Teach You About
Knowing Your Customers..54
Don't Ignore Government Markets 56
SIDEBAR 12 Government Market Facts at a Glance 58
Nonprofit Marketing...59
Know the Lifetime Value of Your Ideal Client 60
Know Why Your Client Buys 62
Know What Benefits Mean the Most to Your Client..........................62
SIDEBAR Marketing to GOM (Grumpy Old Men) 63
Know the Steps in Your Clients' Buying Process................................64
SIDEBAR Five Steps to the Perfect Guarantee................................65
Know Where Your Clients Go to Look for Information 67
Know What You Can Learn from Your Current Clients 68
Where Should I Look for Information?..70
ACTION Describe Your Ideal Client 72

Chapter 4
WHO IS THE COMPETITION? **75**

SIDEBAR What They Say About You Online 76
Who Is Your Top Competitor?..76
Look for the Gaps in Service to Your Niche.......................................77
How Do I Learn More About My Competition? 80
SIDEBAR Trade Shows in Your Marketing Mix..................................80
ACTION Write Your Description of the Competition...................84
SIDEBAR Competition for the Information Marketer........................86

Chapter 5
STRATEGIZE: POSITION YOUR BUSINESS **89**

Bull's-Eye: Position Your Business..89
How to Build a Stronger USP 91
Offer Proof for Your Positioning Statement and USP.......................97
SIDEBAR Testimonials: The Quickest and Most Powerful Way
to Support Your USP 99
Describe What You Want to Accomplish This Year 101
Your Business at a Glance: The Capabilities Brochure 102
SIDEBAR Don't Forget the Yellow Pages.......................................106
ACTION Write Your Goals for Your Business for the Next Year..............108

Chapter 6
BUILD OUT YOUR PRODUCT LINE 113

Cost of Customer Acquisition vs. LCV 115

Creating New Products...117

Features and Benefits 118

Turn Product Flaws Into Selling Points 121

Buying Motivations: The FCB Grid 123

Pricing 124

Selling High-Priced Products... 131

SIDEBAR Pricing Strategies for Selling Services..............133

SIDEBAR Sell a Lifestyle, Not a Product...........................134

Chapter 7
ASSESS YOUR TACTICS 137

Determine the Response You Want From Your Target...............137

Decide What Message Will Stimulate This Behavior 138

Decide Which Marketing Tactics Will Best Support Your Strategy 141

Tactics That Reach Your Target Market 143

Inbound vs. Outbound Marketing Tactics....................... 144

The Busy Doctor Syndrome 147

The Silver Rule Of Marketing 149

Choose the Best Three to Five Tactics to Begin...............150

SIDEBAR Keyword Due Diligence 153

Marketing in Larger Companies...................................... 155

ACTION Identify the Tactics You'll Use...........................157

SIDEBAR Selling to the "Starving Crowd".......................158

Chapter 8
INTEGRATE ONLINE AND OFFLINE MARKETING 161

E-Mail Marketing 161

SIDEBAR Five Ways to Get Your Website Ranked Higher on Google 164

Writing and Publishing a Free E-Newsletter....................165

SEO Your Website 167

SIDEBAR Add a "Recommended Vendors" Page to Your Site 171

SIDEBAR How I Find Fresh E-Zine Content for 50 Cents per Article........ 177

Increase E-Mail Address Capture 177

Blogging 180

Social Media 182

SIDEBAR Getting Started on the Right Foot at Twitter........................... 184

Chapter 9
PUT YOUR MEASUREMENTS IN PLACE 187

What Metrics Should You Measure? 188

Calculating Marketing RDI... 190

Calculating and Measuring ROTI.................................. 192

SIDEBAR Doubling Hour and Doubling Day 194

Measuring Web Metrics 197

Marketing Performance Reporting................................ 204

Create the Tracking System 206

Determine How Often to Review the Data 206

ACTION Write What and How You'll Measure............................. 207

SIDEBAR Predicting the Probable Success or Failure of a
New Product or Marketing Idea 208

Chapter 10
WRITE YOUR PLAN.. 211

Write It Down to Get It Done.. 211

SIDEBAR Use a Swipe File to Write Promotions Better and Faster 213

Create a One-Year Plan 215

Budget 217

Plot Major Campaigns First 220

Break It Down 222

ACTION Write Your Plan 223

SIDEBAR 10 Ways to Stretch Your Marketing Budget................................224

Chapter 11
WORK IT!—IMPLEMENTATION 229

What Stage Is Your Business In?................................... 230

Copy: The Foundation of Implementation.................... 232

Write the Way Prospects Talk....................................... 234

Writing Great Headlines 237

More Copy Tips 240

Make Liberal Use of Free Offers................................... 242

SIDEBAR Promote Yourself by Writing Articles............................... 247

Schedule Your Action Steps for the Next 30 Days 249

Follow These Keys to Success...249

Chapter 12
REVIEW AND TROUBLESHOOT YOUR PLAN 251

SIDEBAR How Good a Marketer Are You?....................................... 252

What You Should Review 254

A Sales Tactic for Overcoming Price Resistance........................... 254

Good, Better, Best.. 256

SIDEBAR The Psychology of Pricing 257

Testing Your Marketing Campaigns 259

What Price Pulls Best?...262

How To Troubleshoot Your Plan 264

What to Do When It's Not Working..265

Non-Marketing Causes of Marketing Plan Failures 266

Honor Your Refund Policy Pleasantly 269

SIDEBAR Don't Waste Your Customer's Time 274

Appendices
A   GLOSSARY 277

B   FORMS & WORKSHEETS 287

C   MODEL MARKETING PLAN 305

D   MARKETING CONSULTANTS 315

E   SOURCES & RESOURCES... 321

INDEX 325

PREFACE

Most people, when they go into a business, think that if they are good at what they do, they will be successful. For instance, if they are a photographer, they believe that all they have to do is take good pictures and they will have more business than they can handle. Unfortunately, it usually doesn't work out that way.

There are legions of small business owners, especially in service industries, who are technically competent or even excellent at their professions, yet earn only a modest living at best. That's because they don't know the ultimate secret to achieving outrageous success in any business: those who make the most money in any profession or service business, from accountants and ad agencies to window washers and web designers, are those who are the best at marketing and selling themselves—not at performing the actual function or service.

Doctors, attorneys, and other professionals have traditionally held the opposite point of view. They criticize competitors who advertise, saying, "If your product or service was any good, you wouldn't have to promote it with such hype." Nice to think so, but naive. Sad to say, it doesn't work that way in the real world. "The expression 'If you build it, they will come' is not true," said Steve Murphy, CEO of Rodale Inc., in an interview with *Fast Company* magazine (3/05). "We had lots of great properties at Rodale, but not enough of them were known. We needed to expose them to the mass market."

My colleague DH agrees: "I'm not torn about whether one should promote one's product or service. Mr. Murphy from Rodale is right. There are just too many options for our customers today. If you're not in front of them with an intelligent, compelling message, they won't go looking for you."

So, how do you make the transition from struggling or average entrepreneur to the top of your profession in terms of income, success, clientele, and prestige? Well, you can start with the simple, common-sense 12-step process for creating and implementing a winning marketing plan presented in this book! Over the years, I've shared my battle-tested marketing methods—in books, articles, blogs, seminars, consultations, and countless promotions and campaigns—with thousands of copywriters, graphic designers, consultants, self-employed service professionals, small business owners, marketing professionals, and corporate clients. Those who apply these techniques consistently enjoy a number of benefits, including increased income, elimination of slow periods, greater cash flow, and enhanced prestige and status within their market or industry.

I do have one favor to ask. If you have a marketing method or campaign that has worked particularly well for your business, why not send it to me so I can share it with readers of the next edition of this book? You can reach me at:

Bob Bly
590 Delcina Drive, River Vale, NJ 07675
Phone: (201) 505-9451, Fax: (201) 573-4094
E-mail: rwbly@bly.com, Web: bly.com

Acknowledgments

First, thanks to Lura Harrison for researching, writing, and editing significant portions of this book. This is truly our book, not just my book—a total collaboration.

Second, as always, thanks to Bob Diforio, my literary agent, for finding a great publisher to produce this book with us.

Thanks to Mark Amtower, Roger C. Parker, and others who permitted me to reprint their writings or otherwise share their marketing expertise in this book.

And thanks to my editor, Jere Calmes, for believing in our idea and for making the book much better than it was when it first crossed his desk.

ABOUT THE AUTHOR

Bob Bly is an independent copywriter and marketing consultant with 30 years of experience in direct response marketing. McGraw-Hill calls Bob Bly "America's top copywriter" and he was AWAI's 2007 Copywriter of the Year. Clients include IBM, the Conference Board, PSE&G, AT&T, Ott-Lite Technology, Intuit, ExecuNet, Boardroom, Medical Economics, Grumman, RCA, ITT Fluid Technology, and Praxair.

Bob has given presentations to numerous organizations including: National Speakers Association, American Seminar Leaders Association, American Society for Training and Development, U.S. Army, American Society of Journalists and Authors, Society for Technical Communications, Discover Card, Learning Annex, and New York University School of Continuing Education.

He is the author of more than 75 books, including *The Copywriter's Handbooks* (Henry Holt), *The White Paper Marketing Handbook* (Thomson), and *Business-to-Business Direct Marketing* (NTC Business Books). Bob's articles have appeared in *Cosmopolitan, Writer's Digest, Successful Meetings, Amtrak Express, Direct,* and many other publications. Bob is a columnist for *Early to Rise, The Writer,* and *Target Marketing.* The *Direct Response Letter*, Bob's monthly e-newsletter, has over 80,000 subscribers (bly.com/reports).

Awards include a Gold Echo from the Direct Marketing Association, an IMMY from the Information Industry Association, two Southstar Awards, an American Corporate Identity Award of Excellence, and the Standard of Excellence award from the Web Marketing Association. He is a member of the Specialized Information Publishers Association (SIPA) and the Business Marketing Association (BMA).

Chapter 1

HARNESS THE POWER OF VISION

Too many business owners and managers have no clue about their future. Are you one of them?

If so, what you need is a clear picture of your destination. You need a vision. Your vision, or mission statement, declares where your business is headed and what it will look like when it has arrived.

A mission statement tells you what success (for you) looks like. How else will you know when you've achieved it? Your marketing plan refocuses everything you do in your business into a series of planned, coordinated actions to create your vision.

Why are goals important? You've heard the old saying: "If you don't know where you're going, you'll never get there." This is true both for travel, for life, and in business. People say, "I want a business in which I make a lot of money," but they can't tell you what "a lot of money" is and have no specific income goal. They say, "I want to be successful in business," but when you ask them exactly what that means, they can't say.

Years ago, I was asked to speak at a conference attended by college seniors. Hundreds were in the audience to hear my talk. I looked out at the college seniors and asked, "How many of you want to be successful?" Every hand in the room shot up. I then asked, "How many of you can give me a clear definition of what success is?" Every hand in the room went down. I said, "If you do not know what success is, then how are you going to be successful?"

The conventional definition of business success is money and size: how much money you earn per year, the gross annual sales of the business, number of employees, number of customers served, number, of locations, and the net worth of the owner. But is that really accurate? Does it work for you? Or are your values different?

I have a colleague, DM, who earns a lot more money per day than I do as a top professional speaker. But he spends his life on airplanes going to speaking engagements. DM loves that. "I get to travel around the world and surf the best waves all at someone else's expense," he told me recently. "Then I get a five-figure paycheck for doing something I love—giving a talk—about subjects that fascinate me. How can it get better than that?"

But I would be miserable with DM's jet-setting existence. I have designed my life to stay home and avoid travel, which I loathe with great intensity. Summer evenings, I can come home while it is still light out and spend time in the front yard talking with neighbors or the back yard reading the paper. Winter evenings, I want to be in my own home in front of a fire, not sitting in an airport waiting for my connecting flight.

DM and I are two different people. His idea of success is not mine. Your happiness will come from designing a business that delivers your definition of success—not from pursuing goals you feel pressured to achieve because of the opinions of others.

What about money: the amount of money you make in your business? Isn't that a measure of success or failure that cannot be debated? Well, I don't know. On the one hand, society sees the entrepreneur driving a BMW, living in a mansion, and making a million dollars a year as successful, and it's hard to argue with. But what price did he have to pay for that success? Was he on airplanes on business travel while his children were young, so as a consequence he wasn't there

for the soccer championship, the school play, and their other important days?

On the other hand, I know a number of internet information marketers—a business I am in today—who make a few hundred thousand
dollars a year, not millions. Their businesses are relatively small. They
are well off, but not wealthy. But to earn that six-figure annual income,
they work only a few hours a day. They do not have an outside office or
a staff. That means they can do what they want to do, when they want
to do it—and that includes spending time
with family. They are not rich, but their six-
figure passive income streams give them a
lifestyle that most Americans would envy.

So while income is one metric by which
business success is measured, it is not the
only one. You have to combine it with other
factors. One of those is time invested as it
relates to income earned. Would you rather
make a million dollars a year working 12
hours a day, six days a week, or $400,000 a year working two hours a
day, five days a week?

> **While income is one metric by which business success is measured, it is not the only one. You have to combine it with other factors.**

There is no right or wrong answer. The answer is to choose what
works for you, and then design a marketing plan that enables your
business to deliver both the income and the lifestyle you seek from it.

Design Your Business to Deliver the Lifestyle You Seek

The ideal business is one that delivers the income and lifestyle you
desire, while enabling you to attain it doing work you enjoy and find
both meaningful and satisfying, with and for people you care about.

Many businesspeople spend their days doing work they either actively dislike or do not care about so that they can afford a big home or
luxury car. But during the work week, you spend more than half your
time working. True happiness comes from being happy both at work
and in the life you enjoy from the fruits of your labors.

To write a marketing plan for your business that enables you to achieve optimum reward both at work and at home, you need to visualize what you want in both venues. At work, do you want to be part of a team of bright, creative, enthusiastic professionals? Or do you dream of spending the day alone at your PC, in quiet and solitude, writing programs or balancing numbers on spreadsheets? At home, is it important that you are the envy of your friends and neighbors for your obvious wealth, living in the biggest, fanciest home on the block, or driving the most expensive cars? Do you desire with all your being to dine in five-star restaurants and join the swankiest clubs? Or is your idea of happiness grilling franks and hamburgers with neighbors in your backyard?

> **To design a business or career that allows you to live each day of your life as close as possible to your ideal day, you must first have a clear picture of what that ideal day would be.**

Valerie Young, of ChangingCourse.com, asks her coaching clients to write a one-page essay describing their ideal day. The idea is that to design a business or career that allows you to live each day of your life as close as possible to your ideal day, you must first have a clear picture of what that ideal day would be.

Here's the brief essay I wrote for Valerie a number of years ago, when I engaged her as a coach. It described how I envisioned my ideal day at the time. Remember, this is not how I actually lived: it was my ideal description of how I would like to live.

I would live in a small house on the water, specifically on the lagoon at the Jersey shore. But of course I cannot move, since my kids do not want to leave their school, and my wife does not want to leave her friends.

I work in a small, inexpensive rented office in town, about a mile from the house. Office hours are roughly 8 a.m. to 6 p.m. weekdays, with a half-day Friday. I might put in a few hours on Saturday if the mood strikes me. But I often take a day off if I feel like it, to read as I sit by the water.

I am writing copy only for clients I like (essentially my practice now), but instead of 20 to 30 projects, I handle only six to eight at a time. I do not negotiate fees or deadlines. Clients have to pay my price and work to fit my schedule, or I turn them away (I do this largely now, but not totally).

Cutting down in this manner will have lowered my annual income from a gross of $600,000 to $700,000 a year to just $300,000 a year, although the lower income is offset by a reduction in expenses: my wife is working with me in this scenario, so I can let some of my helpers go. I have also increased my internet business to gross sales of $7,000 a week minimum, and assuming a 75% profit margin, this puts another quarter of a million dollars a year in my pocket with very little labor on my part.

I am traveling once a month on average, not very far, to give one-day seminars in copywriting or technical writing to corporate clients who pay $5,500 for the day plus expenses. Half the jobs are local in NYC and NJ, and the out-of-town ones are no farther than Chicago.

I continue to write regular columns for Target Marketing and Early to Rise, and may have started writing an occasional article for a major consumer magazine, like AARP or Men's Health. I write one or two books every one to two years—a combination of science books for young readers, social issue nonfiction, and an occasional novel. These are published by major NY publishers, as my other books have been.

I feel relaxed enough that, for the first time in decades, I am starting to think about a hobby. Maybe I buy a clarinet and start playing music again, even joining the local community orchestra if I get good enough (haven't played in 30 years).

My wife Amy and I spend more time together, though I still like to be alone at times. The kids, ages 17 and 20, are close to us.

I realize the reason I couldn't answer your question about how I want to help others is that I already have a full-time job helping one disabled person get the opportunity to lead a normal and happy life: Alex, my older son, who is bipolar and has ADD. Until that job is done, my ability to volunteer to help others will be limited or nil.

Valerie read my essay and sent me the following response:

On the money thing and downsizing, I don't see you necessarily following the steps of the book Your Money or Your Life, *but it does make one think about what we are paying in what he calls "life hours," or in other words the cost of earning money. Life is too short not to play the clarinet.*

I especially like the parameters around travel and picking clients that work for you. Whenever I hit some kind of "should or have to" like I have to be a coach, my mantra is "Who says you have to?" John Madden the football commentator doesn't fly—so, who says you have to fly to be top in his field?! There are more than enough Fortune 500 companies in your own backyard.

Just a thought on outsourcing—rather than taking on a client and then having another copywriter do the work, what about just having a referral agreement with someone you respect. The client knows you are referring them to another copywriter you endorse, and obviously that copywriter does and they agree to give you a referral fee of some kind since they got the job through you. Or ... you can just pass on the referral as a professional courtesy but at least you know as you start turning away work that the client is well cared for.

> **Does this exercise of writing down your ideal day pay any dividends, or is it just theoretical, touchy-feely nonsense?**

My only suggestion is to at some point go back and apply what I call the airplane test ... you're chatting on a plane with a stranger telling each other about your lives (I know you're an introvert, so this would not be you in real life, but bear with me), and as you both get up to leave, that person says, "Wow, Bob, I can't believe that's your life—how wonderful!" You might throw in things like "My wife and I spend the month of January on a Greek island or in Tucson (or wherever would make you happy), where I work on my new book part-time and explore shops and vintage bookstores in little towns the rest of the time," or "I co-wrote a book on parenting a challenged child and all of the proceeds go to an institute that seeks a cure," or "I won an award from the National Science Foundation and AiChe for my innovative approach to getting kids into chemistry and am asked to speak to teachers about how to engage kids—even those with learning disabilities—in science and engineering, which I gladly do for free since I have a lot more free time." It looks great just as you wrote it, but I always encourage people to take what they wrote and then "bump it up."

I just got the copy this morning for my Get a Life Fast Track *program. If you think it would be a fit for some of your customers who are looking to transition from having a j-o-b to freelance or another form of self-employment, I haven't finalized the pricing or the affiliate share, but will be happy to pass that along when I do. No wrong answer on this one.*

Does this exercise of writing down your ideal day pay any dividends, or is it just theoretical, touchy-feely nonsense? When I did it, I was skeptical, as I have never been a fan of self-talk or journaling. I wrote the essay for Valerie, saved it to my hard drive, and promptly forgot about it, though I felt the exercise in itself was worthwhile and the fee I paid her well spent. Just the act of doing this small bit of planning energized me, and that's another advantage creating a marketing plan for your business can give you: the act alone of thinking about your marketing and putting your thoughts down on paper can get you excited and enthusiastic about going out there and promoting your product or service to the hilt.

Even better for me, somehow the goals contained within my ideal day description implanted themselves in my brain. Not everything in my ideal day essay has come true, but I have moved toward it in several significant directions. A couple of years ago, I started an internet marketing business that generates a six-figure income and gives me significantly greater financial freedom. With the profits, we bought a weekend home with a dock on a beautiful lake in northwestern New Jersey, making the dream of living on the water come partially true.

Another useful exercise Valerie has her coaching clients do is write a list of five lives they might enjoy living. My list was:

1. A science writer
2. A novelist
3. A freelance magazine writer
4. A college professor
5. An internet information marketer

Again, after writing the list, I promptly saved it to my hard drive and never looked at it again. Goal-setting programs would tell you that's a huge mistake: you need to post, review, and revise your goals frequently. Yet, again, just the act of writing the list must have implanted the goals in my subconscious and led me toward their achievement. For goal #1, I didn't change my career from copywriter to full-time science writer, but I did write a hardcover science book and get it published, a lifelong dream of mine (*The Science in Science Fiction,* published by BenBella and available on amazon.com).

I also didn't switch from copywriting to magazine writing, yet today, I write two magazine columns, one for *Target Marketing* and another for *The Writer.* Goal #5 I pursued in a big way, and I now co-own, with Fred Gleeck, a membership site dedicated to internet marketing called The Information Marketing Club (infoproductcentral.com). I also have more than 50 information products I publish and market on the internet, each with its own website.

My colleague MM is a huge advocate of having a list of a few important written goals. Many years ago, MM decided that he wanted to be rich. He designed his professional life to make him a multimillionaire many times over. Far wealthier than I, he owns property worldwide, has a huge net worth, and lives in a beautiful home on the ocean.

My personal definition of success is less ambitious than MM's, but it suits me perfectly. For me, success is a business that allows me to do what I want to do, when I want to do it—and conversely, avoid the things I don't like to do—and get paid very well for it.

The key to happiness, in my view, is to figure out your ideal lifestyle and design a business that enables you to live that lifestyle, or as close to it as you can get. That includes both what you do to earn a living and how you spend your time outside of work.

"Money is a result, not a cause," says Russ Whitney in his book *Millionaire Real Estate Mentor* (as cited in *Early to Rise,* 12/8/08), "If you get into business solely for the money, chances are you will never be great at what you are doing. Get into a business you like, learn it thoroughly, and do it right. The money will come."

Write Conversational Copy for the Best Marketing Results

We copywriters are taught to write conversational copy. Many marketers erroneously think "conversational copy" means "write like you talk." But what it really means is "write the way your *prospects* talk."

A public radio station in my area, featuring eclectic rock and pop, sent me a fundraising letter. It began: "Dear Neighbor: I know you are a savvy media consumer."

Now, I don't know about you, but if you ask me why I listen to the radio, I would not say because I am a savvy media consumer; I'd say, "I like music."

Here's my rewrite for the fundraising letter lead:

"Dear Fellow Music Lover: Do you ever wish, when you turn on the radio, that they'd play *our* music?"

While my rewrite hasn't been tested against the original, I believe it's an improvement, for two reasons.

First, it talks about something the reader cares about: hearing music I like when I turn on the radio.

Second, it establishes an empathy-based bond through a common interest between the reader and the writer: we share similar musical tastes—which is why I said "our" music instead of "your" music.

"In most cases, you should write in a conversational, intimate voice," says copywriter Susanna K. Hutcheson. "You should talk as if you're having coffee with the reader and use her language. Many copywriters, and just about all people who write their own copy, don't understand the concept of writing in the language of the reader. It's truly an art."

Is there any situation where you should use language other than conversational copy? What about writing to sophisticated audiences? Don't specialists prefer jargon when discussing their industry or trade?

Some argue that jargon is appropriate because it's language used by specialists in your target audience. But I think they confuse jargon with technical terms.

Technical terms are words or phrases that communicate a concept or idea more precisely and concisely than ordinary terms. For example, using "operating system" to describe the software that controls the basic operations of a computer.

Jargon, on the other hand, is language more complex than the ideas it serves to communicate.

For example, I worked for a company that made industrial equipment. In one of our products, a door opened at the bottom of a silo, allowing powder to fall into a dump truck underneath. Our chief engineer insisted that in our copy we replace "dumped" with "gravimetrically conveyed."

For a client, I wrote that the dental brace they manufactured helped keep loose teeth in place. The product manager rewrote "keep loose teeth in place" to "stabilize mobile dentition." To me, this is like calling the seashore an "ocean-land interface."

Mark Twain said "I never write metropolis when I get paid the same amount of money to write the word city." But is there an exception to the rule of writing the way people talk? A situation where you would deliberately use language more complex than the idea it serves to communicate?

Yes, and the one case in which you might consider replacing ordinary language with more sophisticated phraseology is when you want to set your product *above* the ordinary.

Take a look at a Mont Blanc catalog. They don't describe their products as pens; they sell "writing instruments." Why? Because Mont Blanc pens start at about $100 ... and, while that's too much to pay for a pen, it's not too much to pay for a "writing instrument."

Go Confidently in the Direction of Your Dreams

The year was 1952, and 65-year-old Harland Sanders was facing the loss of his beloved restaurant in the small town of Corbin, Kentucky. You see, the new highway had been routed away from his restaurant and travelers no longer stopped in to eat. Eventually, he was forced to sell and retire. At 65, he didn't have much. But he did have an idea, a *vision* of what he could do with that idea, a plan, and a little recipe using 11 herbs and spices.

His vision was to sell his recipe to restaurants all around the country and be paid a nickel for every piece of chicken they sold. His plan was to franchise his chicken business by traveling from town to town and cooking batches of chicken for restaurant owners and employees. He planned to get started just as soon as his Social Security check came in. And that's exactly what he did. As soon as his SS check arrived, all $105 of it, he packed himself and his wife into their 1946 Ford and set off around the country.

By day, he knocked on doors and sought support for his idea. By night, they slept in their car. They'd go to the restaurant owner and offer a free demonstration of their recipe. The restaurant provided the chicken and spices; Sanders cooked it using his recipe.

> **By the time Sanders sold his interests in more than 600 franchises 12 years later for $2 million, he had built an empire.**

Not only did it demonstrate the product, but the Sanders ate hundreds of free chicken dinners after their sales pitch, provided courtesy of the restaurants that tested the recipe.

Along the way, Sanders learned from his experiences and adapted his idea to something akin to the modern-day franchise. Still, 1,009 times he knocked on doors and heard, "No. Sorry. It's not for us. I don't think so." 1,009 times.

And then, something miraculous happened. He knocked on the 1,010th door. After demonstrating the recipe, the owner said, "Look, I'm not really interested in selling more chicken. I make my money here selling beer. If this chicken were saltier, my customers would drink more beer, and then I'd be interested."

Sanders cooked another batch. This time, he added a secret 12th ingredient: salt. Sanders didn't like the new recipe himself; he was on a low-sodium diet, and he found it too salty. But the restaurant owner said it was perfect and bought on the spot. Colonel Sanders and Kentucky Fried Chicken were in business.

By the time Sanders sold his interests in more than 600 franchises 12 years later for $2 million, he had built an empire, amassed a fortune (for 1964), and forever changed the eating habits of Americans. All because a 65-year-old retiree had a vision, a plan, and persistence.

If a 65-year-old man living on Social Security could change a nation's eating habits with a vision and a simple plan, imagine what you can do. That's the power of vision!

Begin With the End in Mind

In the book *Counterintuitive Marketing,* authors Kevin Clancy and Peter Krieg define a vision as "a dream" and write that a "powerful vision looks outward ... [it] expresses *the end.*" Visions speak to our most passionate, deeply felt reasons for why we do what we do.

Your vision is your mental "big picture" of what your business can become. It clarifies your direction and presents clearly what the business is striving to become. In the process, it should instill a sense of purpose in everyone within your business. If it doesn't, either the vision is not vivid enough or you have failed to express it clearly and passionately enough. Tip:

> *Imagine the day has come when you'll turn the business over to a family member or sell it. Describe in detail the business you're turning over. These are the outcomes you're seeking; this is what the business is striving to become.*

It's the vision of one day holding that heavy gold medal around her neck that drives the Olympic athlete to crawl out of a warm bed on cold mornings to skate on a freezing cold ice rink, or to strive to run faster than yesterday around a track for years before the opportunity to even try out for the national team becomes a possibility.

When Thomas Watson, the founder of IBM, was asked to what he attributed the phenomenal success of IBM, he described three things. First, he created a clear image in his mind of what he wanted his company to look like when it was done. Next, he asked himself how a company like that would have to act on a day-to-day basis. And then from the very start of building his company, he began to act that way. The rest is history. That's the power of vision.

Your vision statement allows you to answer the question, "What do I want this business to be when it grows up?" It should detail what you want the business to become within the next three to five years.

Paint a Picture of the Possible

Let's look briefly at what you need to create a powerful vision statement:

Paint a picture of the possible. Paint your vision powerfully. Shakespeare wrote, "In dreams begin our possibilities." Ask yourself, "If I could create my business to be anything (and you can), what would it look like? When I dream about this business, what do I see? Why am I so passionate about this business?" Answer these questions in as much detail as you can, and then write it down.

Describe your vision as if it has already come true. Write it in the present tense. Describe what you see as you look around. How does it feel? You're developing a mental picture of your business as a success, so make it as vivid as possible. Describe whom you see, the sounds and smells around you, and the colors you're experiencing. What are you thinking? What words capture this experience for you? Are you working alone? If not, describe the people who surround you. How has your company contributed to society or your local community? Have you tackled and changed a particular problem in your industry or community?

> **Search yourself to gain an understanding of your main values. In corporate language, these are called your core values.**

Search yourself to gain an understanding of your main values. In corporate language, these are called your core values. Your vision should not only inspire you; it must stretch you beyond your comfort zone. as well. If necessary, rewrite your vision statement to ensure that it is consistent with these values.

Communicate your vision to everyone involved in growing your business. Do it in a manner that inspires people and builds their commitment to the goals of the vision. As they share in the vision, it will evolve from something that is just your vision to "our vision."

Realize that your vision isn't cast in stone. Expect it to evolve as your business evolves.

Why is a vision important for a small or solo professional business? Because it forces you to really know your ambitions for your business. A vision cannot be vague. It declares the outcomes you expect and becomes a guiding light that will lead your business forward. So make sure your vision statement clearly states the outcomes you intend to create.

The more vivid your experience, the greater permission you give your subconscious to dream big on your behalf. Webster defines *dream* as "something that fully satisfies." Is your vision fully satisfying? It will be your secret weapon on those days when you feel frustrated or are sure you can't go any further with this business. You'll live the power of your vision.

Here are a few examples of actual vision statements:

- **Microsoft (original):** A personal computer in every home running Microsoft software.
- **eBay:** To provide a global trading platform where practically anyone can trade practically anything.
- **North Point Church:** To create a church that unchurched people love to attend.
- **Canadian Cancer Society:** Creating a world where no Canadian fears cancer.
- **Amazon:** To be Earth's most customer-centric company; to build a place where people can come to find and discover anything they might want to buy online.
- **EABS Bank:** A bank account for every Kenyan.
- **Milwaukee Public Library:** Every person's gateway to an expanding world of information. Providing the best in library

service, we guide Milwaukeeans in their pursuit of knowledge, enjoyment, and lifelong learning, ultimately enriching lives and our community as a whole.

- **Sunset Playhouse:** [To be] the distinction between community and professional theater and ... the region's destination for experiences of artistic excellence, whether traditional in nature or daring and innovative in choice.

- **Bowling, Inc.:** More people, bowling more often, having more fun.

- **American Red Cross:** We are the pacesetter and benchmark for excellence in nonprofit management and human service delivery for charitable organizations around the world.

- **Chiropractic Marketing Plans, Inc.** (our fictional company): To be the planning resource that chiropractors in Southern California think of first when looking for tools to grow their practice, because they know we know their industry even better than they do.

Action...

Write Your Vision Statement

It's time to create your own vision statement. Don't worry about trying to make it perfect. What's important at this point is to begin the conversation with yourself about the business you're trying to create. Do this no matter how long you've been in business.

Begin with a clean sheet of paper. Imagine your business three to five years in the future, and answer the following questions.

- What service(s) do you perform? What products do you sell?
- For whom? (What types of clients? If you have specific clients in mind, list them.)
- Where is your business located? Do you work at home or in an office? Describe everything.
- You've just met yourself on the job. What do you do in the business? Are you an owner or a hands-on employee? Do you

render the actual service clients buy or hire employees to do that while you manage and mastermind your business? What is your life like? What about your life makes you happy?

- How much do you and the business earn? (The amounts won't be the same.)
- Do you have employees? If so, how many? What do they do? What value do they add to the business? What skills and training do they have? Be as specific as possible.
- What does this business look like when you sell it or turn it over to relatives?
- What does this business do better than any other? What are you known for? What makes you unique or different from your competitors? What is your **unique selling proposition**?
- How do you feel about this business? What inspires you about this business?
- What are the four or five keywords you use when describing your business to others? What are the words your clients use when describing what you do for them to others?

Now, pull out the strongest words in your descriptions. Look for those words that trigger emotions for you. What jumps out for you? What words generate anticipation and passion for you when you read them on the paper? (See Chapter 8 for instructions on how to find out whether the keywords you think are the correct ones are in fact the terms and phrases internet users search on Google to find your product or service.) These words inspire you, and they belong in your vision statement. Your words should reference the type of client you serve, the service you provide, and the geographic coverage of your service.

Note, for example, that Chiropractic Marketing Plans, Inc.'s vision statement, "To be the planning resource that chiropractors in Southern California think of first when looking for tools to grow their practice," refers to CMP's clients and the extent of the geographic area Perez wants to serve. The statement is equally clear that the company plans to earn chiropractors' loyalty by "know[ing] their industry even better than they do." Further, her desire to be a "planning resource for growing practices" opens the possibility for providing services beyond marketing plans down the road.

Don't use puffery like "We want to surpass what clients expect of us." Come on, dream! If nothing excites you, go back and redo the exercise. You haven't dreamed big enough yet.

Use a Vision Board to Make It Clearer

If you're still having problems, try creating a "vision board." Gather about a dozen magazines that you don't mind ripping apart. Now, go through the magazines looking for pictures and words that speak to you. Don't overanalyze this. If it speaks to you, rip it out and set it aside. Remember, our subconscious minds work in images, so all you're doing here is working with something that comes naturally to your built-in problem-solving processes. Give yourself about a half-hour to do this exercise.

The reason to do this exercise is that seeing images is an aid to helping us visualize everything about our ideal business, including the lifestyle it will allow us to live and the customers we want to serve. If being able to drive a luxury car is important to you, find a picture of the car you want to own in a magazine and pin it up on your vision board.

Bestselling author Sam Sinclair Baker used this technique to help visualize the audience he was writing for. He would find several pictures in magazines that he felt were representative of who his readers would be. He would then clip these and tape them to the edges of his PC monitor, so he would always be looking at them when he typed. In that way, he was better able to simulate having a conversation with them, and indeed, he is known for his conversational style of writing.

Now, place the images and words you ripped out in front of you. Using a poster board, take the words and images that speak most

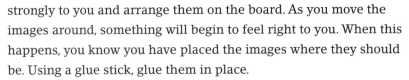

strongly to you and arrange them on the board. As you move the images around, something will begin to feel right to you. When this happens, you know you have placed the images where they should be. Using a glue stick, glue them in place.

Step back and look at what you have created. Write down any words, thoughts, and emotions that occur to you as you look at the images you created. Certain words will begin to recur as you work through this process. Include them in your vision statement.

Write your vision statement here:

_____

_____

_____

Remember, it's not etched in stone. You'll review it monthly, and tweak it when it makes sense. Post your vision board some-place where you'll see it daily. As your vision evolves or your goals change, update your vision board.

Crafting Your Unique Selling Proposition (USP)

In 1961, Rosser Reeves published his classic book, *Reality in Advertising*, in which he introduced the notion of the Unique Selling Proposition, or USP. Today, the book is out of print and difficult to get. As a result, most businesspeople don't know the original definition of a USP. Their lack of knowledge often produces USPs that are weak and ineffective.

According to Reeves, there are three requirements for a USP (and I am quoting, in the italics, from *Reality in Advertising* directly):

Each advertisement must make a proposition to the consumer. Each must say, "Buy this product, and you will get this specific benefit." Your headline must contain a benefit—a promise to the reader.

The proposition must be one that the competition either

cannot, or does not, offer. Here's where the "unique" in Unique Selling Proposition comes in. It is not enough merely to offer a benefit. You must also *differentiate* your product.

The proposition must be so strong that it can move the mass millions, i.e., pull over new customers to your product. The differentiation cannot be trivial. It must be a difference that is important to the reader.

Why do so many advertisements fail? One reason is that the marketers have not formulated a strong USP for their product and built their advertising on it.

Formulating a USP isn't difficult, but it does take some thinking, and many people don't like to think. When you start creating direct mail and advertising without first thinking about what your USP is, your marketing is weak because there is nothing in it to compel the reader to respond. It looks and sounds like everyone else's, and what it says isn't important to the reader.

In general advertising for packaged goods, marketers achieve differentiation by building a strong brand at a cost of millions or even billions of dollars. Coca-Cola has an advantage because of its brand: if you want a cola, you can get it from a dozen soda makers, but if you want a Coke, you can only get it from Coca-Cola. Intel has achieved a similar brand dominance, at an extraordinary cost, with its Pentium line of semiconductors.

Most direct marketers are too small, and have too strong a need to generate an immediate positive return on investment (ROI) from their marketing, to engage in this kind of expensive brand building. So we use other means to achieve the differentiation in our USP.

One popular method is to differentiate your product or service from the competition based on a feature that your product or service has that they don't. The common error here is building the USP around a feature that, while different, is unimportant to the prospects, and therefore unlikely to move them to try your product or service.

For example, in the pump industry, it is common for pump manufacturers to attempt to win customers by advertising a unique design feature. Unfortunately, these design twists often result in no real performance improvement and no real advantage that the customer cares about.

Realizing that they could not differentiate based on a concrete design principle, the pump company Blackmer took a different tack: to create a USP based upon *application* of the product. Their trade ads showed a page from the Yellow Pages ripped out of an industrial buying guide, full of listings for pump manufacturers, including Blackmer. Their company name was circled in pen. The headline of the ad read, "There are only certain times you should call Blackmer for a pump. Know when?"

The body copy explained (and I am paraphrasing here), "In many applications, Blackmer performs no better or worse than any pumps, and so we are not a particularly advantageous choice." But, the ad went on, for certain applications (viscous fluids, fluids containing abrasives, slurries, and a few other situations) Blackmer was proven to outperform all other pumps, and was the logical brand of choice. Blackmer closed the ad by offering a free technical manual proving the claim.

My old friend, the late Jim Alexander of Alexander Marketing in Grand Rapids, Michigan, created this campaign and told me it worked extremely well.

The easiest situation in which to create a strong USP is when your product has a unique feature—one that competitors lack—that delivers a strong benefit. This must be an advantage the customer really cares about, not just a trivial difference.

But what if such a proprietary advantage does not exist? What if your product is basically the same as the competition's, with no special features? Reeves has the answer here, too. He said the uniqueness can either stem from a strong brand (already discussed as an option 95 percent of marketers can't use) or from "a claim not otherwise made in that particular form of advertising"—that is, other products may have this feature, too, but advertisers haven't told consumers about it.

An example from packaged goods advertising: "M&Ms melt in your mouth, not in your hand." Once M&M established this claim as their USP, what could the competition do? Run an ad that said, "We *also* melt in your mouth, not in your hand"?

In his book *Scientific Advertising*, Claude Hopkins gives an example of a USP that has become a classic story. The short version: An ad man walking through his beer client's brewery was fascinated by a machine that blasted steam into beer bottles to sanitize them. "Don't use that in advertising," the brewer told the ad man. "It is nothing unique; every brewer does the same."

"Maybe," the ad man replied, "but I had never heard of it before, and neither has any of the beer-drinking public." He then created a successful ad campaign for a beer advertised as "so pure the bottles are washed in live steam."

One more point: As direct marketers, we—unlike most general advertisers today—are compelled to create advertising that generates net revenues in excess of its cost. Reeves believed all advertising had to do this. He defined advertising as "the art of getting a USP into the heads of the most people at the lowest possible cost." If I were to modify his definition, I would change it to "getting a USP into the heads of the people *most likely to buy the product*, at the lowest possible advertising cost." But who am I to quibble with the master?

Let Your Vision Protect You From Making Bad Decisions

How does having a vision statement help you in day-to-day operations? It creates an easy test: Does this action move us closer to our vision of what we're trying to become? Yes? Then do it. No? Then don't.

This applies to decisions about clients; investments in equipment; whom you network with; organizations you may join; PR and marketing; new services you consider adding; new niches you consider serving; conferences, workshops, and boot camps you may attend; business books you may read; courses you might take; degrees or certifications you could pursue; and new skills you want to develop—literally, every aspect of the business. Let your vision guide you.

Now that you've painted a vision for your business, it's time to clarify what business you're in. But what does that really mean? It means defining exactly who you are, what you do for people, your primary product or service, and your business's key streams of income.

It is possible for two entrepreneurs to do pretty much the same thing, yet see themselves in different businesses. For example, my partner in many internet marketing ventures, Fred Gleeck, is my age and we have similar interests and backgrounds. More than that, when we list what we do to make a living, our activities are virtually identical (see chart).

Yet, even though our activities are nearly identical, Fred and I are in different businesses. I identify myself as a writer—specifically, a freelance writer. I communicate, sell, and provide content in other ways, but what I love to do—my primary skill and service—is writing. Fred also writes, but doesn't love to do it, and would say it is not his primary skill. Although he is a successful writer, internet marketer, and entrepreneur, he primarily sees himself as a professional speaker whose main speaking venue is public seminars, often promoted by him, sometimes by others.

Bob Bly	**Fred Gleeck**
◆ Write books	◆ Write books
◆ Give talks	◆ Give talks and promote
◆ Publish an e-newsletter	seminars
◆ Create and sell information	◆ Publish an e-newsletter
products online	◆ Create and sell information
◆ Write articles	products online
◆ Provide freelance copywriting	◆ Write articles
and consulting services	◆ Provide coaching and
	consulting services

You can look at any business and see it in different ways. For instance, it's been said many times that the reason for the decline of the railroads in America was that they saw themselves in the train business, not the transportation business. Therefore, they did not have the flexibility to adapt to changing times and successfully compete with the airlines.

When I was a kid, we thought of McDonald's as being in the hamburger business. The chain's original mission was to sell a good hamburger cheap and fast. In the 21st century, McDonald's saw Starbucks and Dunkin' Donuts making great money in coffee, and decided to get into the act. To do that, McDonald's management could not continue to think of the company as being in the "hamburger business," but rather in fast food or even convenient fast food for busy people on the go. But some business writers have noted that the real business of McDonald's is not food at all, but real estate. The company owns a huge amount of real estate for its locations, making it one of the largest real estate companies in the country.

Another example is what's happening to one of the industries in which I am active as a freelance copywriter: newsletter publishing. For years, the industry was served by one trade association, the Newsletter Publishers Association (NPA). But the computer and the internet have changed the face of publishing forever, and newsletter publishers were among the most affected. In the good old days, the main products of newsletter publishers were newsletters—printed, content-rich, text-heavy, advertising-free specialized publications, most typically monthly, from 8 to 12 pages per issue. A classic example is the *Kiplinger*

Letter. However, with the computer, publishers have more options and formats for making information available. Readers can get content on CD, with access to a database, on a website, in e-mails, via fax, and in many other ways. In many cases, these methods are cheaper, faster, and more convenient than a traditional printed newsletter sent in the mail.

Therefore, the NPA realized its members are no longer in the newsletter business per se, but in the business of publishing specialized content. To reflect this, it recently changed its name from Newsletter Publishers Association to Specialized Information Publishers Association (SIPA). The reaction was split between favorable and unfavorable, not because one is right or wrong, but because different member publishers see themselves in different businesses. Publishers who are more advanced in electronic publishing and marketing truly see themselves as purveyors of specialized content for niche audiences. However, publishers for whom a monthly newsletter is still their main product continue to see themselves as in the newsletter business, even though they may offer other products like webinars and CDs.

> **The most obvious benefit of deciding and defining what business you are in is that it enables you to explain to others what you do.**

The most obvious benefit of deciding and defining what business you are in is that it enables you to explain to others, whether in a sales presentation, in marketing copy, or at a networking luncheon. The concise answer to the question "So what do you do?" is called the elevator pitch, so named because you should be able to clearly describe your business to someone in the time it takes to ride in an elevator with them.

A more important benefit is that, when you have clearly defined the business you want to be in, you can more easily plan a marketing campaign that helps you attain that goal. For instance, an entrepreneur who sees herself as being in the computer hardware business will likely have a different marketing program, reaching a different audience, than the entrepreneur who thinks of himself as in the small business computing solutions business.

Crafting Your Elevator Pitch

An elevator pitch is a 30-second answer to the question "What do you do?" You need an elevator pitch because the question "What do you do?" is usually asked by complete strangers in casual circumstances. In these situations, you do not have a captive audience watching you go through your PowerPoint sales presentation, so your answer must be pithy and to the point.

Why does it matter how you answer the question "What do you do?" when speaking to someone you don't know? Because you never know when the person you're speaking to is a potential customer or referral source.

Most elevator pitches, unfortunately, don't work—because they are straightforward descriptions of job functions and titles, generating not much else aside from disinterest and a few yawns. For example, a fellow I met at a party told me, "I am a certified financial planner with more than 20 years' experience working." Okay. But who cares?

My friend, sales trainer Paul Karasik, has an antidote to the deadly dull elevator pitch. Karasik's three-part formula can enable you to quickly construct the perfect elevator pitch. By perfect, I mean an elevator pitch that concisely communicates the value your product or service offers in a manner that engages rather than bores the other person.

What is the formula? The first part is to ask a question beginning with the words "Do you know?" The question identifies the pain or need that your product or service addresses. For a financial planner who, say, works mostly with middle-aged women who are separated, divorced, or widowed and possibly re-entering the workplace, this question might be, "Do you know how, when women get divorced or re-enter the workforce after many years of depending on a spouse, they are overwhelmed by all the financial decisions they have to make?"

The second part of the formula is a statement that begins with the words "What I do" or "What we do," followed by a clear description of the service you deliver. Continuing with our financial planner, she might say, "What we do is help women gain control of their finances and achieve their personal financial and investment goals."

The third part of the formula presents a big benefit and begins "So that." Here's what the whole thing sounds like: "Do you know how when women get divorced or re-enter the workforce after many years of depending on a spouse, they are overwhelmed by all the financial decisions they have to make? What we do is help women gain control of their finances and achieve their personal financial and investment goals, so that they can stay in the houses they have lived in all their adult lives, have enough income to enjoy a comfortable lifestyle, and be free of money worries."

Action step: Construct your elevator pitch today or tonight using Paul Karasik's three-part formula:

First part: Ask a question beginning with the words "Do you know?" that identifies the pain or need that your product or service addresses.

Second part: Describe your service, beginning with the words "What I do" or "What we do."

Third part: Explain why your service is valuable by describing the benefits it delivers, beginning with the words "So that."

Creating a Business to Fulfill Your Vision

Your *vision* might include helping everyone in your town who has back pain feel better, but then you have to decide whether you will open a chiropractic center, teach courses on managing pain, or invent a back brace to do it. You still have to define your business.

An entrepreneur called me for a consultation about his new business. He had been injured playing sports and suffered from chronic back pain. His vision was to help everyone in America with back pain to place less strain on their spines and therefore avoid more back pain. His product was a mechanical device with a claw at the end of a telescoping wand for grabbing objects at a distance. The person with back problems could use the product to pick up an object from the floor without bending over.

His vision was to help people who suffer from back pain reduce their suffering. His business, however, was device manufacturing and marketing.

Who are your clients and prospects? Who will buy from you?

Who is the right match for the particular expertise that you and your company offer? Everyone? Think again. Unless your product is money, realize that only a limited number of people will want to purchase what you offer, no matter what it is. To prosper, you must figure out who those people are, what their need is, and whether you can offer a clear advantage to them while meeting that need. Many small businesses thrive by serving profitable market segments that larger companies ignore. This is known as *niche marketing*.

What Is a Niche?

Your *niche* describes the service you perform, for whom you perform it, and the results they can expect. A statement of your niche might take the following form:

I (We) _____ ,
    (describe the service you perform)

for _____ ,
    (describe the group you perform your services for)

so they _____ .
    (describe the results they can expect)

For example, our fictional company, Chiropractic Marketing Plans, Inc. (CMP) serves the following niche:

> *We develop marketing plans for chiropractors located in our state, so they know how to refocus their actions and resources on the clients most likely to help them achieve their vision for their business.*

Why is it advantageous to find a niche rather than be a generalist? It's simple. Today, there is more competition in almost everything. That means consumers have more choices than ever, which is good for them, but bad for you. With more suppliers offering similar products and services, the consumer is in control. In addition, the internet makes it easier for consumers to price shop, as well as giving companies the ability to outsource to India or other nations where cheap labor makes it impossible for American vendors to match their price.

The more products or service providers available in your category, the more of a commodity your product or service becomes. When you are selling a commodity, competition is mainly on price, which is a terrible position to be in. Lowering your price means lowering your profit margin until it is no longer worth your while to continue providing the product or service.

The solution is either to offer a product or service that is not widely available (difficult) or to specialize in providing a more common product or service tailored to a specific niche market (easier).

The Hancock Shoe company competes in the first category. If you are a man and, like me, have a shoe width of EEE or larger, you know how difficult it is to find good stylish shoes that fit. Hancock is a leading direct marketer of these hard-to-find sizes, offering a catalog of over 200 shoe and boot styles in EEE to EEEEE widths. They succeed because you just cannot get what they sell anywhere else—or at least, not easily.

Grow Rich in Your Niche

Why is it important to have a niche?

- ◆ It's easier to specialize.
- ◆ You'll have less competition.
- ◆ You can perfect your expertise.
- ◆ You can more easily become recognized as the expert in your field.
- ◆ You'll have loyal clients because your service is tailored to their needs.
- ◆ You can focus your time and resources on the area where you're most likely to succeed.

As a small business, you don't have the kinds of resources the big players can rely on. They tend to ignore niche markets because they see the returns as too low, but the same $10 million market that's not worth their while can be gold for you. Equally important, once you decide what niche you'll serve, you can stop wasting your resources pursuing clients that don't make sense for your focus.

The groups you target can be consumers, businesses, nonprofits, affinity groups (groups of consumers with shared interests), or governments, but a good niche market has a few basic qualities:

- It's easily defined and accessible.
- Its members can afford your product or service.
- It's being ignored by most of your competitors.
- It has a need you can meet while offering a clear advantage.
- Its members are passionate about the service you provide.

For example, if you want to make money in advertising as an entrepreneur, an obvious way is to open a small ad agency. And because the startup costs are small, many marketing-minded entrepreneurs of decades past did just that. Some of them made nice livings. A few got rich. Many others scraped by. As time went on, there were too many tiny ad agencies competing for the same clients, with none offering a distinct advantage or having a clear USP.

When one ad agency competes against another, they typically say they are more creative or their advertising gets better results. But rarely can they document and prove the "better results" claim. And "more creative" is subjective. Worse, since every small ad agency made these same claims, it gave them no competitive advantage in selling their services, and in fact made them all look alike.

As the ad agency industry evolved, specialized ad agencies began to evolve. One ad agency would specialize in medical advertising. Another would handle only high-tech clients. For a time, this gave these specialized ad agencies a strong competitive position. After all, if you were a medical device manufacturer, all else being equal, would you pick a general ad agency or a medical ad agency with a huge portfolio of successful ad campaigns for medical devices?

What happens, of course, is that competitors see your success in the niche you have picked and decide to move in. The number of medical ad agencies grows, and your competitive advantage begins to evaporate. A solution is to micro-niche. That means specializing in a small area within a niche market. For example, I met a guy, PS, who has a small ad agency that only produces marketing for franchise owners of a hearing aid manufacturer and dispenser—that's a narrow niche. Now, I am sure other ad agencies tell potential clients they will do a great job marketing their hearing aids, but it would be impossible for them to compete effectively with PS and his ad agency. By virtue of specialization and experience, he simply knows more about marketing hearing aids than practically anyone else in the ad agency business. Therefore, he wins the lion's share of the new business in the hearing aid industry he pitches.

Niche marketing, or market segmentation, divides markets into groups based on similar buying habits or a geographic area. It means focusing on a group of clients who buy similar services to meet similar needs in similar ways. For example, in defining a niche for your medical billing services, you could begin narrowing your focus in this manner:

- Doctors are a market.
- Doctors who take care of babies, pediatricians, are a niche market.
- Pediatricians in Southern California comprise a smaller, more narrowly focused niche.
- Pediatricians practicing in Los Angeles County comprise an even smaller, more focused niche.

You might further define the pediatricians you want to focus on by a few zip codes within Los Angeles County, the size of their practice, hospitals they're affiliated with, the insurance they accept, or other factors.

Let's say you're trying to identify a niche for your service that helps women with children start their own businesses:

- Women 18–35 with children are a market.
- Women 18–35 with children under age six are a niche market.
- Women 18–35 with children under age six and who earn $50,000 or more per year are a smaller niche market.

Similarly, depending on the needs you have identified and how well your service meets them, you might want to refine this niche further.

Micro-Niche Your Way to Success

Over the years, I've met dozens of people who want to become speakers, consultants, coaches, TV show hosts, or bestselling book authors. Nine out of ten have told me the area in which they want to speak, write, or coach people is leadership, success, motivation, or some similarly broad topic. These people are thinking big—pursuing broad areas where millions of potential readers, clients, and customers are seeking advice. And I can virtually guarantee you that most of these wannabe speakers, coaches, and gurus are going to fail miserably. The problem is that they are thinking big when they should be thinking small.

What do I mean by "thinking small"? Micro-niching. My friend, speaker Wally Bock, defines a micro-niche as "the intersection of a skill or discipline with an industry." So "customer service" is not a micro-niche, and "banking" is not a micro-niche, but "customer service skills for bank tellers" *is* a micro-niche.

Why should you narrow the focus of your business and target a micro-niche rather than offering a big idea, service, or product that everyone wants? There are two reasons why micro-niching is a smart business strategy. The first is competition. If you want to position yourself as a customer service guru, there's a lot of competition: everybody and his brother are trying to cash in on the need for customer service training, and the barriers to entry are low. On the other hand, if you want to become known as a customer service guru in the banking industry, there's a lot less competition, because it's a narrow niche.

The second reason why micro-niching is a good strategy is credibility. If you proclaim yourself to be an expert in customer service, I'm going to be skeptical. And more than likely, you'll have a difficult time proving your claim to me, your skeptical prospect. But say you have worked as a bank teller for the last 11 years. If you proclaim yourself to be an expert in customer service for the banking industry and tell me that you have over a decade of experience in retail banking ... you're instantly credible and believable.

Generalists are going the way of the dodo and the dinosaur.

Customers want to deal with vendors who are perceived as experts in their field.

A few years ago, I opened the newspaper and saw that, in the Dear Abby column, a reader had written to express his disapproval of the way Abby had answered a particular question. His letter began with this wonderfully sarcastic line: "Dear Abby: How nice it must be to know everything about everything!" Your customers are smart. They realize that no one can possibly know everything about everything, or even about most things. So the broader the areas of expertise you claim for yourself, the less believable you are.

By micro-niching, you become the "credible expert." People believe you more readily and want to do business with you because you're a specialist in exactly the service they need. It's a win-win situation. They get more accurate advice, better service, and confidence in you, their expert advisor. You get more business, at higher fees, with clients who respect you and listen to what you tell them.

By the way, the narrower and more specialized your micro-niche, the higher the fees you will command—and the easier it will be to get leads and close sales. For instance, offering your services as a marketing consultant is a tough field to break into, because so many people peddle marketing advice. Positioning yourself as a software marketing consultant is a great micro-niche, except more and more people are doing it, and the field is getting crowded. So you'd be better off finding a smaller niche with less competition. Example: my friend Fred Gleeck positions himself as a marketing consultant for the self-storage industry. There is little or no competition, and Fred owns most of that market. After all, how many marketing advisors are interested in self-storage, or even know anything about marketing self-storage services? Precious few, of course. So the demand for self-storage marketing advice greatly outweighs the supply—and Fred can pretty much name his own price.

Now, maybe micro-niching won't bring you the fame of a Dr. Phil or a Dr. Ruth. But other than that, what's not to like? So take my advice and find yourself a micro-niche today. It's a smart business move.

Why Is This a Good Niche for Us?

How do you know what niche is right for you? A great niche matches your knowledge, skills, and passion with the needs or wants of a narrowly defined group. How can you find a niche that is right for you?

Steps...

1. Begin at the beginning—with your mission.

Your mission statement answers the question, Why does my company exist? The best niches are consistent with your mission and your values. Ask yourself, What do I do well? and What do I really enjoy? There's no sense in growing a business you're not going to enjoy. Then consider your vision. Your vision statement answers the question, What do I want my company to become? Now, you can begin the search for the type of clients who can use your expertise.

2. Research.

Where do you begin? Here are some questions to help you narrow your focus:

- Do I have expertise in a particular industry?
- Do I have specialized knowledge or education?
- What is my professional experience?
- Am I an expert in performing a specific task?
- What interests me?
- What do I have an aptitude for?
- What do I enjoy doing and learning?
- What is the most common problem the people I usually work with (or want to work with) have? Is any business addressing this problem well? Is there some expertise I can bring to it that others are not?
- If their most common problem is being addressed well by

others, what other challenges or opportunities do they
have that no one seems to be addressing well?

For example, EN, a guy with whom I went to college,
wasn't sure what he wanted to do. He ended up managing
a Chinese restaurant, which was hard work with little pay.
Bored, he responded to a help-wanted ad for entry-level
employees in a large corporation's IT department. When he
was hired, he had little idea of what he would actually be
doing and didn't care. It was just a way to escape what was
for him a dead-end job. Arriving at work, he discovered that
he would be part of a team responsible for implementing
SAP, a large enterprise software application, at the company.
When the implementation was a success, EN got an idea.
Surely many other large corporations needed help implementing SAP. He now had a credential, having worked for
18 months on a major, well publicized SAP project. He put
out a shingle as an independent SAP consultant, and was
successful in that business. But he had not studied computer science in college. In this instance, his choice of niche
was arrived at solely based on his work experience.

Okay. How do you research a niche for you? Start at your
local library or bookstore. Better yet, visit both. At the library,
begin your search by asking a librarian for assistance. Explain
that you're trying to narrow the focus of your business and
want to know more about the issues in the industry you've
chosen or issues related to the service you offer. I've loved and
read books my whole life, and worked in the book industry for
more than 20 years, and I still never fail to be impressed by
how much more librarians know about books and information
sources than I do. They are an invaluable resource. Use them.

The larger chains, such as Barnes & Noble and Borders,
are great for studying titles that are hot sellers right now.
Go to their business shelves, and see what topics you find.

Pay attention to "How To" and "Dummies" titles. Find several books that draw your attention, and scan their tables of contents. Look for overlap in the topics they cover. Again, these are great indicators of the topics people are interested in. Magazines and hobby books also offer great niche ideas. One of the tests for whether you have a viable niche is that it will almost always be served by a magazine devoted to people with that specific interest. Study the ads in hobby and trade magazines, and you'll learn a lot about what matters to the members of that niche.

Go online to Amazon or Barnes & Noble and study their bestseller lists. *The New York Times'* Business, Health, and Self-Help lists are especially helpful looks into what people are interested in right now. If you already know what field you want to focus on, then study books related to that area.

The internet offers several great tools for researching niches. Remember, you want people who are interested in what you want to offer. Search.com tells you the 200 most frequently searched subjects on the internet during that week based on Google, Ask.com, and other search engines. Click on any term in the list, and it will take you three to five layers deeper into what people were searching for related to that topic. You'll learn a lot about the issues and challenges people searching for that term are addressing.

Keyword selection services, such as Google AdWords, SEO Book, Keyword Discovery Free Tool, Spacky.com, and Wordtracker all offer free tools that let you get search totals for topics you type in. If you're clueless about what you want to focus on, go to any of these sites and, one at a time, type in the words "learn," "teach," "guide," "how to," "tutorial," "want," "buy," "purchase," and "problem." You'll gain lots of insight into what people want to buy or learn more about.

For example, if you go to SEO Book and type in "guide," you'll find there were more than 200,000 searches for guides last month. As you study the list of searches for specific types of guides, you'll find people were seeking information on travel, finances, sex, relationships, health, real estate, knitting, and more. Dig deeper into any of those categories, and you'll get increasingly more specific details on the topics people searched.

Go to eBay, create an account if you don't have one (it's free), and then type in pulse.ebay.com. This will list the most popular searches on eBay. You can narrow the search by categories and subcategories. You can search anything from services related to real estate, magazine subscriptions, weddings, audiobooks, automobiles, graphic design, and travel to insurance. Remember, businesses and individuals from all over the world shop on eBay. There may be no better pulse for what people are looking for right now than eBay.

Go to Meetup.com, where you'll find a group for people with just about any interest under the sun. The topics page breaks down the meetups by categories, popularity, and growing popularity. For example, if under Categories, you click on Work & Career, you'll be taken to a list of more than 195 careers and a sidebar with the most popular ones. If, for example, you provide services to small businesses, you'll find more than 840 small business meetups in which like-minded people are meeting face to face. Let's say you serve entrepreneurs in the Chicago area. Click on "Small Business," and go one layer deeper to find an Entrepreneurs group meeting in Chicago. If that's your target market, you can contact the person listed as the organizer of the group and ask to interview her about the issues her more than 800 members bring to their meetups. You can also attend the meetups and learn more as a member. Most of these meetups are either free or cost less than $25 to attend.

Yahoo! Groups and Google Groups also have scores of online groups meeting and sharing information with one another. Focus on the active groups—they have activity level ratings—to get the best insights. One is sure to provide knowledge about the challenges facing members in the niche you're considering.

Here's one more niche research tip: look at the successful niche businesses and niche markets that are successful in your field. Is there an adjacent area of interest or related niche, close but not identical to theirs? You can pick that niche as your own, then emulate the business model they use. If it works in their niche, most likely some modified version of it will work in yours.

3. Identify the largest and most profitable of the underserved segments.

For a market to become a viable niche for you, you must be able to make a profit while serving it. Decide which of the segments you identified appeals to you based on your stated mission and vision. Find out how much competition you would face in serving this market. If there are too many competitors, you might have a difficult time breaking in unless you offer something that prospects will identify as a *valuable* advantage. Study the niche to determine whether it's potentially profitable. Ask yourself:

- What's the size of the market?
- Do these people spend money on the products or services I offer?
- What is their biggest problem that I could help them with?
- Is there an urgency to solving this problem?
- What's our potential? (Do you have a realistic chance to generate enough sales in this niche to meet your financial goals?)
- What are the trends in this industry or niche? (Is this a growing or a shrinking market? Is this a niche you'll be able to succeed in for several years, or is this likely to be a short-lived but profitable trend?)

- What are the keys to succeeding in this niche? (Can you master these?)
- Is this niche growing, shrinking, or static?
- Are there trends or technologies that could eliminate the need for your product or service among these prospects?

Before starting her business, Perez, the owner of our model company Chiropractic Marketing Plans, Inc. (CMP), knew she wanted to specialize in marketing plans for health care professionals. But that focus would have created tens of thousands of businesses she could market to. She knew her time and resources would be best served by limiting the business's scope. This is how she narrowed it:

American FactFinder	Health care establishments	740,000	$590 billion
2005 County Business Patterns (NAICS)	Health care establishments in California	93,500	$63 billion
	Health care establishments in Los Angeles County	26,853	$17.5 billion
	Chiropractors in Los Angeles County (621310 NAICS code)	1,091	$74 million
	Chiropractic VSBs (one- to four-person offices) in Los Angeles County	882	~$59 million
	Chiropractors within 10 miles of her office	169	N/A
	Chiropractic VSBs (one- to four-person offices) within 10 miles of her office	143	~$9 million

As you can see, you can get very specific with your niche. Perez chose to focus the first four years of CMP's efforts on one- to four-person chiropractic offices located within 10 miles of her office. Marketing to less than 150 businesses, she still surpassed her revenue and profit goals.

Now it's time to identify your own niche.

Action...

Describe Your Niche

Write a description of your niche. The following formula can help:

I (We) _____ ,
    (describe the service you perform)

for _____ ,
    (describe the group you perform your services for)

so they _____ .
    (describe the results they can expect)

Describe your niche here:

_____

_____

_____

_____

_____

_____

_____

_____

Are You Too Old to Start a Business?

I have thought at various times in my life (I am now 52) that the cut-off age was 50 ... 60 ... or even 70. There were two reasons I believed you'd reach a point where starting over just wasn't practical anymore.

The first, and lesser, was sheer age and lifespan: the idea that when there are many more years behind you than ahead of you, your time to enjoy the fruits of whatever labors you pursue is too limited.

The second reason I believed there was a cut-off date for starting a new career, learning a new trade, or launching a new small business was lack of experience.

For instance, one of the many careers I considered in my youth was the law. But years ago, I decided pursuing that was impractical (not that I was really interested anyway; it was more of a theoretical consideration).

The reason: say hypothetically you were to graduate law school at age 45. You compete against two groups. The first is other 45-year-old lawyers who are the same age as you—but have 20 years of law experience vs. your zero years.

The other group you compete against is your classmates. Like you, they are new to the law. But being in their 20s and single, instead of 45 and having a mortgage and three kids in college, they can afford to work for starting salaries too small to meet your needs.

However, actor Abe Vigoda has changed my mind about all this ... and my opinion today is that it is *never* too late to learn new things, start a new business, switch careers, or go into a different industry.

Abe Vigoda, if the name does not ring a bell, is a dour-faced actor famous for playing the character Fish on the TV show "Barney Miller." On the internet, I read a short interview with Vigoda, who is still a working actor at age 87.

In it, I was reminded that Abe Vigoda's big break was his first movie, *The Godfather*, in which he played Sal Tessio. Well, *The Godfather* was released in 1972. So if you do the math, Abe Vigoda didn't begin his movie acting career until he was over 50.

More impressive is that, at age 87, Abe Vigoda—who, pardon me, has a slightly cadaverous appearance that makes him look ready for the old folks home—is still a competitive handball player.

If Abe Vigoda can get his first movie role at over 50—beating out actors his age who had decades more credentials and experience—then I am convinced that you and I can start a new career or business at any age.

Yes, you may have some disadvantages over younger colleagues, peers, and competitors—including (possibly) less energy, less flexibility, and less adaptability to new technologies and methods.

Then again, maybe not. It depends on your personality—and your circumstances. If you are a retired empty-nester, you may actually have more time, freedom, and flexibility, not less.

On the other hand, if you are still working for a paycheck because you have to and not because you want to, it may take a greater degree of courage and fortitude to make any major business, career, or life change.

As an older entrepreneur or career changer, you will likely have some advantages over your competitors—such as greater life experience and wisdom to draw on when making decisions.

But I know from first-hand experience that 50 is not too old to make a major change, and from that, I am guessing that your age won't stop you, either.

For example, I started a small online information marketing business as I was closing in on my 50th birthday. Today I earn a six-figure passive income selling information products on the internet, "working" only an hour or two a day.

In my case, I kept my day job as a freelance copywriter and still put in long hours on that. But entering a new field—internet marketing—has energized and renewed me in a way I never thought possible. If your gut tells you that you are ready for a change, you probably are.

I close with this piece of wisdom from Milton Hershey, founder of Hershey Chocolate:

I have often been asked—What is the best age for producing? I know only one answer, the age you are now.

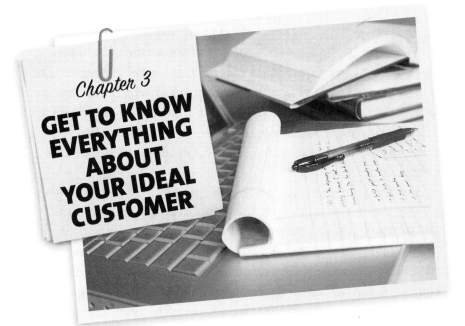

Chapter 3

GET TO KNOW EVERYTHING ABOUT YOUR IDEAL CUSTOMER

In the last chapter, you identified your most promising niche. The people and businesses in that niche are your ideal prospects and clients. But how much do you know about your ideal client? And why does this matter? It matters because meeting your clients' needs better than your competitors do will always be your first job as a business—if you intend to be a successful business.

The closer you are to your market, and the more you understand them, the easier it is to quickly build a stronger relationship with them. Prospects are people who have identified themselves as potential customers through some action (e.g., subscribing to your e-newsletter or requesting your catalog), but have not actually made a purchase. These prospects are obtained by marketing to audiences, through various media and mailing lists, who fit the description of your target market, but who don't know you yet. We can call the people in this vast prospecting universe "suspects."

For example, if you are a chiropractor specializing in relieving back pain, everyone in your town may be a potential patient, but you don't know whom to target, since you don't know who has back pain and who does not. These are your suspects. Now, you run an ad in the local weekly newspaper advertising a free seminar for Tuesday evening on relieving back pain. That Tuesday, 32 people show up. Unless you are serving a free lobster dinner, only people who have back pain or know someone who has it will come. Therefore, your marketing has success-fully completed the first step in the sales process: converting suspects to prospects.

A customer is someone who buys the product now from you. Some business writers separate these buyers into two groups. Users are people who buy the product but are not passionate about it; they are often impulse buyers. Customers are those who buy the product after a deliberate consideration of its benefits; they make what are called "con-sidered purchases," meaning they have considered the buying decision carefully. Beyond customers are buyers so satisfied with your product or service that they proactively recommend it to others; these are called advocates. **Figure 3-1** illustrates this hierarchy of customers.

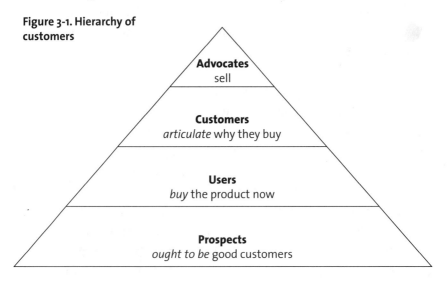

Figure 3-1. Hierarchy of customers

Advocates
sell

Customers
articulate why they buy

Users
buy the product now

Prospects
ought to be good customers

Qualifying Prospects

What's the #1 selling mistake that causes entrepreneurs, executives, salespeople, and professionals to spin their wheels, waste their time chasing after people who don't want to buy, and experience enormous frustration when following up leads?

It's failure to determine whether the person or "suspect" making the inquiry is a genuine, qualified prospect or just someone who likes collecting brochures and wasting salespeople's time. But, how can you quickly, easily, and accurately determine whether a lead is a qualified prospect? By using my "MAD FU" formula.

The MAD FU formula has nothing to do with anger, or any other emotion, or the four-letter F word. Rather, MAD FU stands for the five qualities that differentiate a qualified prospect from a time-waster or tire-kicker: *money, authority, desire, fit,* and *urgency.*

MAD FU says that to qualify a lead, you have to ask them questions. These questions determine whether they have the money to afford what you are selling, the authority to buy it, and a strong desire to own it. In addition, are they a good fit for your business? And do they have a sense of urgency?

Let's look at how to quickly assess all five factors. First, money: Can the prospect afford what you are selling? The easiest way to determine this is to ask, "Do you have a budget for this?" Without a budget, how can they possibly buy your product or service? If they say they do have a budget, ask, "Would you mind sharing with me what your budget is?" Their answer tells you whether they can afford you or not.

Second, authority: Can the person you are talking to write a check or purchase order?

You can determine this by asking, "Who else in your organization is responsible for making this purchase decision?"

The third factor is desire. How intense is their desire to own your product or get your service? How important is it for them to take care of the problem your product would solve for them (e.g., reduce energy costs, control inventory, etc.)? You can gauge their desire through the content of your conversation with them as well as tone and body language. The best prospects have a burning desire to own your product or have you solve their problem.

The fourth factor for qualifying prospects is fit. Is this person a good fit for your business? Is there good personal chemistry between you and them? Does your product or service best meet their needs, or in truth, would they be better off using another vendor?

The fifth and final factor is urgency: What is the prospect's time frame for taking possession of this product or having this service performed? The more the prospect is in a hurry, the easier the deal will be to close. But if the prospect has no sense of urgency, you may spin your wheels for months—even years—chasing after her.

The lesson? When your marketing generates a phone call or e-mail inquiry from a potential customer, don't get too excited. Instead, immediately qualify the lead with MAD FU. Does the person have the money, authority, and desire to buy? Are they a good fit? Is their need urgent? The more "yes" answers you get to the MAD FU questions, the better your chances of making the sale.

Create a Customer Database

One of the marketing tasks you face is to create a list or database of your customers. A database stores all your customer and prospect records on your computer. Each record contains basic information including customer name, address, city, state, zip, phone number, and e-mail address.

The more information you have in each record, the more useful your database is as a marketing tool. For example, say you sell gourmet condiments. In the customer file, you can indicate which type of condiment each customer has bought (e.g., relish, hot sauce), the dollar amount of the purchase, and the date. Now, when you get a new brand of hot sauce you think is terrific, you can send a postcard announcing the new hot sauce just to customers who bought hot sauce from you within, say, the past 24 months.

Why do we want customers who have previously bought hot sauce instead of all customers? After all, someone who buys other condiments may buy hot sauce in the future. And why only customers who have made a recent purchase of hot sauce? The answer is contained in a direct marketing principle called RFM, which stands for "recency, frequency, and monetary."

The first element, recency, refers to how recently the person made a purchase through direct response. According to RFM, those who purchased the most recently are most likely to buy.

This is why it's usually worth paying a premium to rent the "hotline" names on any mailing list—the names of customers who have bought via mail order within the last 12 months or so. The hotline names invariably outperform the other names on the list, because of recency.

The F in RFM is frequency—how often the customer buys. Here, we know that the more often someone buys, the more responsive they are to additional offers. This is why some mailing lists offer a selection called multi-buyers for customers who have bought more than once. Invariably, multi-buyers outperform one-time buyers on the list.

The M in RFM is monetary—how much money the customer spends, or the size of their average order. Here, you want to look for mailing lists where the average order is in the same range as your product's price.

> **Does your product or service best meet their needs, or in truth, would they be better off using another vendor?**

Let's say you are selling a video program called *Overcoming Infertility: How to Have a Child When You've Been Trying Without Success*. The price is $79. You rent a list of people who have subscribed to an infertility magazine for $12. You mail to the list, and the mailing doesn't pull. Why not?

The problem is this: While the people on the list have demonstrated (a) an interest in infertility and (b) that they buy information by mail, they have *not* demonstrated that they will spend $79 to buy something by mail. Twelve dollars, yes; $79, no. The solution? Find a list of people who have, say, attended a workshop on infertility or bought a test kit via mail order for $50 or $100. This might work, because you know not only that the people on the list are mail order buyers and interested in infertility, but that they will shell out a large amount of money for the right offer.

Monetary and frequency make sense, but the principle of recency is counterintuitive. When I first got into direct marketing, I took a course in direct mail copywriting with legendary copywriter Milt Pierce at New York University. One day a student (not me) asked, "Professor

Pierce, why is it that, as soon as I give a donation to a charity, they immediately send me another letter asking for more money?"

Milt replied, "Because they know, from experience, that the person who just made a donation is the one most likely to give again."

The student said, "But Professor Pierce, if I just gave money to a charity, then I would feel I'd fulfilled my obligation for at least a while. And I might even be annoyed that they are coming back to me asking for more."

"Nonetheless," Milt replied, "experience proves that the person who just gave is the most likely to give again." He explained that this phenomenon was called recency, that it held for commercial direct response as well as nonprofit, and that it was part of a formula called RFM, for recency, frequency, and monetary.

To track RFM and other customer activity, you need to build a database. You can hire a programmer to write a custom database manager for your business, or choose from a variety of off-the-shelf database programs; these are listed in **Appendix D.** The data you want in each customer record include:

- Name
- Address
- City, state, zip
- Phone number
- E-mail address
- Gender (male/female)
- Recency—date of last purchase
- What they have bought
- Frequency—how often they buy
- Monetary—size of average order
- Source of order or inquiry—web, e-mail, print ad, billboard, etc.
- Method of inquiry or payment—phone, e-mail, PayPal, credit card

You have several options for maintaining this database. A few businesses still do it manually, recording purchases in a notebook or on index cards. This limits the value and usability of your data, since it is difficult to retrieve and even more difficult to analyze.

For a brick-and-mortar business like a retail store, or a service business like our chiropractic marketing consultants, you can keep your database on your PC. There are database programs you can buy. If there are software vendors who sell business solutions targeted to your vertical niche, those solutions most likely incorporate a customer database as one of the modules.

The maintenance of a database for internet marketers can be performed on their back-end software using an integrated system such as 1shoppingcart.com or Infusion.com. If you use a subscription-based web application such as 1shoppingcart.com, you pay by the month to use the software but do not own it. Therefore, technically, if they went out of business tomorrow (unlikely), your database might be gone. The solution is to export a copy of your database on a monthly or weekly basis to a back-up database management system so you have a copy just in case.

When you build your database, you will input as much of this data as you have for your advocates, customers, and prospects. Suspects are not added to the database until they have made an inquiry and been qualified using the MAD FU formula (see **Figure 3-2**).

Figure 3-2. What to include in your customer database

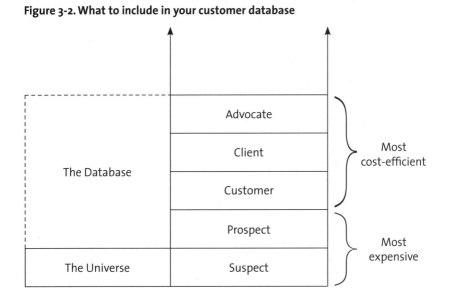

Know Your Customers' "Core Buying Complex"

Big corporations routinely spend thousands of dollars on expensive and elaborate market research studies designed to help them get inside the minds of their customers. These can include mail and online surveys, telephone interviews, and focus groups (see **Table 3-1**).

Entrepreneurs running small businesses worry that if they don't do this kind of expensive market research, they won't know how to reach their prospects and will fail miserably. But for many small companies, the cost of even one study from one of the big market research companies would wipe out their entire marketing budget for the year. Fortunately, there's a low-cost alternative to focus groups and other formal market research studies: the BDF formula.

BDF stands for beliefs, desires, and feelings. The BDF formula says that you can understand your prospect by asking yourself three simple questions:

- What do my prospects believe? What are their attitudes?
- What do my prospects desire? What do they want?
- What do my prospects feel? What are their emotions?

There's no market research required, because you already know these things about your prospects, or else you wouldn't have chosen to start a business that caters to them. Or, to quote Dr. Benjamin Spock, "Trust yourself. You know more than you think you do."

For instance, a company that provides soft skills training to Information Technology (IT) professionals was promoting a new on-site seminar. They sent out a flier where the headline was the title of the program: "Interpersonal Skills for IT Professionals." It generated less than half a percent response. (The offer was more detailed information about the program.) So the marketing manager and the owner brainstormed and asked themselves the BDF questions.

Here's part of what they came up with:

- IT professionals *believe* that technology is all important and that they are smarter than the non-techies they serve.

◆ IT professionals *desire* recognition, respect, continuing opportunities to update their skill sets in new technologies and
platforms, job security, and more money.

◆ IT professionals *feel* an adversarial relationship with end users:
They are constantly arguing with them and they resent having
to explain their technology to us ignoramuses.

Based on this BDF analysis, the company rewrote the letter and
tested it. This time, it generated a 3% response, outperforming the old
mailing six to one. And one-third of those who responded purchased
an on-site one-day training seminar for $3,000. That means for every
100 pieces mailed, at a total cost of about $100, they got three leads and
one order for $3,000—a 30-to-1 return on their marketing investment.

The headline they came up with based on the BDF analysis: "Important news for any IT professional who has ever felt like telling
an end user, 'Go to hell.' Says the company owner, "The BDF formula
forced us to focus on the prospect instead of the product (our seminar), and the result was a winning promotion." Amount of money
spent on market research before the mailing? Not a dime.

The great sales expert and motivational speaker Zig Ziglar always
says, "You can have anything in the world you want if you'll just help
enough other people get what they want." But how can you help your
clients and prospects get what they want if you don't know their needs
and wants? Knowing your ideal client will help you determine what
services to offer, when to offer them, how often, and how to price
them. Who are the people that characterize your niche, and how will
you find and recognize them? To answer this question, you need to
develop demographic and psychographic profiles of the group.

Table 3-1. Key market research methodologies (source: Pranses Research)

Type	Uses and benefits
Telephone survey	Survey projectable sample to get a feel of where consumer attitudes currently stand.
Mail survey	Survey projectable sample by receiving large numbers of responses while holding down costs.

Table 3-1. Continued

Mail survey	Have 50+ respondents see ad prototypes or sample products to measure interest.
Tracking study	Measures attitudes and awareness over time. Provides gradation of interest and readings on trends. Can be done by mail or phone.
Fax or e-mail survey	Used when speed is crucial.
Focus groups	Used when ideas and creative solutions are needed. Gives ability to observe and ask questions. Captures the language in which consumers discuss the product and application.
In-depth one-on-one interviews	Outreach for senior executives, doctors, and other hard-to-reach, high-level consumer audiences. Can uncover their personalities, motivations, and outside buying influences.
Ethnographies	Slides or videos of decision-makers in their work or home environment.
Library and online secondary research	Get background information at minimal expense. Provides a foundation for new learning.

What Do I Want to Know About My Ideal Client?

For most businesses, selling is a multistage process. You:

1. Get leads on people or businesses who might be interested in your service.
2. After qualifying those leads, nurture a connection with those prospects in which you learn more about their challenges and generate interest in your ability to solve them.
3. Follow up. Follow up. Follow up.
4. Make a presentation with an offer.
5. Close the sale.
6. Grow your relationship in an attempt to serve and sell them again.

Ask yourself, "How do I appeal to my ideal client at each stage of the selling process?" (see the Selling Stages form in **Appendix B**). At every stage of the sales process, there's a dance going on between you and your prospect. Selling requires getting and staying in step with your client. To do that, you need to know your ideal client.

Demographic data answers the question, Who are they? You'll want to know information such as age, race or ethnicity (because ethnic marketing might be profitable for your business), gender, education, marital status, occupation, and income. Psychographic data answers the question, What do they want? Psychographics are psychological elements that might impact customers' purchasing decisions, such as personality, values, lifestyle, attitudes, interests, and opinions. Taken together, demographics and psychographics offer insight into your clients' hopes, fears, needs, desires, and aspirations, and how they might govern their purchasing behavior.

Questions that might affect how you serve your niche clients include:

- Are the clients you want to serve international, national, regional, or local in scope?
- What percentage of the decision-makers are male? Female?
- What's their average age? Generally, what generation do they belong to? Are they seniors, Boomers, Gen Xers, Gen Yers, Gen Zers?
- What's their average educational attainment?
- What do they have in common?
- How do they differ?
- How do they get their information?
- To what social class do they belong? To what social class do they want to belong?
- Are they conservative, liberal, or independent thinkers?
- Are they environmentalists?
- Are they healthy, active, sports-minded people?
- What are their purchasing habits? How do they decide what to buy? Who decides? How many people influence the decision?
- How large are their expenditures? How often do they buy?
- Have they used a service similar to yours before, or will you need to educate them?

If your clients are businesses, you'll also want to know details about their organizations:

- ◆ What business are they in?
- ◆ How large is the business? Is it home-based?
- ◆ Who are their best clients?
- ◆ What is the company's niche, or what is it known for?
- ◆ What are its sales?
- ◆ Where is it located?
- ◆ How many locations does it have?
- ◆ How many employees?
- ◆ What are its NAICS codes (replaced SIC codes as government classification of what businesses specialize in)?
- ◆ How stable is the business financially?
- ◆ Does the business spend on advertising and promotion? How much? Where?
- ◆ Why do they buy? To increase revenue? To reduce expenses? To maintain the status quo?
- ◆ What criteria do they use to evaluate the service they purchase?

What 'The Apprentice' Can Teach You About Knowing Your Customers

I never thought of Donald Trump as a direct marketer. In fact, from what little I had seen, he seemed largely ignorant of the principles of DM. For instance, on the first season of "The Apprentice," the two teams had to each come up with an ad campaign for a company that made corporate jets (complete with flight crew) available to clients who wanted to fly in private jets, but did not have the budget to buy their own. Trump praised one team's campaign that featured slick color photos of various parts of the jet shot at angles that made them look like phallic symbols. "Idiot!" I complained to my wife, who was also watching. "The ads should have offered a membership card entitling the recipient to take their first 30 minutes of any flight *free!*" That's how we direct marketers think: offer, offer, offer.

But an episode in the second season of "The Apprentice" was much more encouraging in its demonstration of direct response principles. This time, two teams each had the task of putting together and running, for one evening only, a bridal shop in NYC. The content was simple: whichever team had the highest gross sales for the evening would be the winner.

Team A printed huge stacks of pink fliers inviting people to the sale. They distributed these fliers by handing them out at Penn Station as morning commuters got off the trains to make their way to work. Trump correctly questioned the wisdom of Team A's marketing strategy, asking, "How many people are thinking about getting married when they're commuting to work in the morning?" Team B took a more targeted approach: they rented an e-list of thousands of women who were planning to get married and e-mailed them an invitation to the bridal sale.

I think you can guess the result: Team A had only a handful of customers in their shop, sold only two dresses, and grossed around $1,000. Team B had customers lining up on the sidewalk to get into the store as if it were an exclusive Manhattan nightclub. They sold 26 dresses, for gross revenues of more than $12,000, outselling Team A more than 12 to 1.

The project manager of Team A was fired by Trump that night. The marketing lesson is clear: targeting the right prospects is all-important. In this case, Team B knew that everyone on their list was planning to get married. Team A, by comparison, handed out their invitations to anyone and everyone at Penn Station. How many of those people had any interest in getting married? Was it one out of 100, or maybe one out of 1,000?

The "list" used by Team A had maybe 90 percent to 99 pecent "wasted circulation," meaning the promotion went to the wrong people: those not interested in buying the product. The list used by Team B had maybe 1 percent or as little as 0 percent wasted circulation, because virtually everyone on the list had indicated a planned wedding. And the result? B outpulled A by approximately 12 to 1.

Using the best mailing list versus the worst mailing list can increase your response rates by 1,000 percent or more—which makes testing different mailing lists perhaps the best investment you can make in your marketing.

Don't Ignore Government Markets

Most small business owners concentrate on selling to either consumers or business customers. But there are two alternative markets that may apply to you, depending on your type of business: government sales and nonprofit marketing.

Federal, state, and local governments represent about one-third of the annual gross domestic spending in the United States, spending about $2.5 trillion for goods and services. Though much of this is spent through specific contracts, tens of billions are also spent at the "micropurchase" level (for federal buyers, anything under $3,000; for state and local government buyers, somewhat less). These purchases are made via government credit cards. The federal card is the SmartPay card; there are currently about 300,000 in use, and in FY (fiscal year) 2009 almost $20 billion was spent using SmartPay. No reliable statistics are available for state and local government credit card usage, as there are so many state and local governments.

Government customers are loyal. Once they like you, they will continue to buy from you whenever possible. Mailing to the government is similar to mailing to businesses, but there are nuances you need to be aware of. The following are a few quick tips to get you started. These tips also apply to your website, space ads, and other advertising material.

◆ Know your audience. Who are the users of your product or service, and who are the buyers? These are not always the same people. Is the purchase a team decision? Develop a profile of the person who uses your product, and where possible include the position function, office mission or function, and agency mission. For commodity products where there is broad usage, you need only figure out who the buyer is for each office.

◆ Like all direct marketing, the list is the key factor. Work with a mailing list broker who has experience in business-to-government as well as your product or service niche. Many B2B publications have small segments of government readers, so do not overlook these segments if the list works for you in your business mailings.

- The mail package needs to be well suited to the audience. Catalogs and line cards go to procurement offices and end users. Procurement offices only care about price, source, and what contracts you are on. Collateral material with success stories, features, and benefits go to end users and decision-makers.

- The message is critical. Government decision-makers still receive lots of mail every day, so you need to get their attention quickly. The key messages are features and benefits for users and others on the decision-making team, and price and contracts for procurement offices.

- If you have a GSA Schedule contract, clearly say so.

- Make it as easy as possible for people to respond to your offer. BRCs and BREs still work, so use them in your mailings. Boldface your 800 number and your website address. If you have dedicated government reps, give the direct line(s). Always offer multiple response devices.

- Government mailing addresses often have internal routing codes. Ask for these on all response devices.

- Avoid over-mailing to military bases. All military base mailrooms strictly limit the amount of incoming promotional mail from the same mailer. If you have lots of people on military bases, stagger the mailings by a week.

- Use the SmartPay logo everywhere you use the Visa and MasterCard logos. If you have a special cover for catalogs going into government offices, include the SmartPay logo on the cover.

- Survey your active customer base to better understand how they gather information during the buying process. Ask them what they read, what they attend, what they belong to, and what their favorite business-related websites are.

- Be in front of your buyers during the end of their fiscal year. For feds, September 30 is the last day of the FY; for most state and local governments, it is June 30. Government agencies are not rewarded for thrift. If they do not use their budget, it does not roll over for them to the next FY—it goes back to the general funds. So they spend whatever is left at the end of the FY. It is good to remind them 60, 30, and 10 days out that you are available to help them spend those last dollars.

12 Government Market Facts at a Glance

1. There are over 80,000 governments in the U.S.—one federal, 50 states, 3,042 counties, 14,566 school districts, 31,131 special districts, 35,963 cities and townships, 512 Native American tribes, and five territories.

2. There are over 20,000,000 full-time government workers in the United States, including federal, state, and local governments.

3. Over 33 percent of the Gross Domestic Product is government spending.

4. Over 40 states would qualify for the Fortune 500 if you replaced sales with revenue.

5. There are over 600,000 businesses registered to do business with the federal government and tens of thousands more doing business with state and local governments. Probably less than 10 percent make real money (significant portion of their company business) in this market.

6. Many types of contracts are available at the federal level, but GSA Schedules are the most popular, accounting for one-third of all transactions, though only 10 percent of sales volume.

7. FY 2008 GSA Schedules accounted for $38 billion, and there are over 12,000 GSA contractors on 43 GSA Schedules.

8. 23 percent of all government contracts are *supposed* to go to "small businesses." SBA size standards can be found here: sba.gov/size/indextableofsize.html.

9. The federal SmartPay card accounted for over $19 billion in FY 2008.

10. Credit card orders under $3,000 do not require federal contracts. Many state and local governments also use credit cards for purchasing, usually with a smaller per-purchase threshold.

11. There are 35,000 occupied federal civilian sites in the continental United States, not including post offices or military bases.

Nonprofit Marketing

A reader recently asked me, "I am working on increasing the success of a nonprofit American Cancer Society telethon in my home town. This telethon runs from noon to 11 p.m. on Saturday and noon to 10 p.m. on Sunday. I am hoping to use effective marketing to increase its profit and success, and I have a year to do so. As a marketing expert, do you have any advice or can you offer any assistance in this project?"

Unfortunately, my combined experience in the areas of telethons and fundraising could fit easily in a thimble. So I turned to my erstwhile colleague Jerry Huntsinger for some help. Jerry, considered by many to be the top fundraising copywriter on the planet, specializes in direct mail for nonprofits. According to him, it's important for fundraisers to know their audience, which he defines as "65-year-old women." Decades of experience show that you should aim your message, entertainment, and programming toward women in their 60s, because they are the viewers most likely to donate.

Offering a response premium—a free gift you get when you make a donation—works well in fundraising in general and is especially effective in TV. You rarely see a public television fundraising campaign that doesn't involve tote bags, books, videos, and other prizes given for varying levels of donation.

Keep in mind that people give money primarily to feel good about themselves. "When I write a fundraising package, I interweave two subjects in the copy: the benefits to those who will be helped by the donation, and the benefits to the person giving the donation, which is primarily that they will feel good about themselves," says Jerry.

Appeal to both the viewer's emotions and her intellect during the program. Tell moving stories of struggles with cancer and how your nonprofit has helped so many cope with the disease.

If you can focus on the stories of a few individuals who have been helped rather than statistics, so much the better. Joseph J. Kelley Jr., a former Eisenhower speechwriter, observes,

"If a newspaper reports the sad story of a youngster dying of cancer and how the family is planning an early Christmas for him, letters, money, and gifts will come to them from perfect strangers. People sympathize with and are saddened by the plight of an individual." At the same time, inject positive news into your marketing materials; e.g., breakthroughs in cancer research, hope for a cure, important research funded through the Society, how the donation will be used.

It is emotion that prompts the urge to donate, says Huntsinger, but people often rationalize the decision to give money intellectually before mailing the check or picking up the phone to pledge. So have both emotional and logical appeals in your program. Emotional: Timmy's family has new hope thanks to the American Cancer Society, and your pledge can help more families like Timmy's. Logical: 3,727 cancer researchers receive funding from the ACS.

Celebrities can increase results in fundraising; look at MD and Jerry Lewis. Last year, the 38th annual Jerry Lewis Telethon for the Muscular Dystrophy Association raised a record-breaking $60 million in 21½ hours. If you have a local celebrity you can use, even a local news anchor, recruit him or her to the cause.

Can the American Cancer Society agree to time its fundraising mailings to your city with the telethon? Response rates to its direct mail fundraising efforts will be higher if they are mailed during this time. (Publisher's Clearinghouse always gets its best direct mail response rates when mailings coincide with the airing of its TV commercials.)

Know the Lifetime Value of Your Ideal Client

Think about it. You have only three ways to increase your sales:

1. Increase the number of clients you have.
2. Increase the frequency of their purchases.
3. Increase the amount of their purchases.

Strategies for growing your business must focus on how to do one or more of these things while keeping costs down. So, to meet the goals you set for your business, you need to understand how much money your average ideal client is going to spend with you throughout the course of your relationship. This will also tell you how much you can afford to spend to acquire a client.

To compute the lifetime value of a client:

1. Determine, on average, how much your ideal client will spend with you each year.
2. Determine, on average, how many years this client will buy from you.
3. Determine, on average, how much additional income you'll make from the referrals this client makes to your business.

For example, if your ideal client spends $2,000 a year with you and buys from you for three years, that client has spent $6,000 with you. If that client refers two others to you, who repeat that pattern, that's an additional $12,000. So your ideal client has a lifetime value of $18,000. If 50 percent of that were profit, would you spend $1,000 to acquire that client? Yes. Would you spend $5,000?

Obviously, the longer you've been in business, the more data you'll have to determine a client's long-term value and a reasonable investment for acquiring that client. If you're just starting out or don't have a track record yet, make sure this is one of the measurements you use to evaluate your business success. A monthly client report, such as the one shown in **Figure 3-3**, can help you collect the information you need to summarize the value of each client to your business.

Figure 3-3. Monthly client report

Client Report (Month/Year)								
	Services Purchased	Problem Solved	Date	Amount	YTD $	Last Purchase Date	Client Since (m/d/y)	Lifetime Value to Date
Client 1								
Client 2								
Client 3								
Totals				$	$			$
Comments:								

Know Why Your Client Buys

Look for clues to how your clients' behavior might lead them to use more of your service. Specifically, why would this client buy this type of service? What need or want is he or she trying to satisfy? Consumers and businesses buy for different reasons, summarized in **Table 3-2**.

The more you understand the reasons for buyers in your niche to purchase, the more successfully you can speak to their values as you market to them.

Table 3-2. Why consumers and businesses buy

Consumers	Businesses
Improve the family or home	Become a market leader
Advance in their jobs	Increase productivity
Pursue hobbies	Save money
Feel safe/security	Maximize cash flow
Increase their knowledge	Increase quality
Participate in community activities	Cut overhead
Feel good about achievements	Be perceived as innovative
Enjoy entertainment/recreation	Increase employees' satisfaction
Increase their fitness	Be community-oriented
Enjoy a vacation	

Know What Benefits Mean the Most to Your Client

The more your service appears to be what customers want, the more likely they are to purchase it, but you can't know what that looks like unless you ask them. You have multiple ways to uncover what clients want:

◆ Call and ask them.
◆ Survey them.
◆ Use focus groups.
◆ Do face-to-face interviews.

- ◆ Survey your employees.
- ◆ Invite comments from clients.
- ◆ Have a regular group of client advisors.
- ◆ Review feedback forms from salespeople, who often have new insights about what the market needs.
- ◆ Attend events and conferences your client group attends.
- ◆ Get input from clients on new programs, prospects, and services.

Marketing to GOM (Grumpy Old Men)

For a free 16-page special report on marketing to the over-50 male market, "Marketing to GOM" (cover price: $9), click below now: **marketing2goms.com**

This report outlines 10 characteristics of the older male that marketers need to factor into their promotions aimed at this audience. Among the findings:

- ◆ Men over 50 don't think of themselves as "old," but they increasingly worry about health, weight gain, going bald, and finding meaning in their lives.

- ◆ Men over 50 are approaching retirement, and are therefore highly focused on either accumulating enough wealth to retire or not having their retirement nest eggs wiped out by another market crash or economic downturn.

- ◆ Men over 50 are reaching a point where they no longer want to do what other people (bosses, customers, wife, kids) tell them to do, but instead do what they want to do.

Know the Steps in Your Clients' Buying Process

Why is it important to understand your prospects' buying process? Because you want to appeal to buyers at every stage of the process so that, by the time they make their decision, it's clear that you offer the best response to their needs or wants. As a marketer, you want to influence prospects the moment they start thinking about solving their problem or buying your type of service. You want to know:

- Who makes the decisions?
- Is the decision impulsive or deliberate?
- Do consumers view my product or service as a value-added purchase or a commodity?
- How price sensitive is this market? How can I win business without being the low bid? Must I service what I sell? Can I sell my customer an extended warranty or service plan?
- Will my prospects research this purchase online before coming to my store or showroom?
- Are prospects in my industry mainly generated through referrals from their neighbors, relatives, and friends?
- Do consumers feel knowledgeable about my product or are they looking for an expert to guide and advise them?
- Do decision-makers shop around before purchasing?
- Are products and services like mine readily available and do my customers know about them? Or do I have the market to myself?
- Are my competitors as busy or as hungry as I am? How far are they willing to go to take business away from me?
- How do they pay? Can they purchase outright or do they require financing?
- How much is it worth to them to solve their problem?
- When and how do they purchase? Seasonally? Locally?
- Are they loyal to their current supplier?
- If I get them to buy, how long will they remain my customer, and on average what will they spend with me during that time?
- What warranty or guarantee is standard in my industry? Can I afford to offer a stronger one, and would it make any difference to my prospects?

Five Steps to the Perfect Guarantee

"Using a strong guarantee" is standard operating practice in many markets. And with good reason: without a strong guarantee, your sales will slow to a trickle. That's especially true in direct marketing, since buyers are loathe to buy products over the internet, phone, or by mail sight unseen.

But what exactly makes for a "strong" guarantee? A strong guarantee has five defining characteristics—and your guarantee should possess these qualities, too:

1. Length. As a rule of thumb, the longer the guarantee, the better. Typical guarantee periods are 10, 14, 30, 60, 90, 180, and 365 days. Of these, 10 days is the weakest, because it requires the prospect to act too quickly for comfort. The buyer is afraid that, if he puts the product aside, the guarantee coverage will expire, and he'll be stuck with a product he can't return. And so he doesn't order in the first place.

A 30-day money-back guarantee is standard, and certainly adequate. But 60 and 90 days are better. I personally do not like to offer life-time guarantees, because it creates a financial liability on the books that may be problematic when it's time to sell your business.

A six or 12-month guarantee may be worth testing, but won't work for some products—for instance, a one-year guarantee doesn't make sense for an annual directory.

2. The conditionality of the guarantee. Are there strings attached? Or is it unconditional?

A conditional guarantee might say: Return the product in salable condition for your money back. The buyer is concerned that you will quibble with him over "salable condition." That is, you will refuse to issue a refund for a book he returned because, say, the dust jacket has a smudge on it.

Another conditional guarantee is the one used by many sellers of small business and investment home study programs. The say: If you are not satisfied, send back the course for a refund; just "prove to us that you made some effort to follow our system." When you ask for a refund, they ask for more and more proof—and whatever you send, the seller counters that "you didn't do what we said" (or do enough of it)—and denies your refund on that basis.

Much better is to offer an unconditional guarantee. Tell the customer all he has to do is return the product for a full refund—no ifs, ands, or buts—without question or quibble.

3. Clearly state and spell everything out. Be careful about wording that the consumer can misinterpret. For instance, a performance-based guarantee—"If you do not earn extra money trading options with our program, return it for a refund"—sounds good but contains a potential concern: Does it mean that if I *do* make some extra money with the product, I *can't* return it? Even if I only made 10 bucks? Rewrite the guarantee so there is no condition or ambiguity stated or implied; e.g., "If you do not make extra money trading options with our program, or you are not 100% satisfied for any other reason—or for no reason—just return the program within 90 days for a full refund."

4. The guarantee should be graphically emphasized within the promotion. Don't bury it in body copy or put it in an asterisked footnote in 8-point type. Print the guarantee in 12-point copy with a large, bold headline. Put a box or even a certificate-style border around it to make the guarantee stand out.

5. how generous is the guarantee? The best guarantees are un-fair—but unfair in favor of the buyer, not the seller. That means if the customer takes advantage of the guarantee, the seller is, in a sense, getting ripped off.

Example: For regular books sold via mail order, the guarantee is simple: Return the book and we will return you your money. But think about the same guarantee for e-books: Can the customer really return you the e-book? Do you expect them to send back the copy they printed out ... or sign an affidavit that they erased the e-book from their hard drive ... or shredded the print-out? (Some online marketers have done just that!)

Most information marketers skirt the issue of returning e-books in their guarantees. They say: If you are not 100 percent satisfied, let us know within 90 days for a full refund. No discussion about returning or erasing or not using the e-book takes place.

In the landing pages I write to sell the e-books I publish (see for examplemyveryfirstebook.com), I go a step further: I turn the fact that the customer does not have to return the e-book to me into a benefit. I say, "If you are not 100 percent satisfied, let us know within 90 days for a full refund. And keep the e-book free, with my compliments."

I always suspected that this overly generous offer boosted my sales, but never split-tested it. But in a recent internet marketing seminar, David P., who heard me talk about this point in my presentation, said that he, too, tells his customers to keep the e-book even if they ask for a refund. David has split-tested it, and says that "keep the e-book free" increased his conversion rates on average by 21 percent.

The bottom line: when writing copy, make sure your guarantee is:

◆ **Long**—90 days is ideal for most offers.

◆ **Unconditional**—no strings attached.

◆ **Clearly stated** with no ambiguity or possibility of misunderstanding.

◆ **Highlighted** with bold typography, color, and graphics so it really stands out on the screen or page.

◆ **Overly generous**—so that if the consumer exercises the guarantee, he is essentially taking almost unfair advantage of you, the seller.

The overriding principle of a strong guarantee is to take all the risk off the buyer's shoulders and place it on the seller's shoulders—as it should be.

Know Where Your Clients Go to Look for Information

It's important to put your information in places where your target market either searches for information or makes its buying decisions. This is where your demographic and psychographic profiles will pay off. Learn what outside factors might influence their purchasing behavior (the economy, the price of oil, new businesses moving into the area, executive leadership, availability of skilled workers, availability of manual workers, production of certain goods, overseas competition, local competition, environmental concerns, tax changes, etc.). Remember, the things that rock their world can rock yours as well.

Know What You Can Learn from Your Current Clients

Once you determine who your ideal client is, take a second look at your current clients. Have you been pursuing the types of clients that are best for you? Take some time and review your roster of clients with the intention of profiling them demographically and psychographically to learn as much as you can about them. Do you know what they value? What benefits are important to them? What is their buying process? Where do they go for information?

Start with what you already know about them. Learning your clients' needs and tastes is something you'll do throughout the duration of your business—if you're wise. So don't wait to know everything about your client. This is a recipe for analysis paralysis. Get started with what you know, and use every opportunity to learn more.

Create a client profile for each of your clients, and add to it any time you have any kind of contact with that client. A sample profile you might build in Access or another database is shown in **Figure 3-4**. Link this to your client report to keep both updated. Remember, knowing and understanding your clients' wants and needs better than your competitors do is one of the keys to successful niche marketing. **Appendix A** contains a blank Client Profile form.

Figure 3-4. Client profile

Client Profile	
CONTACT INFORMATION	
Client name	
Title	
Company	
Phone number	
Fax number	
Address, city, state, zip	
PURCHASING HISTORY	
Client since	
Services purchased (dates and amounts)	
Biggest challenges	
Perceived value of solving their challenges	
Client's competitors	
Their main clients	
Year-to-date purchases	
Referrals given	
Lifetime value	
CLIENT PREFERENCES	
Preferred method of contact	
Frequency	
Birthday	
Anniversaries	

Figure 3-4. Continued

Favorite restaurant(s)	
Spouse	
Children	
Hobbies	
Likes/dislikes	
WORLD NEWS	
Issues affecting them	
MARKETING EFFORTS	
Type/dates/results	
Next action (schedule it)	

Where Should I Look for Information?

Where do you find this kind of information? Free or low-cost sources of information include the U.S. Census Bureau, the Bureau of Labor Statistics, the Department of Education, industry journals, business magazines, trade associations, chambers of commerce, community websites, city planning departments, the Small Business Development Center, universities, business schools, libraries, annual reports, press releases, clients' websites, their competitors' websites, your competitors' websites, and market research departments at newspapers.

Case Study...
Chiropractic Marketing Plans, Inc.

Using the listed resources, Perez decided to redefine CMP's ideal clients as family wellness chiropractic practices that emphasize care for parents and children. This type of clinic focuses on nutrition, exercises, and massage as part of its care.

She also learned the following about the chiropractors located within a 10-mile radius of her office:

- 70 percent are in private practice.
- 28 percent specialize in family practice.
- Another 1 percent specializes in pediatric practice.
- They see an average of 127 patients per week.
- The average patient spends $1,200 first year.
- The average patient visits 30 times per year and spends $40/visit.
- New patients make up 60 percent of their patient load.
- They retain 40 percent of old patients.
- They average seven new patients each week.
- The average practice billings are $350–500K per year.
- The average practice earnings are $110K.
- The average chiropractor's age is 42.
- They are 80 percent male.
- **Trigger:** They want more acceptance of what they do by the public and MDs.
- They get information from the state trade association, association magazines, health magazines and journals, business magazines, and the internet.
- They sell pillows, vitamins, and massage services to complement treatments.
- **Hot buttons:** Revenues are stagnant; they need to increase

their new-patient average; dependence on health insurance payments is growing; they want more referrals from and joint ventures with MDs; and they feel the public still lacks understanding of how much chiropractic treatment can benefit them.

Action...

Describe Your Ideal Client

Write a description of your ideal client. Add as much detail as you need to be clear about who this client is. What is your client's most pressing problem? What aspirations does he or she have that might drive buying habits? What influences your ideal client's purchasing decisions?

_____

_____

_____

_____

_____

_____

_____

_____

_____

_____

_____

_____

_____

_____

Describe your current clients:

_____

_____

_____

_____

_____

_____

_____

_____

_____

_____

_____

Comment on how closely your actual and ideal clients match. Describe what they have in common. Describe how they differ. If there is a wide disparity between the two, describe the changes you intend to make to bring them closer together.

_____

_____

_____

_____

_____

_____

_____

_____

_____

_____

What does your ideal client want to experience when doing business with you? Is it the same as what your current clients want?

_____

_____

_____

_____

_____

_____

_____

_____

_____

_____

What do you need to do to find more of your ideal clients?

_____

_____

_____

_____

_____

_____

_____

_____

_____

_____

_____

_____

Chapter 4
WHO IS THE COMPETITION?

It's tough to do a better job than the competition if you don't know anything about them. That should seem obvious, but too often service businesses launch without asking, Who else does what we do? and What can we bring to the game that they don't? Deciding who your competitors are, what they offer, and whom they serve will help you position your business at a more competitive advantage.

Some businesspeople, either through pride or ignorance, believe they genuinely have no competition. This is seldom if ever truly the case. Since the prospect is not on his deathbed and does not yet own your product, he has at least one alternative: not to buy it and carry on as he has been doing all these years. So one alternative to your offer is inaction, and it is actually the easiest alternative for the consumer to take: People like doing nothing, and enjoy not spending money or dealing with salespeople even more.

Other entrepreneurs tell me their product or service is truly superior, and therefore they have no real competition. The problem is that the consumer does not share the view that your product is unique and superior, and is not inclined to believe you. You may genuinely offer advantages your competitors don't. But their marketing campaigns and salespeople are out there telling prospects that in fact they can offer everything you can and more. Lying? Maybe. But the consumer can't tell.

In other product categories, the opposite situation is true: marketers are surrounded by swarms of competitors, which both they and their prospects are acutely aware of. In these situations you obviously need to know how the top competitors are positioning themselves, the products and services they offer, and even what they say about you.

What They Say About You Online

Is your business being hurt by competitors, dissatisfied customers, or disgruntled former employees who are trash-talking about you or your product on blogs and websites? To find out what is being said about you online, do a full search using your company name, brand, and product names on Google, Bing, and Yahoo! twice a month, advises marketing communication strategist Dianna Huff.

On Google, open a Google account and set up Google Alerts. These are e-mails that Google sends you whenever a specific keyword or phrase you specify—like your name—is used online.

Use the images, books, maps, and more links at the top of the Google search page to see how your company and product names are being used. Then click on "more options" to see online reviews, forums, and related searches. Also check for mentions of you on Digg, Delicious, YouTube, Twitter, Facebook, and LinkedIn.
Source: Marcom Strategist, 7/10/09.

Who Is Your Top Competitor?

Do you know who your top competitor is? Is this your top competitor because you think so or because your ideal clients see the business that way? How does this company stack up on the things that matter to your ideal client?

Clients perceive differences among competitors, and you need to know what your clients' perceptions are of you and your competition. That way, you can highlight the positives in your marketing and look for ways to overcome both perceived and real negatives.

Look for the Gaps in Service to Your Niche

You want a clear snapshot of your competitors as they are today. But you'll also need to stay on top of your competitors' activities in the future. So start building files on them now. Look for changes that pose an opportunity for you or a threat to your business.

First, categorize your competition. Who is comparable to you in their service offerings, quality of service, and price? These are your most direct competitors. Identify the top five or 10.

Don't forget about your indirect competitors. These companies don't offer the same service you do, but your ideal clients see their offerings as an alternative to yours. For example, two movie theaters showing the same movies are direct competitors. However, for consumers looking for entertainment, indirect competitors might be live theater, sporting events, theme parks, and nightclubs. They're all vying for entertainment dollars.

Here are some questions to consider when analyzing your competition:

- ◆ What service(s) do they offer?
- ◆ What is their chief focus?
- ◆ If your niche can be divided into categories (beginner, intermediate, and expert, for example), which group do they focus on? Can you profitably target the ones they do not?
- ◆ What advantage do they offer? Don't try to duplicate your competitors' advantages unless you can do it better.
- ◆ What is the main message they communicate in their marketing materials? How do they position themselves?
- ◆ What is their reputation or image in the industry? Can you own a position differentiated from theirs? For instance, if they are the 800-pound gorilla with vast resources and experience, can you be the nimble spider monkey willing and able to do more? Think Avis vs. Hertz.

A positioning statement tells prospects and clients what the business wants to be known for. In their 1981 book *Positioning: The Battle for Your Mind,* Al Ries and Jack Trout define "positioning" as "an organized system for finding a window in the mind." For example, an office equipment salesman was demonstrating a new copier in my office. I liked the copier, but balked at the price, which was more than I wanted to spend. He told me, "But this is the Rolls-Royce of copiers!" This metaphor instantly tells me the photocopier is positioned as a high-end premium machine.

> **Make a list of your favorite businesses. Ask yourself why you choose to shop with them over their competitors.**

Make a list of your favorite businesses. Ask yourself why you choose to shop with them over their competitors. Is it their offerings? Quality of service? Reliability? Courtesy? Prices? What else? How are they positioned in the market versus their competitors? What can you learn from these businesses and apply to your own?

Now, think of businesses that you'll never do business with again. Why? What made you *feel* this way? What can you learn from these experiences and apply to your business?

You're trying to find a window for your business in your clients' and prospects' minds. Examine your competitors' websites, press releases, case studies, articles, and other promotional presentations to identify how they position their business with clients.

For example, State Farm's commercials present a now-familiar positioning statement: "Like a good neighbor, State Farm is there." Their commercials always show an agent stepping in to help a family in need—just like a good neighbor. Their niche: middle-income, upwardly mobile families. Positioning: They're a neighborhood business you can trust.

Questions to ask about your competitors:

◆ What do your competitors do well?
◆ What strengths do they have? Do they offer guarantees? Strong offers? Are they financially stronger?

- What segments, needs, or opportunities within your niche do they ignore?
- What do they do poorly or less than well?
- Why do clients like doing business with them?
- What criticisms do naysayers make about them?
- Why don't former clients do business with them any longer?
- What can you learn from them?
- What can you do better than they do?
- What do you do that your competition can't copy or improve?
- What do you do that they can do better?
- Are they doing anything that could take business away from you?
- What trends or changes might create an opportunity for you?
- How do they price their services? How do your prices compare? If you charge more for the same services, can you demonstrate the added value you bring? If you charge less, can you demonstrate that you bring as much value as those charging more?
- How do they package their service to make it most attractive to clients? (With special offers, bonuses, guarantees, payment plans, longer service hours, more service providers?)
- What weaknesses do they have?
- Do their business practices present any opportunities for you?

Here's an example: Dave, an insurance agent, carried a line of auto insurance for teens. He advertised a deep discount on auto insurance for new drivers who got good grades in school. Unfortunately, all his competitors offer the same good-student discount. So parents asked him why they should have their teen insured with him rather than other agents in town.

One day he wrote his home phone number on the back of his business card, handed it to a prospective customer, and said: "Your child may be out one night, drunk, and be unable to drive. Give him this card with my home phone number on it. He can call me at any time of the day or night. If he should not be driving, I will pick him up and drive him home safely." No other agents in the area were willing to go this extra mile, giving Dave a unique selling offer he could use to close more sales.

How Do I Learn More About My Competition?

Some of the tools you can use to analyze your competition include:

- Yellow Pages
- Google and other search engines
- Libraries
- Websites
- Clients
- Trade magazines
- Networking
- Annual reports, press releases, sell sheets, and any other promotional materials
- Better Business Bureau
- Newspapers
- Suppliers
- Government filings (open to the public)
- Online forums
- Trade shows
- Association meetings
- Competitive intelligence research firms
- Market research studies

Trade Shows in Your Marketing Mix

Early in my career, I worked as advertising manager for Koch Engineering, a company that made mixers and other equipment for the chemical process industry. I liked a lot of things about the job, but one thing I didn't like was managing our trade show exhibits. Unpacking and setting up the booth was a pain, and staffing the booth was boring—a lot of standing around waiting and hoping real prospects would come into the exhibit and express interest in our products.

But I did learn a few tricks about trade show exhibiting during my tenure with Koch (I also handled trade shows for Westinghouse in an earlier job) that I'd like to pass on to you:

1. Nothing attracts people to your booth like action, whether it's motion, an activity, a model, or a demonstration. At Koch Engineering, we sold "internals"—devices that went into the innards of chemical plants where they helped liquids react. We made a crude working model of a miniature chemical plant (about the size of a large desk) out of transparent Plexiglas, filled it with our internals, and ran water through it so visitors could see the liquid drip, bubble, and mist. It was a fantastic attention getter—and more than that, it gave a live demonstration of how our products worked, which was exactly what our audience, chemical engineers, came to see (but rarely got at other booths in the show, which featured mainly enlarged color photos of chemical plants and exhibitor products).

2. ROI—return on investment—is critical. Yet most companies spend thousands of dollars on trade shows without measuring ROI to see if it's all worthwhile. A common reason for companies to continue to exhibit at major shows is, If we drop out this year, people will notice we are not there. Another is, If we drop out this year, we will lose our seniority and our preferential booth location at future shows. Neither is a valid reason for spending time and money on a trade show. The only reason you should be at a show is that you think the business you will write—at the show if they permit it, or with follow-ups to show leads after—will more than pay back the cost of exhibiting (including booth space, travel and lodging, and exhibit design and production).

3. Surveys repeatedly confirm that the number-one reason your prospects come to industry trade shows is to see new products. So make sure your newest products (or at least the new upgrades and versions of old products) take center stage in your display. Use the word "new" prominently in booth graphics.

4. As you know if you visit trade shows, they can be dull and boring. Anything you can do to liven up your exhibit will draw a crowd. Example: To promote a new weapons system for a tank code-named The Gunfighter, Westinghouse hired a real-life gunfighter—a professional cowboy whose specialty was quick-draw shooting—as booth entertainment. As the gunfighter demonstrated how to rapidly pull a gun from its holster and accurately hit the target, he talked about how our weapons systems could do the same thing for a tank (using a script we had given him). It was the hit of the show, and every important buyer we wanted to reach came to the booth to see him.

In another trade show (and remember, this was the sexist 70s, way before political correctness became politically correct), we wanted to demonstrate a new Aqualung—an underwater breathing device designed for military applications. We had a gigantic clear Plexiglas tank built, and hired an attractive, fit female model to demonstrate the product while swimming about in the tank—wearing a bathing suit, of course.

Other things that work well at trade shows (even though you may find them hokey):

- **Giveaways** of free gifts such as key chains, luggage tags, squeeze balls, or Frisbees.
- **"Put your business card into the fishbowl"** for a drawing to win a bigger prize.
- **Free food**—typically candy and popcorn.
- **Short marketing videos** shown on an endless loop. People get hypnotized and drawn in by anything on a TV screen.
- **Sleight-of-hand magicians** and similar live entertainment in the booth.
- **Product demonstrations.**

One more tip: When people approach your booth, give them space. Don't pounce on them like a hungry piranha attacking a cow swimming in the river. Let them look around a bit. Once they are comfortably inside your space, it's appropriate to say something. Don't say, "Is there anything I can help you with?" or "Do you have any questions?" The prospect will say no to deflect you and quickly vacate your booth area. Instead, say, "What brings you to the [name of show] today?" The prospect's answer— e.g., "We need to find a way to control air quality in our office building"—will help you direct conversation toward any solutions you can offer.

Case Study...
Chiropractic Marketing Plans, Inc.

Using the listed resources, CMP found four chiropractic coaching businesses within its niche area. However, none emphasized marketing plans.

Analyzing Yellow Pages ads, card deck and newspaper ads, and other sources, CMP learned that these competitors' messages addressed the same desired outcomes for prospects—growing their practices. So they were indirect competitors, because, even though they didn't offer the same service, prospects could view them as a solution.

Three of the coaching services were new, whereas CMP had a successful four-year track record. The coaching was done over the telephone, whereas CMP worked one-on-one, in person, with clients to develop their plans. The in-person conversations created opportunities for more in-depth discussions and often led to growth approaches the owner had not considered.

So, clients saw value in the personal meetings. The disadvantage is that they were more time-consuming than telephone consultations. Still, if the meetings resulted in more satisfied clients, and those clients referred others, this would be an advantage and clients would perceive it as one.

The main advantage the competitors offered was a promise to help chiropractors implement change. This was a more costly alternative. CMP could appeal to those who believed they could carry out their own implementation once they had a plan. Another option would be to team with one of the coaches.

So, their main opportunity lay in serving those who wanted to do their own implementation. For those wanting full-service practice-building assistance, they could team with one or more coaches.

Action...

Write Your Description of the Competition

Use the table to identify strengths and weaknesses of both you and your competitors. Think back to the things you identified as important to your ideal client in the last step. How well are competitors addressing those issues? Do you see any gaps? Opportunities?

Feature	Your Business	Competitor 1	Competitor 2	Competitor 3	Competitor 4	Competitor 5
What service(s) do they offer?						
Primary focus						
Perceived advantage						
Message						
How do they position themselves?						
What do they do well?						
Strengths (other)						
Segments of your niche they ignore						

Things you can learn from them						
Things you do better than they do						
Things you do they can't copy or improve						
Things they do that can take business away from you						
How do they price their services?						
How do they package their service? (With special offers, bonuses, guarantees, payment plans, longer service hours, more service providers, etc.?)						
Weaknesses						
Opportunities for you						

Write a summary of what you found in analyzing your competitors. Where are the opportunities for you?

_____

_____

_____

_____

_____

_____

_____

Competition for the Information Marketer

Many people who contact me for marketing advice these days are entrepreneurs who want to get into the booming field of marketing information products on the internet. Perhaps the idea of selling information products on the internet has crossed your mind from time to time.

It does for GL, one of my subscribers. But she is hesitating about whether to even start. That's because GL is worried that there are already more than enough people hawking e-books, DVDs, and courses on the internet. "Isn't the internet already overcrowded with a million info marketers selling look-alike products on everything from dating to real estate?" GL asked me. "Aren't I getting into the game too late to carve out a piece of the internet profit pie for myself?"

It's a fair question. And the answer is: yes and no. Yes, GL may be getting into the game a little later than some of her peers. But so what? The old saying—better late than never—is true. And in fact, there is still a huge opportunity for GL—and you—to make your fortunes online.

Newbie internet marketers despair that there is too much competition on the web—and therefore no room for them. What they do not understand is that the information business is not competitive in the way most other businesses are.

For instance, a consumer shops and makes a decision to buy a certain model washing machine when her old machine breaks down—just as my wife did last year. If the consumer chooses your brand—or buys from your store—you have her money. And all the other washing machine manufacturers and retailers have lost the chance to sell to her for at least a decade. That's because she only needs one washing machine—and new machines typically last at least 10 years.

But the buying of information products is a bit different. It's more like the video game market than the appliance market. Kids just don't buy and play one video game: they buy game after game and never stop.

They are video game junkies. And they'll spend a small fortune feeding their "habit."

It's the same with buyers of how-to information products. Consumers of info products are information junkies. They buy many information products—including books ... e-books ... DVDs ... tele-seminars ... and e-courses—on their favorite topics. That means customers will buy your information *in addition to* your competition's info products—not instead of.

The first thing you should do if you are thinking of selling information products online about a particular topic is to Google that subject. If there is no one else selling information products on that topic, you have no competition. But that's actually a bad sign. Why? Because the fact that there is no one else doing it probably means others have tried and found no demand.

On the other hand, there are some topics that, when you Google them, it seems like there is an almost infinite number of sources for information on those topics ... and you despair of how you can ever break through the clutter.

The answer is to narrow your focus: find a niche within that broad topic—a subtopic that (a) people want to study and (b) about which there is a scarcity of good content. For instance, "make money on the internet" is an overcrowded topic—one I would not recommend you go into as a generalist today.

But there is still room for niche products centered around making money on the internet. For instance, I saw one product recently that told everything you need to know about marketing yourself and your product on Facebook. If you are an internet marketer, doesn't that sound like something you should learn?

Let's say you come up with a narrow niche topic that you don't think is overcrowded. Do some research to make sure internet users are searching for information on that topic. You can do this by checking keyword phrases related to that topic (e.g., marketing on Facebook)—and seeing how many people searched those keywords on Google this month. You can use one of the many keyword research and discovery tool like spacky.com or wordtracker.com to see whether there is an active interest in the topic among internet users.

Chapter 5

STRATEGIZE: POSITION YOUR BUSINESS

Let's summarize where we are now. We have a clear, powerful *vision* of where we intend to take our business. We've defined our *niche*, so we know whom we're focusing on. We've analyzed our *client* base and prospects to understand why and how they buy our services and how this benefits them. We've scrutinized the *competition* to learn how they position their businesses to gain trust and attention from prospects.

Now it's time to *position* our business to gain a "window in the minds" of prospects, define our goals for the next year, and begin building a *strategy* that will implement our vision.

Bull's-Eye: Position Your Business

As discussed in the previous chapter, a positioning statement tells your clients and prospects how you want to be perceived in the marketplace. It tells them the benefits of doing business with you and why the value you'll provide them is unique.

You'll use your positioning statement as the basis for all the messages you send your prospects about your business. It will be reflected in your website content, in every press release, in speeches you give, in articles you write, and even in your PowerPoint presentations. It's how you'll "brand" your business. It's what you'll be known for. However, just making a positioning statement means little if you don't integrate the unique value it identifies into every aspect of your business.

Here's how to develop your positioning statement:

1. Remind yourself of what's important to your prospects. What value or criteria do they use most to choose their vendor?
2. Review the comparisons you made between your business and your top competitors in **Chapter 4**.
3. Choose the one thing that makes you distinctive from your competitors that your prospects will value most.
4. Tell your prospects how this distinction will benefit them (also called your **unique selling proposition**, or **USP**).

FedEx's positioning statement, for instance, is "FedEx: When it absolutely, positively has to be there overnight." As a business owner whose ability to win contracts has from time to time depended on my bid absolutely, positively getting there overnight, I liked this positioning statement. Since the advent of e-mail, of course, FedEx has become much less critical to information workers, because our product (documents) can be transmitted instantly to customers over the internet at virtually no cost.

A general format for writing a positioning statement includes the following:

WE OFFER
[Your service type]
FOR *[Your ideal client type]*
THAT NEED/WANT TO *[The problem you solve
and why your solution is different]*

Here's CMP's positioning statement, as an example: "Action plans for the family chiropractic practice that wants growth without pain: because the right alignment with the right plan should never hurt."

The statement is simple, but it identifies the target (chiropractors) and what they do for them (create plans that help them grow). It speaks in language common to their targets, who specialize in relieving pain by realigning vertebrae. It also contains an implied promise: if you take the time to plan and align your actions, you will succeed. Further, it will be painless—an important promise because so many small business owners fear planning. Other chiropractic practice-building specialists, CMP's competitors, are not focusing on the planning or the alignment of actions aspect of growing a practice.

Now you try it. Remember, your positioning statement should focus on what you do, for whom you do it, and the unique benefit for your clients. Focus on just one promise.

Write your positioning statement:

_____

_____

_____

How to Build a Stronger USP

Here's a trick question: What's better: chopped liver or filet mignon? Most people answer "filet mignon." But that's the wrong answer. The correct answer is that filet mignon isn't better than chopped liver. Nor is chopped liver better than filet mignon.

If you picked "filet mignon," you should have said "I like filet mignon better" ... and not "filet mignon *is* better." One is not inherently superior to the other. It's a matter of taste: You like filet mignon. So to you, filet mignon is better. But I like chopped liver ... so to me, it's not.

So ... what does this have to do with your business and your positioning USP? Plenty!

Every business needs to have a unique selling proposition, or USP, a reason why customers should buy from you instead of from your competitors.

Do you know what the most common USP is—the one business owners give most frequently when customers ask why they should buy your product instead of the competition's? It is also, strangely enough, the absolute weakest USP you can have: It's "we're better."

Why is "we're better" such a weak and ineffective USP? Because better, you see, is nonspecific ... and it's difficult to prove. You say you're better. I say I'm better. It's difficult to prove ... and just saying it causes prospects to disbelieve you. Also, better is such a general term, that it has little meaning. Same thing with the overused "quality."

So how do you create a unique selling proposition that actually gets people to want to buy your product instead of the competition? There are many methods, but let me describe just three of them here.

> **You say you're better. I say I'm better. It's difficult to prove ... and just saying it causes prospects to disbelieve you.**

The first is to focus on a feature of your product—one that is different or unique, and that delivers an important benefit to the user. Example: Crispix cereal. The manufacturer didn't say it "tasted better." They said Crispix "stays crisp in milk" ... a benefit consumers wanted.

The second way to create a USP with selling power is to narrow the target market—that is, to focus on a specific market niche. For example, there are thousands of business consultants out there, all fighting for clients. But my old high school chum, Gary Gerber, is a consultant who doesn't fight for clients. He has all he can handle ... and potential clients waiting in line to hire him. Why? Because he is not just a business development consultant—Gary is a business development consultant specializing in eye doctors.

It doesn't hurt that, before becoming a business development consultant to eye doctors, he owned the largest and most successful optometry practice in New Jersey. If you were an eye doctor looking to build your practice, with whom who would you want to work—Gary or a consultant who says he can help you but has never worked with an eye doctor before?

The third way to create a winning USP is with branding. The branding approach usually takes a massive, costly advertising campaign that small businesses cannot afford, although there are ways to shortcut this, such as with a celebrity spokesperson. A great example is the George Foreman grill: This is clearly not the world's best grill, nor do I recall the manufacturer making this claim in its commercials. But it is the only grill you can buy with the name George Foreman on it.

So if you want a grill that cooks good food, you can get it lots of places. But if you want a "George Foreman" grill, you can only get it from the George Foreman grill company.

You can't confidently promote and sell yourself without a strong USP. After all, if you don't have the reason why someone should buy your product instead of competing products at the tip of your tongue ... how will you persuade prospects to buy what you're selling instead of going to your competitors?

A good place to start when formulating your USP is by asking yourself these questions:

- What is different about my product that delivers an important benefit to the user?
- Is there an industry, application, or other niche I can specialize in?
- Is there a way to brand my company or product in a unique fashion with appeal to consumers?

The more your positioning statement differentiates you from your competitors, the easier it will be for you to promote and sell your product. Conversely, a positioning statement that does not reflect a strong USP is a handicap in winning sales over competitors. After all, the USP is the reason prospects should buy from you instead of other vendors. If you cannot articulate why they should hire you instead of your competitor across the street, how can you answer the question, Why should we buy from you? when prospects ask it? And they ask it all the time.

Let's take a closer look at the idea of a USP and how to find one that powerfully differentiates you from your competitors while giving consumers a compelling reason to prefer your service, offer, or brand. Here are the three components of a successful USP:

Steps...

BEGIN HERE

1. **Each advertisement must make a proposition to the consumer.**

   Each advertisement must say to the reader: Buy this product, and you will get this specific benefit.

   So to begin with, there must be a compelling benefit. For instance, "The CryoQuad Quiet-Cool air conditioner reduces your summer electric bills by 25% while keeping your house cool and comfortable."

2. **The proposition must be one that the competition either cannot, or does not, offer.**

   It must be unique—either a uniqueness of brand or a claim not otherwise made in that particular field.

   This is the "unique" in unique selling proposition. You must clearly differentiate yourself from the competition. Example: The CryoQuad Quiet-Cool air conditioner features our patented energy-saving TwinStar freon pump that spreads the cool air evenly throughout the room versus other units that only cool the air in their immediate area.

3. **The proposition must be so strong that it can move the mass millions, i.e., pull over new customers to your product.**

   This means the unique proposition cannot be a trivial difference; it has to be something important, something the customer really cares about. Example: The energy savings you get by cooling your home with a CryoQuad Quiet-Cool can pay back the cost of the unit by the end of the summer if you get it now ... and save you hundreds of dollars more in energy costs over the lifetime of the unit.

To sum it all up, the USP says there are only three criteria for effective advertising:

1. **Does the ad project a proposition?**
2. **Is it unique?**
3. **Does it sell?**

The old ad campaigns for Wonder Bread are a classic example of a USP stated clearly, simply, and lucidly: Wonder Bread helps build strong bodies 12 ways. What's interesting is that if you associate your product with a strong USP in the consumer's mind, it's difficult for competitors to take it away from you. After all, could you imagine another brand of bread saying: We also build strong bodies 12 ways? Every time they said it, the buyer would think of Wonder Bread—and nothing else.

Here's another example: a software company sold an application development tool that computer programmers used to develop web-based applications. They needed a USP, but the applications built with their tool weren't really better than applications developed using other methods. But their tool saved time: tests showed that it took one-third the time to develop web applications using their software than other methods.

The company combined this with their money-back guarantee to come up with the following USP: Develop web-based applications three times faster or your money back! Does this meet our criteria for a strong USP? Yes:

1. It has a strong benefit: develop applications faster.
2. It is unique: they are the only application tool developer not merely claiming but promising (with a money back guarantee) to help the buyer develop applications three times faster.
3. Since programmers are always swamped and productivity is a major issue, a tool that helps them produce their work in one-third the time is a strong enough benefit to get them to try the product.

Do you already have a USP that you created and have been using prior to reading this book? Then make sure it meets all three guidelines:

> *Each advertisement must make a proposition to the consumer. Each advertisement must say to the reader:*
> *"Buy this product, and you will get this specific benefit."*

Strong USPs have a benefit, either direct or implied. Weak ones don't. State Farm's "Like a good neighbor, State Farm is there" has a benefit: if you have a problem and are insured by State Farm, they will review and pay your claim promptly, giving you the money you need sooner.

> *The proposition must be one that the competition either cannot, or does not, offer. It must be unique—either a uniqueness of brand or a claim not otherwise made in that particular field.*

Here's where the "unique" in unique selling proposition comes in. To differentiate yourself from the competition, it's not enough just to offer a benefit; you have to offer something that your competition either cannot or does not.

As the first chocolate to feature a hard shell coating, M&M achieved its unique positioning with "Melts in your mouth, not in your hand"—something only it could claim. Yes, other hard-coated candies followed. But by then, M&M already "owned" the position. What would these candies say? We *also* melt in your mouth, not in your hand?

Note that the claim does not have to be a unique feature your competition cannot offer; it can also be something your competition *does not* offer … "a claim not otherwise made" in that field. The classic example is the story in Claude Hopkins' *Scientific Advertising* of the ad campaign for a beer.

The ad agency copywriter noticed that the bottles were washed in live steam, and commented to the brewery master, who replied, "That's nothing; everyone does that." "But the beer-drinking public does not

know that!" countered the copywriter, who went on to write a successful campaign based on the idea "Beer so pure, the bottles are washed
in live steam!"

> *The proposition must be so strong that it can move the mass*
> *millions, i.e., pull over new customers to your product.*

A common mistake in promoting technology is to build some minor,
insignificant difference into the product and then tell the prospect that
only you have it. Since the difference is in fact minor and insignificant,
the market's reaction is likely to be: Yes, you have it. But who cares?

Make sure the difference you are promoting ... the "unique" in
unique selling proposition ... delivers a benefit or performance difference that the reader really cares about—one that creates a significant
advantage over other products in the category.

For instance, a copywriter touring a piano factory noticed that a
metal bar was installed in each piano. The factory foreman explained,
"Wood warps over time. The bar stabilizes the piano to prevent warp-
ing. That way, this piano will sound the same 20 years from now the
same as it does the day it is first played." That unique feature, the
stabilizer bar, coupled with a powerful benefit—preservation of sound
quality—became the basis for a successful ad campaign.

Offer Proof for Your Positioning Statement and USP

Nowhere do some marketers think less like consumers than when it
comes to proving the claims they make in their promotions. And there
is nothing that sticks out like a sore thumb more to the reader than an
outrageous claim that is not backed by one iota of proof.

For instance, I was writing a sales letter to sell subscriptions to a
magazine covering the defense industry. When I asked the subscription manager what made their product different she said:

"We aren't usually the first to report on a story ... TV, newspapers,
and the internet all beat us to the punch, since we are a monthly ...
but we analyze and interpret the news so our readers can make better

decisions based on what the facts really mean."

"That's fascinating," I replied, scribbling eagerly. "Can you give me an example?" Her reply: dead silence. Imagine: the USP was that this publication analyzed military events more accurately and in depth so military people could make better strategic decisions based on this analysis. *And no one at the publication could give me a single example to prove it!*

Finally, we did get a story—just one story—and it was a beauty: One of their editors analyzed a photo from a battle that had been published in the newspapers, and was able to correctly identify the model of tank in the picture—something the newspapers had gotten wrong.

Why did this matter? Turns out, it was an inferior model of tank. The editor explained: "By knowing that a 'cheap' tank had been deployed, we knew the enemy did not consider this a strategically important area ... or else he would have deployed premium tanks there. The enemy's strategy was revealed, and our readers could plan accordingly."

Can you imagine claiming that you could help a general plan victory in battle—or help people get better jobs—or help companies reduce their insurance costs—without producing even one good story or example to prove it? Sounds absurd, but dozens of promotions I see do just that!

Often, these promotions have no proof for their major claim because the marketer has never bothered to collect it. And if you're going to aggressively market your product through the mail or online, collecting such proof from satisfied customers should be your #1 priority.

People are skeptical that your product can deliver the benefits you promise because everyone is promising those same benefits. When you show how a particular feature delivers the benefit, it becomes more believable to the prospect. For instance, if you tell the buyer your computer system never loses data, he thinks, "How can that be?" But when you describe the feature—that there is a built-in tape drive and that the system automatically backs up to that tape drive daily—then your claim becomes more believable.

Fortunately, it's easy to come up with strong proof for product claims, though it will involve a bit of time and effort up front. First, figure out the claim you want to prove or demonstrate, e.g., XYZ is the only prod-uct that does [benefit] for [audience] by [method]." Then, send a simple letter or form to your customers. Ask them: "Has our product [XYZ] ever helped you achieve [benefit] by [method]? We are looking for success stories from customers like you. If you have a success story to share with us, please summarize it below and send this form back to us. If we use your story in our marketing, you will receive a free [name of gift]."

Offer a nice gift in the $50 to $100 price range to anyone whose story you use. This will be sufficient to motivate people to take the time to think about your product and relay the story of how it helped them. Do this until you have, ideally, 12 really good stories you can use. Then use them as follows:

1. In an ad, lead-generating letter, or e-mail, you can build your copy around a single compelling story.
2. In a traditional direct mail package with a multi-page letter, pack your letter with proof. Tell three of the stories in detail, and three to six more in summary.
3. Reprint the 12 as group of testimonials on a single printed sheet you mail in your sales literature or post on your website.

The bottom line: The more thoroughly you demonstrate how your product delivers a particular benefit in a unique fashion, and prove it has done so through user success stories, the more effective your marketing will be.

Testimonials: The Quickest and Most Powerful Way to Support Your USP

Using testimonials—quotations from satisfied customers and clients—is one of the simplest and easiest ways to add instant credibility to your promotions.

Always use real testimonials instead of made-up ones. Even the most skilled copywriter can rarely make up a testimonial that can match the sincerity and credibility of genuine words of praise from a real customer or client.

Prefer specific, detailed testimonials to general or superlative testimonials. On receiving a letter of praise from a customer, our initial reaction is to read the letter and find the single sentence that directly praises our company or our product. With a blue pencil, we extract the words we think are kindest about us, producing a bland bit of puffery such as: "We are very pleased with your product."

Actually, most testimonials would be stronger if we included more of the specific, detailed comments our client has made about how our product or service helped him. After all, the prospects we are trying to sell to may have problems similar to the one our current customer solved using our product. If we let Mr. Customer tell Ms. Prospect how our company came to his rescue, he'll be helping us make the sale.

Don't try to polish the customer's words so it sounds like professional ad copy. Testimonials are usually much more convincing when they are not edited for style. Use full attribution. We've all opened direct mail packages that contained testimonials from "J.B. in Arizona" or "Jim S., Self-Made Millionaire." To increase the believability for your testimonials, attribute each quotation. Include the person's name, city and state, and (if a business customer) their job title and company.

There are two basic ways to present testimonials: You can group them in one area of your brochure or ad, or you can scatter them throughout the copy. A third alternative is to combine these techniques, having many testimonials in a box or buck slip and a smattering of other testimonials throughout the rest of your copy.

I've seen both approaches work well, and the success of the presentation depends, in part, on the skill of the writer and the specific nature of the piece. But, all else being equal, I prefer the first approach: to group all your testimonials and present them as a single block of copy. This can be done in a box, on a separate page, or on a separate sheet.

My feeling is that when the prospect reads a half dozen or so testimonials, one right after another, they have more impact and power than when the testimonials are separated and scattered throughout the piece.

Finally, get the customer's permission to reprint his words before including his testimonial in your marketing campaign. Send a letter quoting the lines you want to reprint. Ask permission to include them in ads, direct mail, brochures, and other materials used to promote your firm. This way, you can use the testimonials again and again.

Describe What You Want to Accomplish This Year

Now that you've staked out your position with a strong USP, how do you become that company to your prospects? And how long will it take to brand you as the company in your position statement? It starts now. Go back to your vision for your business, and think of where you want to be three years from now. Write a list of what you want to accomplish. Be specific about revenues, earnings, the clients you have, services you offer, employees, locations, and anything major that will help define your goals for the next three years.

Ask yourself where you need to be one year from now to accomplish these goals. How will your business be different one year from now? What are your goals for the next year?

A goal is a statement of a result you want to achieve. *Goals* have been defined as ends toward which efforts are directed. Goals tell us what we need to spend our today time on if we're going to accomplish what we say we intend to accomplish by our deadline. Your goals should further your vision.

A goal has several attributes, commonly referred to as SMART:

- **S**pecific
- **M**easurable
- **A**ction-oriented
- **R**ealistic—Make your goals big (shoot for the moon) but reachable to create excitement and a challenge
- **T**ime-bound—Give them a deadline

And if they're going to be met successfully, goals are almost always *written*. The very act of writing a goal sends a set of instructions to our subconscious, releasing it to go to work on accomplishing the goal for us.

Research tells us that those who set goals increase their motivation to achieve, are more self-confident, and are more likely to eliminate habits that hold them back. Pretty strong reasons for wanting to set goals.

So what are your goals for your business this year?

Case Study...

Chiropractic Marketing Plans, Inc.

CMP has one main goal for this year: increase revenues 33%—from $150,000 to $200,000.

Currently, CMP averages 29 clients per year throughout Southern California, with a growth of two to three new clients each month. Perez charges $5,000 to create a plan for a new client and $500 to review the plan in subsequent years. The company has a retention rate of 35%; these clients pay CMP to review their plans every year.

Your Business at a Glance: The Capabilities Brochure

In the pre-internet era, businesses did not have websites to tell prospects all about the company and its services. Therefore, all businesses created what was called a "capabilities brochure" summarizing the business, including its position, mission, vision, capabilities, products, services, benefits, USP, and advantages.

Even in the internet era, it may be a good idea to create such a brochure. You don't have to actually print it; you can post it in HTML or as a PDF on your website. But going through the exercise can help both you and your prospects get a clearer picture of your business and what it offers.

However, I do recommend that you create a print version. When you get an inquiry, you can immediately e-mail a PDF of the brochure or a link to the HTML brochure to the prospect so their questions are answered instantly. However, people tend to forget what is on an HTML website after they click away, and many won't print or save your PDF. Therefore, a good strategy is to put a print version of the same brochure in the snail mail at the same time. A few days after your phone conversation, the brochure arrives on the prospect's desk, reinforcing your message and reminding her of what you offer.

You can use the form shown in **Figure 5-1** to plan and create an effective capabilities brochure.

Figure 5-1. Literature specification sheet

1. Objectives of the brochure (check all that are appropriate):
- [ ] Provide product information to customers
- [ ] Educate new prospects
- [ ] Build corporate image
- [ ] Establish credibility of your organization or product
- [ ] Sell the product directly through the mail
- [ ] Help salespeople get appointments
- [ ] Help salespeople make presentations
- [ ] Help close the sale
- [ ] Support dealers, distributors, agents, and sales reps
- [ ] Add value to the product
- [ ] Enhance the effectiveness of direct mail promotions
- [ ] Leave behind with customers as a reminder
- [ ] Respond to inquiries
- [ ] Hand out at trade shows, fairs, conventions
- [ ] Display at point of purchase
- [ ] Serve as reference material for employees, vendors, the press, investors
- [ ] Disseminate news
- [ ] Announce new products and product improvements
- [ ] Highlight new applications for existing products
- [ ] Train and educate new employees
- [ ] Recruit employees
- [ ] Provide useful information to the public
- [ ] Answer the prospect's questions

☐ Generate business leads
☐ Qualify your company to be on a customer's approved vendor list
☐ Other (describe):

2. The type of literature needed (check one):

☐ Annual report
☐ Booklet
☐ Brochure
☐ Case history
☐ Catalog
☐ Circular
☐ Data sheet
☐ Flier
☐ Invoice stuffer
☐ Newsletter
☐ Poster
☐ Other (describe):

3. Topic

a. What is the subject matter of the brochure? (Describe the product, service, program, or organization being promoted.)
b. What is the theme or central message (if any)?

4. Content

a. Is there an outline of the main points and secondary points that must be included in the brochure and the order in which they should be presented?
b. Is the outline thorough and complete? Does it cover all points?
c. What is the source of this information? Have you provided the copywriter with the necessary background documents?
d. What facts are missing? What additional research (if any) is required?

5. Audience

a. Geographic location
b. Income level
c. Family status (Married? Single? Divorced or widowed? Children?)
d. Industry
e. Job title/function
f. Education
g. Politics
h. Religion/ethnic background
i. Age
j. Concerns (reasons why they might be interested in your

product or service or organization)
   k. Buying habits/purchasing authority
   l. General description of the target audience (in your own words)

6. Sales appeals
   a. What is the key sales appeal of the product?
   b. What are the supporting or secondary sales points?

7. Image
What image do you want your literature to convey to the reader?

8. Sales cycles
How does the brochure fit into your sales cycle? Check all that apply:
- ☐ Generate leads
- ☐ Answer initial inquiries
- ☐ Provide more detailed information to qualified buyers
- ☐ Establish confidence in the company and its products
- ☐ Provide detailed product information
- ☐ Answer questions frequently asked by prospects
- ☐ Reinforce sales message for prospect ready to buy
- ☐ Support salespeople during presentation
- ☐ Close the sale
- ☐ Other (describe):

9. Competition
What images and sales appeals do competitors' brochures stress?

Competitor	Image	Key Sales Appeal
_____	_____	_____
_____	_____	_____
_____	_____	_____

10. Format
   a. Approximate number of words
   b. Number of color photos
   c. Number of black-and-white photos
   d. Number and types of illustrations and other visuals (describe)
   e. Number of pages
   f. Page Size:
      ☐ 8½ x 11" ☐ 7 x 10" ☐ 6 x 9" ☐ 5½ x 8½" ☐ 4 x 9" ☐ Other
   g. Method of folding or binding
   h. Number of colors used in printing:
      ☐ 1-color ☐ 2-color ☐ 4-color process ☐ Other
   i. Type of paper (weight, finish, texture, color)

11. Budget

Use the worksheet below to estimate costs.

Task	Cost
Copywriting	_____
Photography	_____
Illustration	_____
Design and layout	_____
Typesetting	_____
Mechanicals (paste-up)	_____
Printing	_____
TOTAL	$ _____
Number of copies to be printed	_____
Cost per copy	$ _____

12. Schedule

How long will it take to produce?

Task	Number of days to complete
Copy	_____
Copy review	_____
Copy rewrite	_____
Design	_____
Design review	_____
Design revision	_____
Typesetting	_____
Photography and illustration	_____
Mechanicals	_____
Delays, mistakes	_____
TOTAL	_____

Don't Forget the Yellow Pages

Here's one Yellow Pages advertising technique that may work for you. Ironically, I learned it from my dad. I say "ironically" because my father had no interest in advertising or marketing. His expertise was insurance—he was an insurance agent, and he knew the technical aspects of insurance inside and out.

He ran a one-man insurance agency in downtown Paterson using his own name: F.W. 'Dave' Bly Insurance. F stood for Fabian, which he hated. Most people who hate their first names go by their middle names, but the W in F.W. stood for Wolf, which he equally despised. He told me that when he was a kid and he met new kids who asked him his name, he would mumble, "Fabe," short for Fabian, and hope they couldn't hear him clearly. One day, another kid replied, "Did you say 'Dave'?" "Yeah," said Dad, and from then on he went by Dave—for the rest of his life.

His major means of advertising his agency was an ad in the Yellow Pages. As a small independent agent in the rather downscale city of Paterson, NJ, where we lived, Dave Bly couldn't afford the biggest ad on the page; other, larger agencies could always outspend him.

So one year he decided to try something new.

In his small display ad (I can't remember the exact size), he made the headline "INSURANCE" in large, bold type. Underneath, he had two columns of bullets—a laundry list of all the types of items he could insure for you. In the list, he focused on items that people frequently asked about but that other insurance agents did not actively pursue: snowmobiles, I recall, was one of the items in his bullet list. Underneath he had the name of his agency and the phone number.

Well, that bullet list ad was far more successful than any other ad he ever ran, getting him at least one phone call a day from people needing insurance. They told him they were trying to find insurance for a particular item (like a snowmobile), so they opened the Yellow Pages to insurance, and his ad was the *only* insurance ad in the book with the word snowmobiles in it. Of course they called him first.

Other agents, of course, could also insure snowmobiles and the other items in his bullet list.

But if you want to buy a kiwi fruit, which ad will you respond to—the one that says fruits or the one that says kiwis?

Consumer Reports used this technique in a recent mailing to sell subscriptions to their magazine.

The magazine rates consumer products in a wide variety of categories for quality. Many people, however, think of *Consumer Reports* primarily for their new car ratings. A recent mailing used an oversized envelope. Printed on the outer envelope were the names of dozens of consumer products covered by *Consumer*

Reports—everything from loudspeakers and soy milk to treadmills and microwave ovens. There were literally dozens of products listed.

Dad never made a fortune as an insurance agent, but he lifted himself out of poverty (he was a child during the Great Depression) and supported a family of four, and his Yellow Pages ads always paid back their cost many times over. Having won a Purple Heart in World War II, he was a patriotic American, but not a rabid capitalist—he felt insurance costs were getting out of control and that the only way to make it affordable to the masses would eventually be to socialize medical insurance. He was also old-fashioned: computers came into insurance offices, but by then, he was near the end of his career and refused to learn them, never even touching a PC. He left the PC work to his assistant, who by that time was my mother—who now has a computer at home.

Action...

Write Your Goals for Your Business for the Next Year

Try to focus on no more than three to five major goals. You don't want to be overwhelmed.

_____

_____

_____

_____

_____

_____

_____

_____

_____

Describe Your Strategy for Achieving Your Goals

Next, lay out your strategy, or approach, to meeting your goals. You want a strategy that will bring in a steady stream of clients. Make sure your strategy includes the following details:

- Your target or ideal client.
- Your target's primary problem that makes them an ideal client for you.
- Your solution.
- Your proof that you can do what you say you can do.
- How you can differentiate your business in ways that matter to your ideal client.
- The best places to promote your solutions to your ideal client (this is information you identified when doing your client profiles).
- Your message, which needs to interest your ideal client in learning more about your services (whatever you say, it has to be all about them, not about you).
- How much you plan to spend to implement your strategy (expect to spend 2–4 percent of expected sales on your marketing budget).

Remember, CMP has one main goal for this year: increase revenues from $150,000 to $200,000. To reach its goal, CMP's strategy is to:

- Become well known for writing marketing plans for chiropractors, because no one else in its coverage area is doing this.
- Dominate their field within a 10-mile radius of its office.
- Add 15 net new clients.
- Increase its client retention rate to 40 percent.
- Earn income by matching clients with coaches to implement the plan.
- Add a midyear review service to increase the frequency of usage of its services.

Case Study...

Strategy Analysis

CMP's ideal clients are chiropractic practices that focus on services to families. Most have a well defined service to offer families non-prescription, noninvasive treatment for pain and other common health ailments. This is appealing to families who want to stay away from taking medications or giving them to their children whenever feasible.

The problem is, CMP's clients need to educate families about the benefits they can offer, and they don't know how to organize their efforts to accomplish this. Competitors offer telephone coaching services to assist the practices, but they skip or skimp on a well-thought-out marketing plan before jumping into implementation. Many practices are dissatisfied with their coaching results; without a plan to focus their efforts, they never really see the growth they expect.

CMP's solution is to focus practices first on a plan, then work with coaches who can lead them through the steps of implementation. CMP has successfully completed action plans for more than 150 clients. Although the feedback from clients has been positive, CMP hasn't tracked its clients' results as carefully as it should. One of its implementation tactics will be to institute a tracking program.

Chiropractors in their target market obtain information from four main sources: *Chiropractic Economics* magazine, the California Chiropractic Association, ChiroWeb online, and *American Chiropractor* magazine. Word of mouth is also strong among local chiropractors.

CMP's message is "Grow with a Plan for All Seasons," because family practice can remain a profitable niche even during economic downturns for those chiropractors who have a plan for growth. CMP will lean heavily on low-cost tactics, such as e-mail and article marketing, speaking, networking, and direct mail to reach its target market. Perez estimates expenditures of $5,000 in marketing costs for the year.

Write Your Strategy for Meeting Your One-Year Goals

_____

_____

_____

_____

_____

_____

_____

_____

_____

_____

_____

_____

_____

_____

_____

_____

_____

_____

_____

_____

_____

Chapter 6
BUILD OUT YOUR PRODUCT LINE

To be in business, you have to have a product or service to sell. But to *succeed* in business, you have to have multiple products and services to sell. If you only have one product or service, your business is almost certainly not a viable business, but more like a hobby or avocation: you may make sales and get paid, but you will never grow very large or become very profitable, much less make a living. Exceptions? Of course.

Lifetime Customer Value (LCV) Revisited

Why do you need additional products and services to sell people who have bought one product from you? Recall our earlier discussion of lifetime customer value (LCV). LCV is the amount of money a customer spends with you over the period for which she remains an active customer of yours. Say you have a grocery store. The average customer spends $100 a week or $5,000 a year. If the average customer stays with you five years before moving away or switching to another grocery store (because it's closer, has a better selection, offers lower prices, or the customer grows unhappy with your store), that customer has an LCV of $25,000.

The money in most businesses in not made in the initial sale, but in repeat orders from the same customers. The first product you buy from a company is known as the front end product or front end sale. The process of getting a new customer to make their first purchase from you is called acquisition, because you are acquiring that person as a customer. The additional products the person buys from you once they become a customer are known as the back end. And for most businesses, the back-end is where the profit is made.

Why is the back-end so much more profitable than the front-end? One obvious reason is that the front-end is a one-time sale, where the back-end is many sales over an extended period. In addition, the back-end sales are easier and less costly to make.

Customer acquisition through a front-end product offer is challenging and expensive. You are attempting to get a stranger who has never done business with you before to do so, and it takes a lot of sales and marketing effort to overcome their skepticism and get them to risk spending money with you. It is much easier and less costly to sell additional back-end offers to existing customers than to acquire new customers. On average, making a sales to an existing customer is five times less expensive than making a first sale to a new customer.

Therefore, you need a back-end of additional products and services to sell customers who have already purchased their first product or service (for the rest of this discussion, let's use the word product to mean product or service, and product line to mean line of products or menu of services offered).

One of my clients is a large marketer of self-help audio learning systems, sold mainly through direct mail. This client does not make a profit on the first order he gets from you when you become a customer. However, he has a back end of dozens of other programs, which he aggressively sells to existing customers to turn each customer from a loss into a handsome profit.

Cost of Customer Acquisition vs. LCV

Often, marketers will sell the first product at cost or even at a loss to gain as many new customers as they can as swiftly as they can because they know from the LCV the enormous value of each new customer they add to their list.

A product sold at or below cost to acquire new customers is called a loss leader. An example is the mail order magazine ads you see from coin and precious metals companies offering silver or gold coins "at cost." The company makes no money selling the coin at cost, but it does gain a new customer, which has enormous LCV.

> In the service sector, "buying the business" is a derogatory term used to describe the practice of "lowballing" (under-bidding) to win a contract.

In the service sector, "buying the business" is a derogatory term used to describe the practice of lowballing (under bidding) to win a contract. Those who frown on the practice say that if you lowball to get the first contract, you can never charge that client your regular rates—and you have just acquired a highly unprofitable piece of business. But there are two flaws in that thinking.

First, it's simply not true. Just call your low-ball price quotation an introductory special. Make clear that the product or service usually costs more—and will in the future—but that customers can get a great deal when they act now.

Second, buying the business often turns out to be a smart move—especially when you take into account the LCV of the customer you are trying to win.

To determine how much they can afford to spend to get a new customer, many service firms make the mistake of basing that figure on the average size of the first order.

Therefore, if the front-end product or service is $500, they won't spend anywhere near that to acquire the customer, for fear of operating at break-even or even a loss. If they want to double their money on the promotion, the most they'll spend to make the sale is $250.

But smarter marketers know that the amount of money you can spend to acquire a new customer should be based on LCV, not just the revenue from the first order. For instance, if the average unit of sale is $500, the average number of purchases per year is two, and the average customer remains a customer for five years, the lifetime customer value is $500 x 2 x 5 = $5,000.

Based on the average lifetime value, you can see where it would in fact be worth spending $500 to acquire a new customer. The business owner who understands lifetime customer value as it relates to customer acquisition has a tremendous advantage: He is willing to spend more to acquire new business, because he knows its true value.

> **Send each prospect a personal letter telling them they already have an account with you—and that it contains $300 they can use at any time this year.**

Based on an understanding of this principle, marketing guru Jay Abraham frequently advises clients to give salespeople a 100 percent commission on the first sale, instead of their regular 10 percent or whatever. The 100 percent commission gives the salesperson much greater incentive to go out and get new business. And the company gets its usual profit on all the repeat sales. Only the first order is 100 percent commission.

A company selling books to corporate librarians asked me to devise a marketing campaign to get new corporate accounts to start ordering books from it. I asked the owner what he would be willing to spend to get a new account. He said about $300. Forget advertising, I advised. Just open up an account for every company you want as a customer— and put $300 in it! Send each prospect a personal letter telling them they already have an account with you—and that it contains $300 they can use at any time this year. Instead of a sales or marketing campaign, my client gave the money he would have spent to generate leads and make sales calls directly to his key prospects, so they could try the service at no cost. It worked like a charm!

Today online trading services use the same tactic. They send you a letter telling you they have opened an account for you with $75 or so in it. You get the money when you do your first trade.

Need to stimulate business? Calculate lifetime customer value, decide what percentage of that amount you want to spend on acquiring new customers (10 percent is a common figure), and basically just give potential customers the money in exchange for trying your product or service.

Creating New Products

When designing products for your line, keep in mind that a product is not just a physical object made of such-and-such material, weighing so many pounds, and having particular dimensions and colors. A product is much more than that. Marketing writers are fond of noting that consumers don't actually buy products—they buy the benefits the product offers them.

Books are a good example. If you think of a book as a physical product, it is essentially paper and ink. The value of the paper and ink that went into manufacturing this book is much less than the price you paid for it. But you are paying not for paper and ink, or words on a page, or even the information and ideas. You are paying for the value of that information and those ideas, which is their ability to help you improve your business and make you more money. How-to writer Jerry Buchanan once said, "When you sell a man a how-to book, you are not selling him paper and ink; you are selling him a whole new life."

So in planning a new product, you of course have to determine what features to build into it. But you should also think about how these features can deliver the benefits your buyers want. Other aspects of a physical product (i.e., merchandise) you must consider in the design stage include models available, sizes, colors, options, accessories, weight, dimensions, and packaging.

Virtually all products are defined not just by their physical features, but also by the company and service behind them. What kind of warranty or guarantee will you offer? What kind of service and support comes with the product? Does the seller or the consumer pay for shipping and handling? The worksheet in **Figure 6-1** can help make sure you cover all the important points when bringing out a new product.

Figure 6.1. Product definition and description ranking sheet
Fill in the correct information for your product or service.

1   = weak; don't stress this aspect in promotion
5   = strong; stress in advertising
NA = not applicable
Name of product:_____

Category	Comment	Ranking
Packaging		
Description		
Benefits	1.	
	2.	
	3.	
Features	1.	
	2.	
	3.	
Perceived value		
Models, colors, & special features available		
Options/accessories		
Warranty/guarantee policy		
Price		
Ease and method of purchase		
Method of delivery or		
Distribution		
Speed of delivery		
Service and support		
Reputation of the seller		

Features and Benefits

You've heard it said before that when advertising your product, you should stress benefits instead of features. But it's a little more complicated than that. To be accurate, product attributes aren't just divided into one of two categories—features or benefits. Experienced marketers know that there are four levels of production description. These are *features, advantages, benefits*, and *ultimate benefits*, the hierarchy of which is illustrated in the FAB (feature/advantage/benefit) Pyramid **(Figure 6-2)**. The more you understand and use all four levels in your advertising—not only benefits—the more effective your advertising will be.

The lowest level of the pyramid is features. A feature is what a product is or has—the literal physical description of the product. For instance, one feature of a tire is that it is steel-belted. Another might be that it is double-ply. Although experts tell you to "stress benefits, not features," a feature can be a selling point even if the prospect doesn't know what it is! For instance, when I was a kid, brochures for the new car models coming out would boast about "rack and pinion" steering. The car makers hyped it so much, everyone asked dealers, "Does the car have rack and pinion steering?" Yet I bet not one buyer in a hundred really knew what rack and pinion steering was. I still don't, to this day.

Next, there are advantages. An advantage is a feature your product has that competitive products do not have. You know that to get consumers interested in your product, you must show how your product is different than competing products. The advantage is that point of differentiation. For our tire example, it might be that our tire is the only steel-belted radial tire that is also double-ply.

Moving up the hierarchy, the next level of product description is benefits. A benefit is what the product does and how the consumer comes out ahead as a result of this capability.

Going back to our tire example, again, the benefit of a steel-belted double-ply radial might be that the tire grips the road tighter and increases safety while driving, or that it can drive for another 100 miles after being punctured before you have to change it.

At the top of the product description hierarchy are what I call ultimate benefits. An ultimate benefit is "the benefit of the benefit"—the most important way in which the product improves the user's life. Ultimate benefits include saving money, saving time, making money, success, self-esteem, security, safety, joy, pleasure, and happiness. Remember the TV commercial for the tire showing a baby sitting in the middle of a tire? That's an example of showing the ultimate benefit: simply put, it's If you buy our tires, you won't kill your baby.

In business-to-business marketing, a benefit might be "reduces

Figure 6-2. The FAB Pyramid

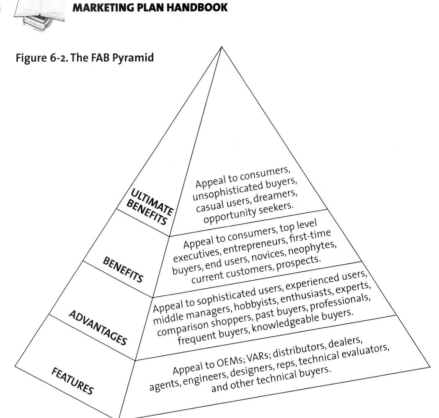

Appeal to consumers, unsophisticated buyers, casual users, dreamers, opportunity seekers.

Appeal to consumers, top level executives, entrepreneurs, first-time buyers, end users, novices, neophytes, current customers, prospects.

Appeal to sophisticated users, experienced users, middle managers, hobbyists, enthusiasts, experts, comparison shoppers, past buyers, professionals, frequent buyers, knowledgeable buyers.

Appeal to OEMs; VARs; distributors, dealers, agents, engineers, designers, reps, technical evaluators, and other technical buyers.

ULTIMATE BENEFITS

BENEFITS

ADVANTAGES

FEATURES

energy costs." The ultimate benefit is often "makes you a hero within your company," meaning that if you achieve the benefit by purchasing the product, senior management will look on you favorably.

To make your copy richer, deeper, and more credible, don't only talk about benefits. Instead, use all four levels of product description: features, advantages, benefits, and ultimate benefits.

Why not just focus on the highest level—ultimate benefits? Well, although ultimate benefits are powerful, they are too generic and not specific enough. To give your advertising specificity, state the specific benefit (e.g., "reduces energy costs 50%") that delivers the ultimate benefit ("you'll be the hero of your company").

To differentiate your product from others that deliver a similar benefit, you need to explain the advantages—how your product is different from or better than the competition. Lots of marketing seminars urge you to stress benefits instead of features, but you should use both.

Reason: Prospects are skeptical that your product can deliver the benefits you promise, because everyone is promising those same benefits. When you show how a particular feature delivers the benefit, it becomes more believable to the prospect. For instance, if you tell the buyer your computer system never loses data, he thinks, "How can that be?" But when you describe the feature—that there is a built-in tape drive and the system automatically backs up to that tape drive daily—then your claim becomes more believable.

Turn Product Flaws Into Selling Points

No matter how well you plan your product or how meticulously you fabricate it, no product is perfect. Your product will have strengths that competitors do not have, but also be weaker in other areas. The trick is to highlight your strengths, of course. But rather than hide your weaknesses, which almost never works (your competitors will be sure to point them out for you), you can actually gain leverage by turning them into an advantage or selling point.

Example: Legendary adman James Webb Young, who started selling fruit by mail around the same time that Harry & David did, tells the story of an apple-growing season where he was nearly ruined. Violent hail storms bombarded his apple trees with ice pellets, causing bruising and pock marks.

He feared massive complaints and returns if he shipped the bruised fruit to his mail order apple buyers. On the other hand, if he didn't ship the damaged apples, he would have to refund all the orders, and his mail order business would be ruined.

However, the apples were damaged only cosmetically. The hail had pockmarked the skin, but this did not affect the flavor or freshness. Young went ahead and filled his orders with the pockmarked apples, and in each box shipped, enclosed a preprinted card that read as follows (I am paraphrasing):

> *Note the pockmarks on some of these apples. This is proof that they are grown at a high mountain altitude, where the same extreme cold that causes sudden hailstorms also firms the flesh and increases the natural sugars, making the apples even sweeter.*

According to Young, not a single order was returned. In fact, when orders came in for next year, many order forms had handwritten notes that said, "Pockmarked apples if available; otherwise, the regular kind."

Young's story proves what experienced marketers know: Often, by being truthful about your weaknesses and flaws, you can gain substantial credibility with your buyer, increasing loyalty, sales, and customer satisfaction.

> **Often, by being truthful about your weaknesses and flaws, you can gain substantial credibility with your buyer.**

Years ago, an industrial pump manufacturer, Blackmer, used the "show your warts" strategy with great success.

As a chemical engineer, I can tell you that not all pumps perform equally in all applications. Instead of hiding this fact, Blackmer made it a primary advertising claim.

Their trade ads showed a Yellow Pages page ripped out of an industrial buying guide, full of listings for pump manufacturers, including Blackmer; the Blackmer name was circled in pen. The headline of the ad read, There are only certain times you should call Blackmer for a pump. Know when? Body copy explained (again, I am paraphrasing), "In many applications, Blackmer performs no better or worse than any pumps, and so we are not a particularly advantageous choice.

But, the ad went on, for certain applications (viscous fluids, fluids containing abrasives, and a few other situations) Blackmer was proven to outperform all other pumps, and was the logical brand of choice. Blackmer closed the ad by offering a free technical manual proving the claim. The late Jim Alexander, founder of Alexander Marketing in Grand Rapids, Michigan created this campaign and told me it worked extremely well.

Another example: James DiGeorgia of 21st Century Publishing was initially concerned that putting disclaimers and fine print required by regulatory bodies would depress response to his e-mail marketing campaigns promoting his stock market and options trading newsletters.

Instead of hiding the disclaimers in fine print, however, he put them in the same size type as the rest of the e-mail promotion. He found, to

his surprise, that being up front about the warnings and cautions actually increased response! The conclusion: Instead of hiding a weakness,
be forthright about it.

How to use this technique: Pick one weakness of your product or
company. Talk about it frankly in your marketing. Show why either (a)
the weakness is not really important or (b) how you have designed
your product or service to either overcome, solve, or compensate for
the weakness.

Buying Motivations: The FCB Grid

Which elements of the FAB Pyramid—features, advantages, benefits,
or ultimate benefits—should you stress in your marketing communications? Which will most effectively motivate the consumer to buy
your product?

One way to determine this is with a tool called the FCB Grid (see
Figure 6-3), named after the ad agency that developed it: Foote, Cone,
& Belding. The grid helps pinpoint consum-
er buying motivation based on two factors.

The first factor is involvement: Is this a
purchase decision you devote much thought
and time to? In the figure, you can see that
the purchase of a new camera is a high-
involvement activity. You might go to several
stores to research it, review digital camera
pricing online, ask friends for recommendations, and so on. An example of a low-
involvement purchase decision would be buying paper for your laser
printer: whenever you run out, you go to Staples and buy more reams
of whatever they happen to have in stock.

> **Which elements of
> the FAB Pyramid—
> features, advantages,
> benefits, or ultimate
> benefits—should you
> stress in your marketing
> communications?**

The second factor determining consumer buying motivation is emotion: Is the buying decision based on cold logic (thinking), or is there a
strong emotional component to it (feeling)? An example of a feeling-
based purchase decision might be when a bride-to-be shops for her
wedding gown, while a thinking-based purchase decision might be
buying blank CDs for your PC.

Determining the degree of involvement and the degree of emotion places the purchase decision in one of four quadrants on the FCB grid, which in turn tells us what elements of FAB to stress in our marketing copy. For a high-involvement, feeling-based purchase like buying a new car, we would be in the upper right quadrant. That would mean marketing copy should stress ultimate benefits and benefits, plus some advantages, with features being a minor part of the copy.

On the other hand, a digital camera would be a high-involvement purchase, but thinking-based, so it would fall in the upper left quadrant. Here our marketing messages would stress features and advantages (e.g., a larger memory for storing more images), but also hit benefits (e.g., you can store more photos of your grandkids to show off to friends).

Figure 6-3. The FCB grid

	EMOTION	
	Think	Feel
High Involvement	• 35mm camera	• Destination vacations • Family car • Eyeglasses Alaska • vacations • Perfume
Low Involvement	Clothes pins •	• Popsicle

Pricing

What should you charge for your product? That too is a component of product development. Are we looking to create a low-priced item we can sell as a loss leader to bring in new customers (a *loss leader* is a low-priced product, often sold at or below cost, to acquire customers)? Or are we looking to create a high-priced product to sell to our existing customers on back end?

As a business owner and marketing advisor, I have a prejudice against the discount business model or any business operating on a tiny profit margin. I agree with internet marketing expert Yanik Silver, who says, "You must charge a premium price so you have a large margin to provide an extraordinary value and experience." To me, it's more rewarding to command a higher price, charge premium fees, and get paid very well for what I sell. Especially if you are in a service business, competing on price means you work harder to earn less. Who wants that?

But in a competitive world where many other businesses seemingly offer products and services similar to yours, how do you command a premium price? There are five factors you can control or exploit to enable you to charge a higher price than your competitors in virtually any field—and have more customers than you can handle waiting in line, cash in hand, to pay it:

> **There are five factors you can control or exploit to enable you to charge a higher price than your competitors in virtually any field.**

1. Supply and demand

According to simple economics, the greater the demand for something and the more limited the supply, the more the seller can charge and get paid for it. Since you're not OPEC, you probably can't control the supply of your product or service available to your customers. So what you have to do is create an overwhelming demand for you, your product, or your service. Perhaps the easiest way to do this is to position yourself as the preeminent expert or authority in your field. If people view you as *the* guru in property taxes, hazardous waste cleanup, or whatever your field is, they will come to you first, knocking each other over to hire you instead of your lesser-known competitors.

2. Market niche

As a rule of thumb, the narrower your market niche, the more you can charge. Specialists can always charge more than generalists. If you are a marketing consultant handling any small business clients you can get, you have lots of competition and great difficulty commanding a premium fee. On the other hand, if you specialize in the marketing of accounting practices, accountants will pay a premium to get your advice because it applies to their own situation.

3. Value

If your competitors all sell audio cassette albums with six cassettes for $79, and you want to charge $300 for an album with six cassettes on similar topics, why should the buyer pay it? One way to differentiate your product is to add value. In the above example, you could include a CD-ROM with software programs of use to the buyer and related to the topic of the audio cassette album (e.g., if the album is about time management, the CD-ROM could contain a personal day planner). The material cost is only a dollar or so per CD-ROM, but the perceived value of software is easily $100 or more, enabling you to charge a premium price for your package. And that's the trick: to add extras that have high perceived value but don't cost you much.

> **"Free" is one of the most powerful words in sales.**

"Free" is one of the most powerful words in sales. In the late 70s, when I took my first marketing job in Baltimore with Westinghouse, we had a secret marketing weapon we referred to as the "junk cabinet." It was filled with all sorts of advertising specialties—favorites were golf balls and golf tees—all imprinted with the Westinghouse "circle W" logo. My first thought was, "Who would want this cheap crap?" Turns out, everybody.

Whenever a salesman was giving a high-ranking general a tour of the plant (our biggest customer was the military), he'd invariably ask us for golf balls and tees. I was fascinated to see that the presentation of these items—which only cost a few bucks—thrilled the customers to no end.

Once, we sent Westinghouse customers a single cufflink with an invitation promising they would get the matching link when they came to our exhibit at a major trade show. We barely had enough room in our giant booth to accommodate those who came—almost all asking for their free cufflink.

Fast forward a decade or so. I am at a meeting of a marketing club. A man who works for a pharmaceutical advertising agency tells me an amazing story. His agency regularly used direct mail to invite medical doctors to symposia on diseases treated by his clients' products.

To see whether he could increase attendance, he decided to offer a free pocket diary to doctors accepting the invitation. Cost of the item: a buck or so. The result? In an A/B split test, mailings offering the free pocket diary outpulled mailings without the free gift offer 6 to 1!

The conclusion: people love to get free stuff. By offering a small free gift to your prospects, you can significantly boost the response to your marketing efforts at minimal cost. If your prospect is an information seeker, then a free information premium—a booklet, a white paper, a special report—can perform well.

If your prospect is not a reader, then use a merchandise premium. The possibilities are almost limitless: coffee mugs, golf balls, T-shirts, golf caps, tape measures, mini-tool sets, pens, key chains, luggage tags, and calculators, just for starters. The cost of the premium depends on what you can afford to spend to acquire a new customer. But in most instances, we're looking for premiums that cost $10 or less.

> **You can improve your response rates by offering a premium that has a perceived value much higher than its cost.**

You can improve your response rates by offering a premium that has a perceived value much higher than its cost. A CD-ROM can be a great premium, because the value of its content, whether images, video, audio, or software, can be extremely high (software sells from $19 to $500 or more per program), but the duplication cost is a few bucks apiece. You can also offer this on a 1GB flash drive, which has a high perceived value, can include a lot of content, and can be reused by the client.

On the other hand, a publisher did a promo that bombed when it offered a deck of playing cards with a famous editor's photo on them.

Perceived value is low: everybody knows a deck of cards costs about 99 cents in CVS.

Advertising Age magazine had spectacular success offering a personalized coffee mug with the subscriber's name on it. What made it work was that the name was incorporated into a headline, "Bob Bly Wins Marketing Genius Award"—that was laser-printed on a facsimile of the front page of an *Ad Age* issue on the mug.

In addition to high perceived value, look for premiums that are unique. The Sovereign Society, a newsletter on offshore investing, had great success offering new subscribers an unusual premium: their own Swiss bank account.

I advise every direct marketer to offer a premium, whether you're generating sales leads or selling a mail order product. Offering a gift with inquiry or order adds perceived value to your offer. It also allows you to legitimately work the word free into your headline or envelope teaser—and in doing so increase your chances of catching the prospect's attention and getting an inquiry or order.

> **I advise every direct marketer to offer a premium, whether you're generating sales leads or selling a mail order product.**

Years ago, when I was selling business writing seminars to Fortune 500 corporations, I charged $3,500 a day. Many other trainers charged anywhere from $1,500 to $2,500 a day for similar programs. To add value so I could get my fee, I offered unlimited free 30-day follow up, where the attendees could call me for advice and ask questions without charge for a full month after the seminar date. While this follow-up service had a high perceived value (I described it as a $1,000 value in my sales literature), and training directors loved the idea, in reality very few seminar attendees took advantage, so it cost me almost nothing to deliver.

4. Return on investment

If you design your product or service so that it generates a large ROI that is easy to see and measure, it will be easier to sell at the price you want to get. As consultant Jay Abraham says, "Will you give me a quarter if I give you a dollar?" If you can prove a 4:1 ROI from your product or service, it's like selling a dollar for a quarter—an easy sale to make. For example, $200 for a high-tech thermostat may seem like a lot of money, but not if the manufacturer can prove that installing the thermostat will save the homeowner $300 to $1,000 a year in heating and air conditioning costs.

5. Customers' concern about whether they will be satisfied with your product.

You can control this by offering a money-back guarantee. Guarantees overcome sales resistance. If you guarantee that customers will be happy and that you will refund their money if they are not, they will be more willing to pay your price, no matter what it is.

We all know that a strong money back guarantee is a powerful weapon for overcoming buyer resistance and boosting your sales. But you can run into problems when your guarantee has flaws. The best guarantees are:

- **Fair**
- **Long-term**
- **Generous**
- **Unconditional**

When any of these four elements is missing, sales are likely to suffer. For example, many of my clients are newsletter and magazine publishers. A number of these publishers offer lifetime guarantees. They permit the subscriber to cancel at any time and receive a pro-rated refund on "unmailed issues."

But if you offer both a bill-me option as well as payment with order—as I often come across—such a lifetime guarantee actually gives the customer an incentive NOT to pay up front. Think about it: Say the customer checks the bill-me option for a monthly magazine, gets his first issue, and then writes "cancel" on his invoice. The publisher doesn't send him a bill for one issue, nor does the publisher ask for the magazine back. So the customer gets a free issue.

But if the customer pays in advance, then cancels after the first issue, he gets a refund for 11/12th of the subscription price (the 11 unmailed issues) and therefore ends up paying for the issue received. Why should the bill-me customer get a free issue, but not the payment-with-order customer? It isn't fair and doesn't make sense, considering a cash-with-order customer is more desirable than a bill-me order. Solution: Offer a full money back guarantee within the first 30 days, then prorated refund thereafter.

Another frequent guarantee problem is wording that says you will get your money back "if you return the product in salable condition." Well, the customer doesn't have any control over the UPS man who brings the box to your door. Your guarantee implies that if the product is damaged in transit on its way from the customer to you, the buyer doesn't get a refund. That would make me hesitate to order from you.

I was in a video game store where a clerk refused to refund a woman's money. She was returning a game her son had gotten as a gift one day late after the 30-day guarantee period expired.

I interfered and explained to the clerk what he was doing was wrong. The woman got her money back, and I got a dirty look from the clerk.

Remember, you benefit enormously from offering a guarantee, because it gets more people to trust you and buy from you. But the customer benefits, too: He gets a chance to try the product risk-free.

Most people won't take unfair advantage of your guarantee. If you sell a quality product, accurately described in your marketing, at a price that's fair in relationship to its value, your return rate will be low—probably less than 5 percent.

That still means one of 20 will ask for a refund. Give them back their money promptly and with good cheer. Few things will cause more customer dissatisfaction and ruin your reputation faster than being difficult, adversarial, and uncooperative when people believe what you said in your guarantee and take you up on it. Don't get angry with these folks. Returning the product is their right—and part of your cost of doing business.

And there you have it. Increase demand for your product or service, target a vertical market niche, add value, generate a good ROI, and guarantee satisfaction, and customers will gladly pay your price, even if it's 50–100 percent or more above what your competitors charge.

Selling High-Priced Products

One risk of charging high prices is that it may induce "sticker shock" in your prospects when you tell them the cost. "Sticker shock" refers to a price so high that when you reveal it to the customer, he or she is flabbergasted and immediately protests that "your price is too high" or "I could never afford this." If your customers experience sticker shock, it means you have not convinced them that the price of the product is a drop in the bucket compared to the value of the product. Even if you've done a good job of communicating value, the prospect may experience sticker shock if the price is extremely high or beyond their means.

Sticker shock reduces your chances of closing the sale: If customers gasp when they learn the price, they're probably not ready to pay it. If, as a marketer or salesperson, you can head off sticker shock before it happens, your odds of closing the sale increase tremendously. But how do you prevent sticker shock?

> **Sticker shock reduces your chances of closing the sale: If customers gasp when they learn the price, they're probably not ready to pay it.**

One way is to show the customer products in your line with higher prices before showing him the product you want him to buy. In his book *Influence*, Robert Cialdini describes how this is done in a retail setting. Say you want to sell $100 sweaters in your store, but are afraid your customers will faint at the price. You put a table in the aisle near the front door and place three stacks of sweaters on it. As a customer walks into the room, she sees the first stack. All of the sweaters in this pile cost $300. "What a rip-off!" she thinks. "No way would I pay that." Then she examines the second pile, which contains $200 sweaters. "Phew," she thinks. "That's a little better." She continues to go down the table until she comes to the third stack—your $100 sweaters. By that time, she is so relieved that a sweater won't cost her $300 or even $200 that the $100 you are asking seems like an incredible bargain.

Breaking the price into monthly installments is another effective way to minimize sticker shock. For instance, the Franklin Mint was selling a collectible chess set. The pieces were each hand-painted pewter miniatures of Civil War figures, sent to you one per month. For these hand-painted collectible figurines, the price was only $17.50. Seems like a bargain for a collectible item, right? But if you multiply $17.50 times the number of pieces (32), the entire chess set cost a hefty $560 (the board was yours free once you bought all 32 pieces). If the Mint's ad had said, "Civil War Chess Set—$560," how many do you think they'd have sold? Not many, right?

Another way to avoid sticker shock is to present the price at the beginning and get any price objections out of the way up front. Most advertising for expensive products builds desire and perceived value, then reveals the price once the customer is sold. An opposite approach is to state the price up front and use the exclusivity of a big number to weed out non prospects. This is illustrated by an old cartoon showing a salesman in an auto showroom saying to a customer, "If you have to ask how much it costs, you can't afford one."

For example, say you are selling a financial service for $2,500 a year. That's on the high end for financial advisories, so you risk inducing sticker shock when you introduce the price at the end of the copy. The solution is to introduce the price at the beginning. The idea is to deal with it up front and get it out of the way, e.g., "This service is for serious investors only. It costs $2,500 a year. If that price scares you, this is not for you." If the prospect continues reading your promotion after seeing that on page one, you know that they are willing to pay the high price provided they perceive high value.

An element of exclusivity and snob appeal is at work here: the more you tell someone they do not qualify, the more they will insist they do and want your offer. The classic example is Hank Burnett's famous letter for the Admiral Bird Society's fundraising expedition. The second paragraph states: "It will cost you $10,000 and about 26 days of your time. Frankly, you will endure some discomfort, and may even face some danger." Once readers have seen the price and decided to continue reading, the possibility of sticker shock is eliminated because they already know what the product costs. Surprise is eliminated, and sticker shock is all about surprise.

Pricing Strategies for Selling Services

A common strategy for small businesses is to undercut the competition by charging lower prices. For instance, if every other graphic designer you know charges $100 an hour, you figure you'll steal business away from them by charging only $50 an hour. Charging low prices, or lowballing, as it is commonly known, is a terrible pricing strategy for service businesses—for several reasons.

First, your perception that a lower price makes you more attractive to clients is not universally true. Yes, some clients are price buyers, and your low price will draw them in like moths attracted to a flame. But there are many other clients who do not buy based on price. These clients value other attributes—such as quality, reliability, speed, customer service, expertise, track record, and reputation—and are willing to pay a premium price to get them. In fact, your low price signals to many of these buyers that you do *not* deliver those desirable attributes ... and that you and your services are inferior. The low price actually turns these prospects off!

This is not theory, by the way. Direct marketers know that, in split tests of price, the low price for a product or service often loses and is less profitable than higher prices, which generate more orders and sales. Low prices create a perception in the client's mind of low value. As John Ruskin, the 19th-century English critic, pointed out, "There is hardly anything in the world that someone cannot make a little worse and sell a little cheaper, and the people who consider price alone are that person's lawful prey."

Second, your low price attracts a less desirable clientele than a premium price, which attracts clients who value good work and don't mind paying for it. Price buyers are the least profitable clients to work for, and ironically, often the most demanding and difficult to please.

Third, in a service business, time is money. The less you charge, the less money you make—and the less profitable your business. Given the choice, wouldn't you rather work for $100 an hour instead of $50 an hour, or earn $200,000 a year instead of $50,000 a year?

If lowballing is a bad pricing strategy, where should your pricing fall in relation to your competition? Years ago, GD, a pricing expert, gave me the following rule of thumb for setting service fees: *Your price should fall in the middle of the top third.* So, if the lower third of service firms in your trade charge $50 to $100 an hour, the middle range charges $100 to $150, and the highest-paid charge $150 to $200, GD thinks you should aim for $175 an hour.

Why? Well, those competitors who charge in the lowest third are the lowballers. They figure they'll get customers by offering the lowest prices in town. As we've seen, that's not a good pricing strategy for service providers. The middle range isn't quite as bad: it can make you a decent living and win you some good clients. But if a low price creates a perception of low quality, a middle price can create a perception of mediocrity. Is that how you want to be seen in your marketplace? So, given that, you should charge somewhere in the top third. In the example given above, GD would say to charge $175 per hour.

Why not go all the way and charge the highest price—$200 an hour? Because at that price level, your fee becomes a huge concern to your clients. It stretches their finances to the limit, and they begin to feel like you're trying to take them for every penny. By backing off the top of the price range a little, you can still command a premium price, but remove price as the foremost concern in the client's mind.

Sell a Lifestyle, Not a Product

MM, a client of mine in the business education field complained to me recently that many copywriters whose work he critiqued seemed to focus on the obvious benefits of the product—and missed the subtler benefits.

"People, especially as the years pass, don't just care about becoming a millionaire or making six figures," he said.

What they are after most, said MM, is a certain kind of lifestyle, and living that life on their own terms. Money for them is mostly a means to that end.

I am convinced he is right, and marketers who simplistically trumpet "get rich" in their ads are not reaching their prospects on a deeper and more powerful level.

I saw this principle in action in a series of TV commercials for ITT Tech, an institute offering career training for adults.

In the old days, these career training ads implied, within the limits of the law, that if you took their program, you'd make a lot of money.

One of my clients in this field back then ran an ad featuring a student standing proudly next to his new Jaguar.

What the copy failed to mention is that he bought the Jaguar with money he won in a personal injury suit after he was injured in an auto accident, not with money he earned as a result of his training.

Anyway, the new ITT Tech ads feature interviews with students who graduated their training and are now gainfully employed. But they don't talk about money.

One of the men talks about how proud his kids are to see him put on a suit and tie and go to work every day (presumably, he had a blue collar job or was unemployed beforehand).

Another graduate whose company sent him on several business trips overseas talked about how he loved to travel, try new foods, see different cultures, and meet new people on the job.

He said nothing about money. His mother also spoke in the commercial, saying how proud she was of her son.

I have coined a name for this type of marketing. I call it "lifestyle promotion."

A lifestyle promotion works like this: you figure out the lifestyle your target prospects would like to have. Then you write the promotion to show how your product helps them achieve this lifestyle.

Lifestyle promotions can be written for almost any product and any market. But I find lifestyle promotions work best with "lifestyle products."

A lifestyle product is a product "reverse engineered." You start with the lifestyle desired by your market. Then design a product that delivers this lifestyle to the buyer.

A good example is that odd exercise machine you see advertised claiming that it can get you fit in only four minutes a day. The machine looks something like Santa's sleigh. It costs $14,615. And the company has been selling them since 1990.

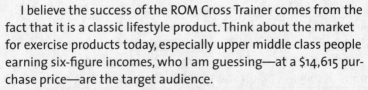

I believe the success of the ROM Cross Trainer comes from the fact that it is a classic lifestyle product. Think about the market for exercise products today, especially upper middle class people earning six-figure incomes, who I am guessing—at a $14,615 purchase price—are the target audience.

To begin with, they want to look and feel better, tone their body, and lose weight. Doctors and trainers tell them to exercise at least 20 to 30 minutes a day—and in some cases an hour a day—anywhere from three to seven days a week.

The most common complaint you hear: "I don't have time to exercise!" They don't have time to go to the Y and swim ... or to take a half hour walk ... or a half hour bike ride ... or to go to the gym two or three times a week. So the ROM 4-Minute Cross Trainer is the perfect fitness solution for their busy lifestyle: you can get all the exercise you need—a complete workout—in just four minutes a day!

Many upper-middle-class consumers have more money than time. Say your time as an executive or entrepreneur is worth $100 an hour. If the ROM Cross Trainer cuts their exercise time by five hours a week, it will pay for itself in less than eight months—making it a good investment instead of an expense.

Instead of taking two hours out of your day to train at the gym, your daily exercise routine is over in less than five minutes—without leaving your home or office.

Instead of going to work out at night, you can get home at a reasonable hour, and have dinner with your spouse and kids.

The reason I think lifestyle promotions work is that many times you are starting with the prospect, not with the product.

You write the promotion first, creating copy you are confident will sell like gangbusters.

Then you design a product to deliver on all the promises you incorporated into your copy.

This is a smarter way of marketing than the conventional method, which is to create a product and then to write copy that tries to convince people to buy it.

Action step: think about the lifestyle your target prospects desperately desire. Write a promotion that offers that life to them. Then create a product that delivers on the promises in your copy.

Chapter 7

ASSESS YOUR TACTICS

Now that you've mapped out your strategy for achieving your goals, it's time to identify the tactics you'll use to implement your strategy. First, you'll need to define your outcomes. What do you want your prospects and clients to do in response to your tactics? Next, what message do you need to give them to motivate them to take the actions you want? Only then can you decide which tactics are most likely to give you the desired responses.

In marketing, rarely will employing only one type of tactic result in everything you want to accomplish. So, first, evaluate the range of tactics available to you. Then, choose the best three to five, so you won't be overwhelmed. Last, you'll write a description of the tactics you've decided to use. Trial and error will let you identify which tactics are actually working for you.

Determine the Response You Want From Your Target

Tactics are the actions you take to implement your strategy. First, determine what response you're trying to generate from your target audience. For example, you might want them to:

◆ Go to your website to get more information.
◆ Fill out an online survey.
◆ Call to speak with a salesperson.
◆ Request that a salesperson call them.
◆ Attend a free webinar.
◆ Download a free white paper.
◆ Call for more information.
◆ Agree to a sales meeting or presentation.
◆ Attend a free seminar or workshop.
◆ Request a free product demo.
◆ Take a 30-day free trial of the product.
◆ Refer your services to others in your target market.
◆ Become an affiliate and sell your products and services.
◆ Buy the product with a credit card.

Decide What Message Will Stimulate This Behavior

Next, ask, What message(s), if properly conveyed and believed by my audience, will stimulate this behavior? Can I support the message with evidence? Do I have testimonials, case studies, thank-you letters or notes, or other support?

Here are some tips on crafting a message to generate the desired action on the part of the prospect:

Steps...

BEGIN HERE

1. The "so what" test.

After you write your copy, read it and ask whether it passes the "so what" test. Copywriter Joan Damico explains, "If after reviewing your copy, you think the target audience would just respond with 'so what,' then keep rewriting until they'll say something like, 'That's exactly what I'm looking for. How do I get it?'" Copywriter's agent Kevin Finn adds, "When copy is being critiqued, you should ask after each and every sentence, 'So what?' It's a technique that can assist in changing copy to be more powerful."

2. Use the key copy drivers.

Make sure your copy hits one of the key copy drivers as defined by Bob Hacker and Axel Andersson: fear, greed, guilt, exclusivity, anger, salvation, or flattery. "If your copy is not dripping with one or more of these, tear it up and start over," says Denny Hatch.

3. The drop-in-the-bucket technique.

"You have to show that the price you are asking for your product is a 'drop in the bucket' compared to the value it delivers," says copywriter Mike Pavlish. Fred Gleeck says this is a function of product quality, not just copywriting. "Produce a product that you could charge 10 times as much for," says Gleeck. "If you really have a product that is so much more valuable than the price you're charging, it becomes much easier to sell it hard."

4. Know your audience.

Understand your target market—their fears, needs, concerns, beliefs, attitudes, desires. "My way to be persuasive is to get in touch with the target group by inviting one or two to dinner for in-depth conversation," says Christian Boucke, a copywriter for Rentrop Verlag in Germany. "I also call 15 to 40 by phone to get a multitude of testimonials and facts, and go to meetings or exhibitions where I can find them to get a first impression of their typical characteristics. Ideally, I accompany some of them in their private lives for years. By this, I understand better their true underlying key motivations."

5. Write like people talk.

Use a conversational, natural style. "Write like you talk," says

Barnaby Kalan of Reliance Direct Marketing. "Speak in language that's simple and easy to understand. Write the way your prospects talk."

6. Be timely.

"Pay very close attention to goings-on in the news that you can and should link to," suggests Dan Kennedy in his *No B.S. Marketing E-Letter* (June 2002). "Jump on a timely topic and link to it in useful communication with present clients, in advertising for new clients, and in seeking media publicity."

7. Lead with your strongest point.

"When I review my writing, or especially others', I find they almost always leave the most potent point to the last line," says John Shoemaker. "So I simply move it to the first line. Instant improvement."

8. The tremendous whack theory.

"I employ Winston Churchill's 'tremendous whack' theory, which says that if you have an important point to make, don't try to be subtle or clever," says Richard Perry. "Use a pile driver. Hit the point once. Then come back and hit it again. Then hit it a third time—a tremendous whack."

9. Build credibility with your reader.

"In my experience, the #1 key to persuasion is this: communicate trust," says copywriter Steve Slaunwhite. "If you do this well, you at least have a chance at engaging and persuading the reader. If you don't do this well, however, no amount of fancy copywriting techniques will save you."

10. Don't use an "obvious lead."

Instead of writing your lead as if you are just starting to talk to the customer, says Bryan Honesty, write as if you were already engaged in a conversation with the customer and are just responding to her last statement. Examples: "You have the gift. You just don't know it yet." "You can't quit on your dreams now." "So why is it so hard for you to lose weight?"

Decide Which Marketing Tactics Will Best Support Your Strategy

Choose only those tactics that support your strategy and positioning statement. Remember, everything should work toward the same outcome. Tactics take many forms, and there are several types. **Table 7-1** highlights some of the most common tactics.

Table 7-1. Common tactics to support your strategy

Product/Service Tactics

- Add value-added features: alterations, overnight delivery, consultants to assist with specialized problems, installation, free repairs
- Introduce a new service to add depth
- Introduce new packages to fit specific markets and applications
- Create exclusive distribution channels
- Package services or products together to make the package more attractive
- Package a product with its accessories

Pricing Tactics

- Introductory pricing (low fees to capture new clients willing to try out your service at a low-risk fee)
- Image pricing (low prices to appeal to fee-conscious prospects; higher prices to appeal to value-conscious prospects)
- Tier pricing (quantity breaks)
- Bundling pricing (if you purchase this item also, you'll pay only $ for both items)
- Value-added pricing (free installation, free training, free e-book, etc.)
- Pay-one price (membership club fees that open up the entire inventory to members)
- Non-negotiating price (e.g., Saturn cars—lowest price guaranteed)
- Free shipping
- Taxes paid for client

Packaging Tactics

- Image (business cards, brochures, product package, IBM blues)
- Demonstrations (Lunch n' Learn sample trainings; food tables at Sam's Club and Costco; clothing sellers do fashion shows)

Table 7-1. Continued

- Displays (DVDs and reports with strong graphics-based covers)

Customer Service Tactics: "Have It Your Way"
- Technical service
- Flexible hours of operation
- Refund guarantees
- Guarantee your estimates (the maximum bill will be 110% of the estimate)
- Flexible delivery times
- No/low minimum order
- Installment payments
- Credit
- More methods to pay

Communication Tactics
- Website(s) for every service you offer
- Include your website URL in all your promotions
- Press releases
- Speaking to groups
- Write articles
- Direct mail
- Postcards
- Telephone calls
- Internet advertising
- Classified ads
- Yellow Pages
- Trade shows

- Viral, word of mouth, referrals
- Social media (YouTube, LinkedIn, MySpace)
- Business cards
- Networking
- Salespeople
- Joint ventures, cross promotions
- Affiliate programs
- Podcasting
- Webinars
- Blogs
- Teleseminars
- Seminars
- Workshops
- Lunch 'n' Learns
- Surveys
- Online courses
- Newsletters
- E-zines
- Gift certificates
- Contests
- Publicity events
- Signs
- Banners
- Pay-per-click (PPC)
- Google AdSense
- Sponsorship
- Sales letters
- Case studies
- E-mail marketing

Tactics That Reach Your Target Market

As you evaluate each tactic, ask yourself whether it will appeal to your target audience. Specifically, how will it help move forward your strategy for meeting your goals? **Table 7-3** shows a variety of marketing channels and their relative effectiveness when targeting narrow niche markets.

In fact, your very ability to conduct a targeted marketing campaign aimed at a narrow niche of buyers depends on whether there are media available that enable you to reach your potential prospects cost effectively.

Years ago, I worked with a company that sold business services to medical group practices. They targeted radiologists, and doctor lists are easy to get.

However, they discovered their target prospect was not the doctor, but the radiology practice's business manager. Their mailing list broker did not have a medical list targeting the radiology manager versus the radiologist.

They found out that, as is often the case, there was a small trade association serving the marketplace they wanted to reach. In this case, it was the Radiology Business Managers Association (RBMA). The RBMA had a monthly newsletter, and the company had good success with full-page ads in this publication, because they could target the radiology practices' business managers directly and write an ad to their needs and concerns.

Table 7-3. Degree of targeting by industry or specialization

Key: 1 = broadly targeted, horizontal media, aimed at mass market
      5 = highly focused, vertical media, aimed at narrow audience
           with specialized interests

Marketing Tool	Degree of Targeting
Newspaper advertising	1
Magazine advertising	4
Broadcast advertising	1
Cable TV advertising	4
Network radio	2
Spot (local) radio	3

Table 7-3. Continued

Billboards	1
Transit advertising	1
Catalogs	5
Direct mail	5
Postcard decks	4
Publicity and public relations	3
Telemarketing	4
Trade shows	4
Websites	3
Pay-per-click advertising	4
Banner advertising	3
Organic search	4
E-mail marketing	4
Social networking	2

Inbound vs. Outbound Marketing Tactics

Which works best—inbound or outbound marketing? By *inbound*, we mean prospects contact us out of the blue, as it were, because they somehow know about us or find us. *Outbound* marketing requires us to reach out and touch prospects proactively; e.g., with a postcard, tele-marketing call, e-mail, or magazine advertisement.

The question of which marketing—inbound or outbound—gener-ates the best leads can't really be answered authoritatively, because it's too broad. If we say the winner is "inbound," does that mean *every* type of inbound communication produces better leads than every type of outbound communication? Such is not the case.

A better way to approach the question is to examine each inbound and outbound marketing channel, and evaluate the quality of leads produced on a case-by-case basis. In Table 7.4, I list the major market-ing promotions used for lead generation, indicate which I consider in-bound versus outbound, and rate them on a scale of 1 to 5 (1 = low, 5 = high) for quality of leads and ROI (you may disagree with some of my choices and ratings). "Quality of leads" mainly measures whether the marketing communication attracts prospects who fit your customer profile, have a need for your product or service, and are predisposed to buy from you instead of your competitors.

ROI measures whether the leads turn into orders, generating revenues far in excess of the time and money spent to obtain them. Note: These ratings are my own and are to a degree subjective, based on three decades of experience; they are not based on statistically valid research.

The biggest controversy in lead generation is traffic generated by organic search. Some marketing writers erroneously tell us that organic search brings you the best leads. They reason that prospects would not be searching your keyword unless they were researching a product purchase. Therefore, organic search brings you good prospects—those in shopping mode.

> **The biggest controversy in lead generation is traffic generated by organic search.**

The quality of organic search leads depends, however, on the keywords being searched. We find that searches performed on broad keyword terms (e.g., limousines) attract visitors who are in the early stages of product research, and therefore not hot leads. When a search is performed on highly specific keywords (e.g., used Lincoln Continental limousine for sale in New York area), the prospect is most likely further along in the research process and closer to making a buying decision.

The reason I do not rate organic search leads higher in Table 7.4 is that, while these prospects may be predisposed to buying, they are in no way predisposed to buying from *you*. Indeed, the very fact that they are doing a Google search on a generic keyword probably means they have little brand loyalty. As a freelance copywriter, some of the worst leads I get are people searching for freelance copywriters on Google. These prospects often view copywriting as a commodity service and are likely to choose low price over experience and quality, as many internet shoppers do in numerous categories.

Conversely, the best leads service professionals get are typically people who call or e-mail us because they know us by reputation and may even be fans of our work. By far the most qualified leads I get are prospects who have read my books and articles, or heard me speak at a seminar, conference, or workshop.

Creating and disseminating content related to your product or industry is a proven technique for establishing yourself as a thought leader in your field or niche. Therefore, a prospect who is an avid reader or student of your writings and talks is predisposed to doing business with you, because they consider you a guru or expert.

I rated social networking a 4 in lead quality. Networking has always produced good leads, and social networks are basically networking moved online. So far, however, most B2B marketers have been unsuccessful in establishing hard metrics to measure social media ROI. Some argue that the ROI has to be high because social networking is virtually free. But they neglect ROTI, return on time invested. A survey by Michael Stelzner of White Paper Source found that experienced social media users spend two to four hours per day using it, which means an investment of up to half their work week.

> **Networking has always produced good leads, and social networks are basically networking moved online.**

Direct mail has long been considered the workhorse of lead-generating marketing communications. Ten years ago, I would have rated the lead quality a 4, because postal list selects enable narrow targeting, so you can mail only to prospects who fit your ideal customer's profile. I downgraded direct mail lead quality from a 4 to a 3, because lately, I find prospects with more urgent needs respond to electronic or phone marketing, while those whose need is not as immediate are more likely to mail back a business reply card requesting your catalog, brochure, or white paper.

ROI of direct mail–generated leads is a 4, because the leads you do close often make significant purchases in the multiple thousands of dollars. You can as a rule get from 10 to 25 percent or more of DM leads to take the next step in your buying cycle, whether agreeing to see your rep or sending you a purchase order. Direct mail that's working usually generates a positive and significant ROI, producing revenues many times greater than the campaign cost.

E-mail gets a 3 in lead quality. You can target the right prospects. But internet users have an element of distrust for e-mail, so a single e-mail isn't going to move prospects very far forward in the buying cycle.

ROI is a 5. That's because e-mail marketing is so cheap, even a few orders can give us an ROI equal to many multiples of the promotion cost. When you are renting opt-in e-lists, your cost per thousand can be $200 or more. E-mailing your own list, depending on what service you use, is a fraction of a cent per name.

I also gave public relations an ROI rating of 5 because the cost is so minimal that any business generated usually pays for the PR campaign many times over. Lead quality of PR is a 4, because people believe and trust editorial content more so than marketing copy.

> **Internet users have an element of distrust for e-mail, so a single e-mail isn't going to move prospects very far forward in the buying cycle.**

The point is that in the debate of outbound versus inbound marketing, you simply cannot make a sweeping generalization about which is better. You must evaluate the lead quality and ROI of each marketing channel individually. Table 7-4 is a starting point. But the quality and ROI for each medium can vary greatly from industry to industry, even from company to company. My recommendation: Test them, track results, do not repeat those that fail, and do more of the ones that do work.

The question boils down to not whether inbound versus outbound marketing is better, but which one is better for you. I do feel that, for small businesses selling technical, trade, and professional services as opposed to physical products, inbound offers the advantage of producing more qualified leads that are easier to close.

The Busy Doctor Syndrome

The most obvious type of outbound promotion for selling services is cold calling. Can cold calling work? Absolutely. I know for a fact that cold calling can work.

How? Because I've tested it. Not in my freelance copywriting. But for another venture—with pretty good results. Also, I personally know a number of people who are very successful with cold calling. Despite this, I dislike cold calling—and I rarely recommend it.

One drawback of cold calling is that it's labor-intensive. Unless you can outsource your cold calling—a viable option, by the way—then it requires you to spend hours dialing the phone. And for every hour you're cold calling, you're losing an hour of billable time.

A second drawback of cold calling is that it's not exactly fun. You are calling perfect strangers, interrupting busy people. If you get a 10 percent response, then for every 10 calls you make, nine people will reject you—right over the phone. Some will be nice about it. A few may be downright mean or abusive. And because you called them unsolicited, and interrupted whatever they were doing, you have to take it. Politely.

But in addition to these drawbacks, there are two bigger problems with cold calling and outbound marketing as business-building methods.

First, it violates the "busy doctor syndrome." This term was coined by the late Howard Shenson, who wrote many books on consulting and seminar promotion.

The busy doctor syndrome says that people would rather hire those they perceive as busy and successful. They do not want to hire those who seem desperate and in need of work.

Well, if you are sitting at a phone cold calling potential clients, how busy and successful do you think you seem to them? Not very, of course.

The second reason I dislike cold calling is that it puts you in a weak position for negotiating anything about your service—terms, scope of work, fee, payments, delivery dates. The reasons prospects agree to pay premium prices are:

1. They want or need what you are selling.
2. They perceive it as exclusive and difficult to get.
3. They believe that if they do not act quickly, it will be snapped up by others and therefore not available.

When you cold call, reasons #2 and #3 disappear. After all, when you call strangers on the telephone to sell them, then obviously you have a surplus of what you are selling.

The Silver Rule of Marketing

To avoid cold calling, I urge you to practice what I call the Silver Rule of marketing and selling. I call it the Silver Rule because I first heard it from my old friend, marketing consultant Pete Silver—although I don't think he actually called it the "Silver Rule."

Peter said:

> **It is better to get them (prospects) to come to you, than to have you go to THEM.**

Cold calling and other outbound marketing doesn't do this. So what type of marketing *does* follow the Silver Rule? Inbound marketing, including advertising, direct mail, e-newsletters, and e-mail marketing.

So do things like establishing yourself as a recognized expert by giving seminars and speeches or writing articles for publications read by your potential clients or writing books.

When you get an inquiry from someone who subscribes to your e-newsletter, you are negotiating the sale from a position of strength—because *they* came to *you*, rather than *you* calling *them*.

When someone approaches you at a conference, says they loved your speech, and asks about engaging your firm's services, you are in a position of strength.

After all, they see you as the expert ... and *they* came to *you*, rather than you going to them.

Why does Tom Peters get $30,000 or so to give a one-hour speech on business—and have more business than he can handle—while other speakers struggle to get bookings for $3,000 or less for a talk? It is largely because, as a best-selling author, he is perceived as an expert. And so prospects come to him, rather than him going to them.

He has become a wealthy entrepreneur simply by practicing the Silver Rule. And so can you.

Table 7.4. Marketing channel lead quality and ROI.

Key: 1 = low; 5 = high

Marketing channel	Category	Lead quality	ROI
Articles	Inbound	4	4
Blogs	Inbound	4	3
Books	Inbound	5	4
Direct mail	Outbound	3	4
E-mail marketing	Outbound	3	5
Organic search	Inbound	3	3
Pay-per-click advertising	Outbound*	4	3
PR	Inbound	4	5
Print advertising	Outbound	4	2
Seminars, live	Outbound	5	3
Social networking	Inbound	4	2
Telemarketing, inbound	Inbound	5	4
Telemarketing, outbound	Outbound	2	3
Tele-seminars	Outbound	4	4
Trade show exhibits	Outbound	2	2
Yellow Pages	Outbound	5	3
Webinars	Outbound	4	4
Websites	Inbound	3	3
White papers	Inbound	4	3

* I rank pay-per-click and other advertising as outbound because you are proactively placing advertisements to attract new business.

Choose the Best Three to Five Tactics to Begin

In the beginning of your marketing program, it's important to focus on just a few tactics to avoid being overwhelmed. This will allow you to study the results of each tactic and decide what is or isn't working for you. At the same time, it's important to try at least a few tactics. One tactic alone is rarely going to allow you to meet your goals. So start with a few tactics. Choose the three to five tactics that you think will most effectively implement your strategy and achieve your goals.

One of the least expensive and lowest-risk tactics is public relations. For a couple of hundred dollars, you can write a press release and send it to magazines and newspapers whose combined readership is in the hundreds of thousands or millions. **Figure 7-1** shows a press release I sent out to a couple of hundred business magazines during the recession of the early 1990s. We sold 3,500 copies of the booklet at $8 each. More important, feature articles about me and the booklet appeared in at least 18 publications, including a major business story in the *LA Times*. This publicity generated at least three consulting assignments and half a dozen paid speaking engagements. My total cost for the promotion, including list, printing, envelopes, and stamps: about $200.

Figure 7-1. Sample press release

From: Bob Bly, 174 Holland Avenue, New Milford, NJ 07646
CONTACT: Bob Bly (201) 385-1220
For immediate release

NEW BOOKLET REVEALS 14 PROVEN STRATEGIES FOR KEEPING BUSINESSES BOOMING IN A BUST RECOVERY

Dumont, NJ—While some companies struggle to survive in today's sluggish business environment, many are doing better than ever largely because they have mastered the proven but little known strategies of "recession marketing."

That's the opinion of Bob Bly, an independent marketing consultant and author of the just-published booklet, "Recession-Proof Business Strategies: 14 Winning Methods to Sell Any Product or Service in a Down Economy."

"Many businesspeople fear a recession or soft economy, because when the economy is weak, their clients and customers cut back on spending," says Bly. "To survive in such a marketplace, you need to develop recession marketing strategies that help you retain your current accounts and keep those customers buying. You also need to master marketing techniques that will win you new clients or customers to replace any business you may have lost because of the increased competition that is typical of a recession."

Among the recession-fighting business strategies Bly outlines in his new booklet:

◆ Reactivate dormant accounts. An easy way to get more business is to simply call past clients or customers—people you served at one time but are not actively working for now—to remind them of your existence. According to Bly, a properly scripted telephone call to a list of past buyers will generate approximately one order for every 10 calls.

◆ Quote reasonable, affordable fees and prices in competitive bid situations. While you need not reduce your rates or prices, in competitive bid situations you will win by bidding toward the low end or middle of your price range rather than at the high end. Bly says that during a recession, your bids should be 15 to 20 percent lower than you would normally charge to a healthy economy.

- ◆ Give your existing clients and customers a superior level of service. In a recession, Bly advises businesses to do everything they can to hold onto their existing clients or customers, their "bread-and-butter" accounts. "The best way to hold onto your clients or customers is to please them," says Bly, "and the best way to please them is through better customer service. Now is an ideal time to provide that little bit of extra service or courtesy that can mean the difference between dazzling the client or customer and merely satisfying them."

- ◆ Reactivate old leads. Most businesses give up on sales leads too early, says Bly. He cites a study from Thomas Publishing which found that although 80 percent of sales to businesses are made on the fifth call, only one out of 10 salespeople calls beyond three times. Concludes Bly: "You have probably not followed up on leads diligently enough, and the new business you need may already be right in your prospect files." He says repeated follow-up should convert 10 percent of prospects to buyers.

To receive a copy of Bly's booklet, "Recession-Proof Business Strategies," send $8 ($7 plus $1 shipping and handling) to: Bob Bly, 22 E. Quackenbush Avenue, Dumont, NJ 07629. Cash, money orders, and checks (payable to "Bob Bly") accepted. (Add $1 for Canadian orders.)

Bob Bly, an independent copywriter and consultant based in New Milford, NJ, specializes in business-to-business, high-tech, and direct response marketing. He is the author of 18 books, including *How to Promote Your Own Business* (New American Library) and *The Copywriter's Handbook* (Henry Holt). A frequent speaker and seminar leader, Mr. Bly speaks nationwide on the topic of how to market successfully in a recession or soft economy.

How do you choose just three to five tactics to start with? Here's how I like to do it when time and budget permit only three; this allocation may work for you too:

One of the three tactics is some kind of traditional direct marketing promotion, most often a sales letter with a reply card or a postcard sent by postal mail. The idea is to generate a steady flow of new business leads, and direct marketing does that well.

The second of the three tactics involves establishing the company's reputation as a thought leader in its industry or market. If it does not already have a white paper, I often recommend that first, so we have something to offer people as an incentive to reply to our direct marketing tactics. If the company already has a white paper, I often suggest that a person from the company—often the owner or product designer—write an article for an industry journal or other publication read by the target audience.

The third tactic is online marketing, It could be a revamp of its website to make it sell and convert traffic more effectively. Or it might be optimizing the existing site for the search engines. Or, it could be redoing the site to increase e-mail address capture rate, allowing the company to build a large and profitable opt-in e-list.

Keyword Due Diligence

Before you optimize your website or buy pay-per-click (PPC) traffic, you should perform "keyword due diligence." That means you must check to see that internet users are actually searching for information on your product or topic using the same keywords you assume they would use.

When I tell this to people, they often pooh-pooh it. "It's not necessary for us to do keyword research," they tell me. "We know our industry; we know our products; and we know what words they would search on."

To which I say: Oh, really?

With the internet, there is no need to guess at which keywords are the right ones. There are software tools that can tell you exactly how many Google or Overture/Yahoo! searches were performed on your keywords this month. Often, the keywords used most often are not the ones you picked. In addition, small variations in keywords can make a big difference in results.

For instance, I need to optimize a website for people looking to buy and maintain aquariums, theaquariumdetective.com. It seems obvious that the keyword to optimize the home page for would be "aquarium," right? And when I used spacky.com to check, sure enough there were 823,000 searches on the term "aquarium" on Google this month.

But, there were 11.1 million searches on Google this month on the term "aquariums," which is the plural of aquarium and has an extra "s" at the end. This result tells me that I should optimize the home page copy on the word "aquariums" and not "aquarium." I would never have known this had I not done my due diligence and checked the actual search volumes myself.

My favorite keyword due diligence tool is spacky.com. It's free, and when you enter a keyword, it shows the monthly search volumes for that term on Google, Overture/Yahoo!, and Microsoft Network. In addition, spacky.com displays a long list of related terms and their search volumes, so you can choose the keywords that are searched most frequently.

Of what use is keyword due diligence? There are at least three online marketing activities that can benefit from keyword research and discovery.

The first, as already noted, is search engine optimization. Each page on the website should be optimized for at least one keyword relating to its topic. This should be the keyword that gets the most search activity.

The second online marketing activity related to keyword due diligence is pay-per-click advertising. Even a good PPC ad will generate mediocre results if you bid on the wrong keywords.

The third keyword-related online marketing activity is determining the feasibility of new products.

Example: you decide to write and sell an e-book on how to set up your first aquarium. You think fish keeping is a very popular hobby, but you aren't sure. But even if you were sure that fish keeping is popular, that doesn't mean the book will sell. Remember, we are not selling in a bookstore; we are selling on the internet.

So for a product to be successful, potential buyers must be searching the internet for information relating to it.

My rule of thumb is that the keyword must have at least 100,000 searches a month on Google to be successful online. "Aquariums" with 11.1 million and "aquarium" with 823,000 both pass with flying colors.

There's another way to do your keyword due diligence. It's to spy on your competitors and see what keywords their websites are optimized on. But don't worry—it's perfectly legal.

Here's how to do it: You can see what keywords your competitors are using by reading the source codes on their website. "Source code" is the programming language used to build their websites. And in optimized websites, the source code for the pages include key word lists in areas of the code called meta tags. The most important meta tags to check are the title tag, description tag, and keywords tag.

To find the keywords contained in the meta tags of your competitor, go to his home page. Click "view" and then choose "source." A window will appear displaying the page's source code with the meta tags clearly labeled as title, description, and keywords. The keywords appear between symbols; e.g. <head> and </head>, <title> and <title>.

In minutes, you can know all the keywords your competitors have optimized their sites for. You can then use spacky.com or another keyword research and discovery tool like wordtracker.com.

Marketing in Larger Companies

Larger companies have an additional challenge: how to allocate resources among different levels of marketing. Should an ad in *Fortune* magazine talk about the corporation as a whole, a new technology, or a specific product?

Table 7-6 provides some guidance in this regard. As you can see, in larger companies marketing resources must be allocated across three levels. At the top is corporate communications. These are marketing programs that promote the company as a brand name. Microsoft TV commercials often promote Microsoft as an entity, and the Microsoft brand, rather than specific software or services.

The second tier is to promote the individual business units or companies operating under the corporate umbrella. When I worked at Westinghouse, I was responsible for marketing the division of Westinghouse that manufactured defense and aerospace products. I had no involvement in refrigerators, transportation systems, or any other area of the company.

The third tier is marketing resources devoted to particular divisions, each of which is responsible for a different product line. While at Westinghouse Defense & Aerospace, I worked for the business unit that manufactured radar systems for airports and military applications. While the company made many other products, such as fire control systems for F-16 fighters, ships, and tanks, others in my department handled those divisions, while I was responsible for the radar division.

Table 7-6. Marketing communications responsibilities

	Mission	To This Audience	Through These Media	To Sell
Corporate	Sell the corporation as a corporation	Business leaders, Financial influentials, Government, Opinion leaders Community Academia Press	Television, Business publications, Major newspapers	Basic strengths of the corporation
Business Units	Present capabilities for markets/ industries	High-level decision makers, Planners/ engineers, financiers	General Business, Horizontal industry publications	Systems capabilities, Broad product & service capabilities
Divisions	Inform prospects of available products & services	Specifiers, designers, purchasers, Purchasing influences	Vertical publications, Functional publications	Specific products & services

Case Study...
Chiropractic Marketing Plans, Inc.

Goal for this year: Increase revenues from $150,000 to $200,000.
To reach its goal, CMP's strategy is to:

1. Become well-known for writing marketing plans for chiropractors because no one else in their area is doing this
2. Dominate their field within a 10-mile radius of the office
3. Add 15 net clients
4. Increase client retention rate to 40 percent.
5. Earn income by matching clients with implementation specialists

6. Add a midyear review service to increase the frequency of service usage

After careful analysis, CMP decided the initial tactics most likely to be effective for them are:

1. Form joint ventures with coaches who specialize in building chiropractic practices
2. Write articles for both online and offline magazines
3. Institute a strong referral program
4. Use direct mail
5. Speak to chiropractic groups

Action...

Identify the Tactics You'll Use

Identify the three to five tactics you'll begin with and why you think they're your best choice given your goals and strategies.

_____

_____

_____

_____

_____

_____

_____

_____

_____

_____

Selling to the "Starving Crowd"

In an interview, *National Enquirer* editor-in-chief David Perel revealed the secret of the tabloid's outrageous success: "The big news organizations tell people what they think they should be interested in, whereas we try to give them stories that they are interested in."

I think Perel has hit upon a key principle that applies to all marketing, not just the selling of tabloid newspapers. Namely, that your sales will be many times greater when you offer your customers information they want to read and learn—instead of information you *think* they should read.

The late Gary Halbert went even further, advising marketers to sell exclusively to what he called a "starving crowd." A starving crowd not only wants what you are selling—but has an insatiable appetite for it. Therefore, even if there are a lot of players in that market, they can all do well, because the market's demand is a bottomless pit.

In particular, there are three "starving crowd" markets that have an especially consistent and unending demand for products and services related to their interests and needs:

Hobbyists. Hobbyists spend money on antique collecting or quilting not because they have to, but because they want to. Those who are heavily "into" the hobby, whether that hobby is calligraphy or macramé, can't get enough of it.

In these hobby niches, a lot of competition is a good sign, not a negative sign, for two reasons: (1) it proves the niche is viable. If others are making money selling to this market, you can too and (2) you can make joint venture deals with these other marketers to sell your products to their lists and vice versa.

Business opportunity seekers. There is an insatiable appetite for information on how to make money in your spare time, start a home based business, change careers, or earn a living without a job.

I believe these business opportunity seekers can be divided into two groups. The first group is doers. These doers are serious about changing their lives, and they actually pursue the course of action you recommend. The second group is dreamers. The dreamers enjoy learning about small business, yet take no action beyond buying and reading how-to information products.

You can't usually distinguish between these segments when marketing. But you really don't have to, because both consume an unending stream of info products purchased online.

Money making and investing. It is a nearly universal desire to make more money and increase one's wealth.

If you sell products, financial services, or advice that helps people get greater returns from their investments with less risk ... or accumulate a seven-figure net worth ... or become financially independent ... you will never run out of eager buyers.

Of course, there are other starving-crowd niches for marketers, including: self-help, relationships, sex, health, beauty, fashion, fitness, and weight loss.

But the three above—hobbies, business opportunities, investing—are by far the largest and most active.

One of the biggest mistakes beginning marketers make is choosing, as their primary niche, a market that is not a starving crowd. The reason this is a mistake: without a starving crowd of buyers, you will always be fighting an uphill battle to peddle your products, services, and ideas.

And you will be forever frustrated that your prospects aren't buying your valuable material when you know it's stuff they absolutely should have.

But people don't readily do what they should do—or what you think is good for them.

They are much more easily convinced to buy what they already want, rather than what you think they need.

And when you select as your primary niche in marketing a starving crowd, like hobbyists, business opportunity seekers, or wealth seekers, you can sell your prospects the stuff they want— over and over again.

Chapter 8
INTEGRATE ONLINE AND OFFLINE MARKETING

Now, let's look at some of the internet marketing methods you can use, in combination with offline marketing, to actively promote your product or service. The main online marketing techniques we will look at include e-mail marketing, e-newsletters, websites, blogging, and social networking.

E-Mail Marketing

E-mail marketing can be extremely profitable. I distribute approximately 400,000 e-mail messages a month for my online business, and it generates a handsome six-figure income in return. Yet, I am worried. E-mail is less effective today than it was a few years ago, and I have grave concerns about its future.

Why has e-mail marketing response declined so dramatically? Spam filters are one reason. But the main reason is probably the glut of e-mail messages each of us receives daily. When you get 100 or 200 e-mail messages a day, just getting through them becomes a drain on your time and productivity. To protect themselves, many people simply delete e-mails from anyone they don't know. They assume it is spam—or don't want to risk a virus infection. So they click Delete and your message is gone.

How do you overcome this obstacle and get your prospects to open, read, and respond to your e-mail marketing messages, then buy the products you are selling? By becoming part of the prospect's e-mail inner circle. Let me explain what the inner circle is and how you can join it. According to a survey by Nielsen/NetRatings, most people regularly open and read e-mails from a maximum of 16 permission-based sources. The only way for you to break into this inner circle of 16 correspondents whose e-mail messages the prospect will read is to displace someone already in that inner circle, according to the survey. An article in *DM News* (10/16/03) concludes,

> **According to a survey by Nielsen/NetRatings, most people regularly open and read e-mails from a maximum of 16 permission-based sources.**

"Marketers will have to enter that emerging inner circle of trusted companies from whom people are willing to keep reading e-mails."

So how do you break into this inner circle of e-mail senders whose messages your prospects will open and read? Despite the proliferation of free online newsletters (e-zines), the best way to become part of a prospect's inner circle is to write and publish a truly valuable e-zine. If you publish your e-zine regularly (at least once a month) and provide content of genuine worth, readers will come to value your publication and establish a relationship with you. You will have entered their e-mail inner circle, because they will view anything with your name in the From line as being from a trusted adviser and worth their time to at least open.

The e-newsletter is free. The money is made by sending, at virtually no cost, e-mail sales messages to your subscribers. Agora Publishing, for example, doesn't charge for a subscription to the *Daily Reckoning*. But by marketing aggressively to the *Daily Reckoning* subscriber list, they generate over $100 million in online sales of their newsletters and services each year—at very little cost.

Similar to e-zines are short news bulletins, which some marketers send to their subscribers on a regular basis. For instance, *Computer-World* magazine (*CW*) sends a daily online update with short items from the magazine. *CW*'s daily online updates have become part of the inner circle for many IT professionals who must keep up with new developments in hardware and software.

If you do not publish your own e-newsletter, you can still break into the prospect's inner circle by advertising in one of the newsletters they subscribe to. You can purchase a short online ad in these updates, thereby buying your way into the reader's e-mail inner circle. For example, CMP, a trade publisher, e-mails a monthly update, *Business Technology Advisor* (*BTA*), to the subscribers of all its publications. For $200 per thousand, you can sponsor *BTA* and have the entire issue devoted to your firm and products. Since CMP subscribers know and look forward to *BTA*, your message gets a higher readership and response than it would if you sent it under your own banner.

Another way to break into the prospect's inner circle is with periodic service and upgrade notices. Software users, for example, will read and open e-mails from the software publisher that contain news about upgrades, technical information, or service policies. If your customers regularly need to receive service and product news from you, get in the habit of delivering it via e-mail. Then they will be "trained" to read your e-mails, so when you send a promotion, it, too will get opened and read.

A survey from quris.com shows that customers also value and read two specific types of e-mails: (a) transaction confirmations and (b) account status updates. So you can get your promotional message read by embedding it into routine e-mails that contain transactional or account status information. A good example is Amazon.com, whose customers open and read the e-mails they send because they might contain news about their orders.

You can also break into the customer's inner circle by offering timely news and updates through free e-mail alerts. When a prospect subscribes to your e-newsletter, you can send them additional content via e-mail to keep them updated on the topic between regular issues.

These alerts must contain useful news and information, not just sales pitches. The most successful marketers keep the information content of the e-mails high, but also liberally promote products and services to these e-mail alert recipients.

Another way to become part of the prospect's inner circle is to form a club and invite them to join it. Reason: Your prospects will read e-mails from clubs, associations, online communities of interest, subscription websites, and other organizations of which they are members. Therefore, if you can create a club or have your e-mail distributed by one of these membership organizations, you can easily enter the prospect's e-mail inner circle.

As a rule of thumb, whenever you can send e-mail to your prospect using one of the above methods, your chances of getting opened and read increase exponentially versus sending a typical promotional e-mail. Remember, people buy from people they know, like, and trust. When you become part of the inner circle, your prospects know, like, and trust the e-mail messages you send, giving you an inside track to getting them to spend their online shopping dollars with you.

Five Ways to Get Your Website Ranked Higher on Google

Search engine optimization expert Don Kaufmann gives these guidelines for getting your website ranked higher on Google:

1. Always be adding new content. Google ranks sites higher when they are frequently updated.
2. List your site on the top niche directories and subdirectories in your industry.
3. Use longer copy—a minimum length of 250 words per web page.
4. Post online videos—since its acquisition of YouTube, Google places greater ranking emphasis on video.
5. Add credibility icons—start with trade association membership icons or the Better Business Bureau logo.

Writing and Publishing a Free E-Newsletter

An *e-zine* is an online newsletter. If you want to market your product or service over the internet, I strongly urge you to distribute your own e-zine free to your customers and prospects. There are several reasons for doing so.

First, the e-zine allows you to keep in touch with your best customers—indeed, with all your customers—at virtually no cost. Because it's electronic, there's no printing or postage cost.

Second, by offering potential customers a free subscription to your e-zine, you can capture their e-mail addresses and add them to your online database. You can then market to your prospects, also at no cost. Whether you are generating leads or direct sales, there are two ways to sell to your e-zine subscribers. You can place small online ads in the regular issues of your e-zine; these ads are usually 100 words or so in length, and include a link to a page on your site where the subscriber can read about and order the product. Or, you can send standalone e-mail messages to your subscribers, again promoting a specific product and with a link to your site.

> **If you want to market your product or service over the internet, I strongly urge you to distribute your own e-zine free to your customers and prospects.**

There are thousands of e-zines published. Examples of successful, money-making e-zines include John Forde's *Copywriter's Roundtable* (SUBSCRIBE@JackForde.com), Paul Hartunian's *Million-Dollar Publicity Strategies* (hartunian.com), and Agora's *Daily Reckoning* (dailyreckoning.com). No two e-zines are the same, and there is no single accepted formula for writing and designing e-zines. However, my e-zine, *Bob Bly's Direct Response Letter*, has been pretty successful for me (you can subscribe at bly.com), and I do have a formula for producing it.

When you are dealing with a free e-zine, people spend just a little time reading it before they delete it with a click of the mouse. I am convinced that most subscribers do not print out the e-zine, take it home, and curl up with it on the couch later to read. Therefore, I use a quick-reading format designed to allow the subscriber to read my e-zine online right when he opens it. In this formula, my e-zine always has between five and seven short articles, each just a few paragraphs long. Every article can be read in less than a minute, so it never takes more than seven minutes to read the whole issue, though I doubt most people do.

I advise against having just a headline and a one-line description of the article with a link to the full text of the article. All that clicking forces your subscribers to do a lot of work to read your articles, and that's not what they want.

I do not use HTML; my e-zine is text-only. This way, it is easy and inexpensive to produce. I don't make a production out of it—it's just straight type. Many readers have told me they like it this way and they don't like HTML e-zines, which look (a) more promotional and less informational and (b) seem to have more to read.

> **I use a quick-reading format designed to allow the subscriber to read my e-zine online right when he opens it.**

When preparing your text e-zine for distribution, type your copy in a single column as a text file. The column should be 60 characters in length, so you can set your margins at 20 and 80. However, to make sure the lines come out evenly, you must put a hard carriage return by hitting "Return" at the end of each line.

I happen to be a freelance copywriter. Let me show you specifically how having an e-zine helps bring in business for me. I recently gave a speech on software direct marketing. It was recorded, so I had audio cassette copies made. In my e-zine, I offered the cassette free to any subscribers involved in software marketing—potential clients for my copywriting services. Within 24 hours after I distributed the e-zine, we received over 200 inquiries requesting the tape, many from qualified prospects who needed copy written for direct mail and e-mail to promote their software. By comparison, most copywriters tell me that when they send postal direct mail to a list of prospects, they average a 1 percent response. At that rate, they would have to send out 20,000 pieces of mail to generate the 200 leads I got in an hour for free.

That's what an e-zine can do for you. Once you build your sub-scriber list, you have an incredibly powerful marketing tool and the most valuable asset your business can own: a database of buyers with e-mail addresses and permission to mail to them at any time.

SEO Your Website

An estimated 80 percent of online purchases begin with prospects using a search engine such as Google to find the products they are in-terested in. Therefore, it makes sense to optimize your website so that it ranks higher in Google and other search engines. How do you go about this?

"My advice is always to write for people, not search engines," says copywriter Dianna Huff. "Yes, it's good to place the correct key-words in the body copy, and yes, it's correct to place your most important keyword at the beginning of the title tag and in the head-line of the page. However, you don't *have* to do this to achieve high rankings. And you certainly should not do it if your copy ends up sounding spammy. If you want a site to rank well, you do have to optimize it, but not at the expense of the marketing objectives. Copy should be written for people, not search engines."

> **So what I found that works is to make a list of the top 10–15 keywords and use these naturally, organically, and in a reader-friendly manner in the content.**

"Over the years, the tactic I found that works best is to have the most targeted keywords towards the top of the page and work your way down, like a reverse pyramid," says internet marketing consultant Wendy Montesdeoca. "The entire page should be keyword dense, and there can be some repetition, but from my understanding of search engine spiders, they like more organic content.

"So what I found that works is to make a list of the top 10–15 key-words and use these naturally, organically, and in a reader-friendly manner in the content. And of course use your top five keywords in the alt, meta, and title tags. For instance, if there's a picture of Bob, don't just have 'Bob Bly'—have 'Bob Bly, freelance copywriter.'"

Okay. Let's say you have a website that has not been optimized, and you want to optimize it now. How do you go about it?

First, determine which keywords are best for your industry or traffic you are looking to generate. Keywords are the terms your prospects and visitors will type into the search field when they are looking for talent. So consider the words and phrases they might use to describe your products or services.

Here are some additional tips for selecting keywords:

- Use plurals for your keywords, but avoid excessive repetition.
- Misspell keywords if misspellings are common. For example, DIRECTV, a digital satellite television service, is frequently referred to as Direct TV. If your name is misspelled regularly, include that spelling in your keywords, as well.
- Don't always use obvious keywords. Include phrases that may get fewer searches but higher results.
- Don't let your combined keywords exceed 1,000 characters. The fewer keywords, the greater impact they will have.

Need help coming up with a list of likely keywords? There are tools that can help. One of these is spacky.com. Another is Wordtracker.com. Spacky shows you the number of searchers performed that month on Google, Yahoo!/Overture, and the Microsoft network. Wordtracker helps you find all keyword combinations that bear any relation to your business or service, and they offer a free 30-day money back guarantee.

Next, create *meta tags* on all pages of your website, based on the keywords you target. These are descriptive text written in HTML code on your site. They are not visible on your web pages, but search engines can read and find them. Before you create your own meta tags, it's a good idea to take a look at those of others, especially competitors and colleagues. Fortunately, you can easily open a window and view the meta tags of any website you visit. From your browser's toolbar, choose the View menu. Then click on Source, and a window will open with HTML text that you can study. The most important meta tags are found near the top of the page in between codes like this: <head> and </head>.

If you are creating your own website, depending on which software you use, all you have to do to add meta tags is type the words you've chosen in the appropriate places. The key meta tags for marketing purposes are title, description, and keywords. These tags control what surfers see when your site is listed in the search engines, which means they will help people decide whether to visit your site.

The title tag is what your visitors see at the top of their browser windows when they visit your site, as well as what they will see in their bookmark lists. So make sure each page has a title that makes sense to visitors, not just to you. Be descriptive; failure to put strategic keywords in the page title is often why web pages are poorly ranked. The title tag can be a maximum 95 characters including spaces, but ideally no longer than six or seven words.

The key meta tags for marketing purposes are title, description, and keywords.

When your website comes up in search engine results, the meta tag identified as the description is often the opening statement people will use to decide whether to access the link. The description should concisely answer the question What do you do? For example: XYZ Design provides client-focused, creative, and effective graphic design, art direction, and project management for marketing communications. The description tag should be a maximum of 220 characters with spaces.

Put your keywords in your meta tags. You also should include your keywords in the first 25 words of your home page. You can use Good Keywords as a meta tag creation tool. Keep adding the keywords you need into the Keyword Pad available within the software. Once you are done, a simple click will get you the required keyword meta tag, ready to be pasted into your HTML file. Now your website is primed for optimum search engine placement.

Write the best copy you can on every page of your website. Write it for the human reader first, and the search engines second. Don't even think about keywords as you write. Concentrate 100 percent on sounding like one human being talking to another about a subject he is enthusiastic about and wants to share. Long copy is OK. In fact, Google prefers webpages that are at least 250 words.

Once you've written the strongest copy you can, go back and insert key words from your keyword list into the copy, wherever and as frequently as you can, without disturbing the style, tone, meaning, or persuasiveness of the copy. If forcing a keyword in disrupts the flow of the copy, don't do it.

For instance, on bly.com, one line of the original home page copy reads Call on freelance copywriter and internet marketing strategist Bob Bly. I like the sound of strategist. But our keywords research showed that people search for internet marketing consultants, not strategists. So we changed the copy to read "internet marketing consultant."

> **Once you've written the strongest copy you can, go back and insert key words from your keyword list into the copy, wherever and as frequently as you can.**

In another paragraph, we talked about my experience as a copywriter, saying that I know "how to craft landing pages that drive conversions through the roof." Once again, I like the variety of using "craft" as a verb. But to optimize the sentence with the keyword "copy," I changed it to "how to write potent, compelling copy for landing pages that drive conversions through the roof." Another keyword phrase that came up in our research was "make money online," and so we added that to the sentence: "landing pages that drive conversions through the roof – and make more money online."

One of the keyword phrases that ranked highly in our research was "online copywriting." Any time you can replace a non-keyword-phrase with a keyword phrase, with no harm to the copy, you should. So we changed "they call on Bob Bly to write their most important online marketing campaigns" (people were not searching for "campaigns") to "they call on Bob Bly when they need online copywriting that sells."

Add a "Recommended Vendors" Page to Your Site

I'm not an original thinker, and I don't think I've invented a single marketing technique in my life. Except one: having a Recommended Vendors page on my website.

Go to bly.com and click on Vendors. You'll see my Recommended Vendors list—a web page with the vendors I recommend to my clients, indexed and organized by category. What's the purpose? To give clients an online resource where they can find vendors you recommend who can provide services they need—in particular, services that complement the ones you offer.

Should you have a Recommended Vendors page on your website? Yes, if you (a) are a service provider and (b) do not provide the full range of services your clients need to solve their problems. For instance, as a freelance copywriter, I only provide part of what clients need for their direct mail campaigns: the copy. They also need mailing lists, graphic design, printing, letter shop services, and other related services to produce DM campaigns—services I don't provide.

Many clients buy services à la carte and don't need a single-source vendor. But, if you sell one or two services and a client needs three or four, you should at least be able to show them where they can get the rest. Why is this important? Some clients may not hire you to provide Service A until they are confident that they can also procure Services B and C.

Having a Recommended Vendors page on your website gives you a number of benefits. To begin with, it makes your website a value-added resource for your clients and prospects, drawing more traffic and repeat visits. Also, potential clients will often ask, "I know you can do A, but I need A, B, and C. Who can handle B and C for me?" I reply, "Are you online right now? Go to my website and click on Vendors." Then I direct them to the vendors who can handle B and C for them.

Somehow, giving them the referral when they are looking at the vendor's name and contact information on the screen makes them more confident. They get the impression that if the vendor is posted on my website, I must refer my clients to them often, which in turn gives them the confidence that they can get all their needs met. It's also convenient: the client doesn't have to hastily jot down a bunch of names and phone numbers—it's all right up there onbly.com. Plus, having a list of my preferred vendors on my website helps cement my relationships with these vendors. My vendors are grateful for the opportunity to get more business, and in return, they give my clients preferred treatment, which further increases the value I provide my clients.

One other point: Having a Recommended Vendors page is not standard website practice. So if you do it, not only will you add tremendous value for your clients, prospects, vendors, and visitors, but you'll stand out from the crowd. To create your Vendors page, model it after my Vendors page on www.bly.com. Group the vendors by category. For instance, if you are a contractor, your vendors page categories might include Architects, Landscape Designers, Appliances, Plumbers, and Electricians. Have an index of categories at the top of the Vendors page, linked to the category headings. This allows your visitors to find what they need even faster without scrolling through a long list of vendors.

Steps…

Five Steps to Building Your E-List

Many marketers want to cut marketing costs by shifting more of their marketing budgets from traditional direct mail and paper newsletters to e-mail marketing and e-newsletters. But if you want to ramp up your online marketing program, you should start building a large opt-in e-list of customers and prospects now.

Why? Because without a significant online house file (list of opt-in subscribers), you can only reach prospects in your niche by renting other marketers' opt-in e-lists, which is hardly cost-effective: each time you want to send another message to your industry, you have to rent the list again, at a cost that can easily reach into the hundreds of dollars per thousand names.

Some marketers buy databases containing e-mail addresses of business prospects in their niche market. This can work if you are sending highly targeted e-mails on extremely relevant topics and offers to narrow vertical e-lists. But when you send e-mail messages to non-opt-in lists, you are mostly asking for trouble. CAN/SPAM does not prohibit e-mailing to people who have not opted in, but people on non-opt-in e-lists are much more likely to register spam complaints than those on legitimate opt-in e-lists—and far less likely to buy from you.

So the best online strategy for marketers is to build your own opt-in e-list of subscribers. Doing so eliminates the cost of renting opt-in lists while preventing the spam complaints and lower response rates typical of non-opt-in purchased or rented lists.

When you own an opt-in e-list covering a sizable percentage of your target market, you can communicate with your prospects and customers as often as you desire or think is appropriate at minimal cost. Being able to send an e-mail to your target market with a few mouse clicks makes you less dependent on costly direct mail, print newsletters, and other paper promotions.

By using a double opt-in process that requires new subscribers to verify their identity before being added to your e-list, you help minimize spam complaints and bounce-backs. Owning a large opt-in e-list of target prospects also decreases marketing costs and improves lead flow and revenues.

So how do you build a large and profitable opt-in e-list of qualified B2B prospects in your field? Here are five ideas:

1. Dedicate a portion of your online marketing budget exclusively to list-building.

Most marketers drive traffic either to their website home page or landing pages relating to specific offers (e.g., free webinar registration, free white paper download, purchase a product). And a lot of the traffic they drive to these pages is existing customers and prospects who are already on their e-list.

You should spend a minimum of 20 percent of your online marketing budget on building your house opt-in e-list. That means getting qualified prospects in your industry who have not yet opted into your online subscriber list to do so. There are many online marketing options that work well for e-list building programs. These include pay-per-click advertising, postcard marketing, banner advertising, online ads in other marketers' e-newsletters, co-registration deals, video marketing, viral marketing, editorial mentions in trade publications, online article marketing, affiliate marketing, and social media, to name a few.

2. Calculate your maximum acceptable cost per new subscriber.

When evaluating marketing methods for e-list building, you have to weigh the cost of acquiring the name versus the value that name has for your business. To determine value, divide the total annual revenues generated by your online subscriber list by the number of names on that list. Example: If your 20,000 online subscribers account for $600,000 in annual sales, your subscriber value is $30 per name per year.

You decide how much you are willing to spend to acquire a subscriber worth $30 per year. If uncertain, use this rule of thumb: list-building campaigns should ideally pay back their cost within three to six months. Therefore, if your names are worth $30 per year each, you can afford to spend up to $15 per subscriber to acquire new names.

Say you drive traffic to a landing page where people can sign up to your e-list. The conversion rate is 50 percent, so for every two unique visitors you drive to your registration page, you get one new opt-in subscriber. Using Google AdWords, you can drive traffic at a cost of $7 per click. Can you afford that? Yes, because that means you get one new subscriber for every two clicks you buy, which works out to $14 per subscriber—within your $15 per new name limit. Would it make more sense to base the allowable acquisition cost per new name on the lifetime customer value (LCV) of online subscribers rather than just the average one-year revenue per name? Theoretically, yes. But you can only do that if you've been marketing online long enough to have reliable numbers on which to base LCV estimates. Until you do, stick with the revenue per year per name figure as the baseline.

3. Publish a free e-newsletter.

As discussed, the best way to build and regularly communicate with an opt-in list of prospects is to publish and distribute a free e-newsletter on a specialized topic related to your product line and of interest to your target prospects.

Publishing a free e-zine gives you two important benefits for your online marketing efforts. First, it gives you a standing free offer you can use in your e-list-building efforts—a free subscription to your e-newsletter. Second, having the e-newsletter ensures that you communicate with your opt-in subscribers on a regular basis. This regular communication builds your relationship with your online prospects while increasing the frequency of branding messages and online marketing opportunities.

4. Build a "free-on-free name squeeze page."

With a staggering number of free e-newsletters on the internet competing for attention, it's not enough to have a simple sign-up box on your home page for your free e-newsletter. You should offer a bribe as an incentive for visitors to subscribe. The best bribe is a free special report the visitor can download as a PDF file in exchange for opting in to your e-list. For instance, if you sell supply chain management software, and publish an e-zine called *The Strategic SCM Partner*, offer a short bonus report called "Seven Steps to Improving Supply Chain Management in

Your Enterprise" as a premium for new subscribers.

Drive traffic not to your home page or standard sub-scription form, but to a special "free-on-free name squeeze page"—a landing page highlighting this offer. We call it a name squeeze page because it extracts or squeezes new names for your list from web traffic. Free-on-free means you are offering free content (the report) as a bribe to get the visitor to accept your primary free offer (the e-news-letter subscription). For an example of a free-on-free name squeeze page, see bly.com/reports.

5. **Capture the e-mail addresses of site visitors who do not buy, subscribe, or register.**

Put in place one or more mechanisms for capturing the e-mail addresses of site visitors who do not buy a product, download a demo, subscribe to your free online newsletter, or take other actions that opt them into your e-list.

Going back to our example for supply chain management, when visitors attempt to leave the site without purchasing or registering, have a pop-up window to capture their e-mail addresses. The headline says, "Wait! Don't leave without claiming your free special SCM report!" Short copy explains they can get a free copy of your special report "Seven Steps to Improving Supply Chain Management in Your Enterprise" by typing their e-mail address in the blank space and click-ing Submit.

If you are not proactively making an effort to capture e-mail addresses of site visitors who do not otherwise register, you are leaving money on the table.

How I Find Fresh E-Zine Content for 50 Cents per Article

Whenever I am in a used bookstore or—even better—a library selling old books, I look for and buy old business books. At my local library, they are 50 cents each. If you are looking for content for your e-zine, I urge you to do the same with books related to your topic. Why?

Thumb through any old business book and I can virtually guarantee that within two minutes, you'll find at least one gem—a great quote, a neat idea, a list of how-to tips—you can use as a short article in your e-zine, on your blog, or in other how-to writings.

Increase E-Mail Address Capture

Did you ever go to a website or landing page to learn more about a product you were interested in and then end up deciding, for whatever reason, against buying it? I'm sure you do this all the time. I know I do.

Next time you do it, watch what happens when you click away from the site without having made a purchase. If you are allowed to leave without further interaction, then you have just witnessed the most common online marketing mistake: namely, the website failed to capture your e-mail address.

Why bother to capture the e-mail addresses of visitors to your landing pages and other websites? There are two primary benefits: first, you can send these visitors an online conversion series—a sequence of follow-up e-mails delivered by auto-responder. The conversion series gives you additional opportunities to convince these prospects to buy, and can significantly increase your overall conversion rate. A landing page may have only a 1 percent to 5 percent conversion rate, but add an online conversion series of e-mails, and conversion rates can increase to 10 percent, 20 percent, or more.

Second, the best names for your e-mail marketing efforts—far better than rented opt-in lists—are in your house e-list. So the faster you can build a large e-list, the more profitable your internet marketing ventures will become. How much more profitable? Internet marketing expert Fred Gleeck estimates online revenues of 10 cents to $1 or more per name per month for small businesses selling information products online (other industries may have different figures). Therefore, a 50,000-name e-list could generate annual online revenues of $600,000 a year or higher. Many businesses do significantly better. Agora Publishing has, as near as I can figure, online sales of more than $100 million a year from about half a million names—a hefty $16.70 per name per month. Hewlett-Packard has 4.5 million e-zine subscribers, from whom they generate $60 million in monthly sales.

> **A 50,000-name e-list could generate annual online revenues of $600,000 a year or higher.**

So how do you maximize capture of e-mail addresses from site visitors? Well, for those who buy something, you require them to give you their e-mail address on the transaction page to complete their order. But what about those who visit but do not buy? Use a "pop-under" window. When you attempt to click away from the landing page without making a purchase, a window appears. The copy in this window says something like, "Wait! Don't leave yet!" and makes a free offer. Typically, this offer is some sort of free content, such as a downloadable PDF report, an e-course delivered via auto-responder, or an e-zine subscription, given in exchange for the visitor's e-mail address.

To see how this works, go to one of my sites, becomeaninstantguru.com, and leave without buying. Unless you have a pop-up blocker, a pop-under window comes up that offers you a 50-page special report that normally sells for $29 for free. In exchange, all I require is your e-mail address.

Some marketers ask for the e-mail address and offer the free content within the actual landing page itself—often in a boxed sidebar. The problem with such an approach is that it gives the prospect a choice between a free option and a paid option for two content offers on the same topic, and by giving that choice, you risk having people take the free offer and bypass the paid offer.

The big advantage of the pop-under is that visitors see it only after they have read to the point where they are leaving without ordering. Therefore, the free content offer doesn't compete with or distract visitors from the paid product offer. Any time you create a landing page or website selling a product without a pop-under or other mechanism for capturing e-mail addresses, you are leaving money on the table.

As Fred Gleeck says, "The two goals of your site are to generate orders and capture e-mail addresses." He notes that they are about equal in importance, but capturing the e-mail addresses may be the more important goal. After all, if you are serious about making money with internet marketing, there is no asset more valuable to your online business than a large, qualified e-list of prospects and buyers. Your future profits are directly linked to how quickly you can build this list.

One other point: a pop-under window is a standard web tool. You don't need to buy special software to create one. Any web designer can do one for you for a nominal fee.

On your homepage, moving the form for subscribing to your list from its current location to the upper right corner of the screen can increase sign-ups considerably.

On your homepage, moving the form for subscribing to your list from its current location to the upper right corner of the screen can increase sign-ups considerably. The home page should also have more than one enticement for opting into your list. In addition to the subscription form in the upper right of the screen, you can add another box offering a free special report, a second featuring a survey, and even a third with something else of interest.

On my site, bly.com, I offer use of a free online tool, Bob Bly's Direct Response ROI Calculator, at: dmresponsecalculator.com. When you click on the site, you can access a free break-even calculator. You enter the mailing costs—postage, list rental, printing, and so on. The tool automatically calculates the response rate you need to break even.

By break even, we mean that the mailing generates net revenues exactly equal to its costs. The Direct Response ROI Calculator determines net revenue per order by subtracting the cost of goods from the purchase price of the product. The mailing cost is calculated by adding up postage, mailing list rental fees, printing, and letter shop fees— what it costs to have a direct mail service assemble the components of the mailing and send it out. Copywriting, graphic design, illustration, and other one-time costs to create the mailing are not factored into the break-even calculation. There is no cost to use the calculator, except you have to opt into my list to access it.

Blogging

A simple, three-step content plan is the key to using a blog to successfully market yourself, your business, your book, or your other information products. The plan doesn't need to be complicated to succeed. Here's an overview of the process Roger C. Parker used to update his *Published & Profitable Writer's Daily Tips Blog* (blog.publishedand profitable.com).

Steps...

BEGIN HERE

1. Identify posting frequency.

Start by asking yourself, "How many times a week do I want to post?" Everyone has to answer this question for themselves. The right answer depends on your marketing goals, how comfortable you are as a writer, and how much time you have available for marketing. If your goal is to immediately gain awareness and search engine visibility, the more you blog, the better.

Some marketers blog once a week. I blog twice a week. More important than the number of posts you add each week, however, are the *consistency* and *predictability* of your posting. You want to create the habit of frequent posting and build it into your weekly schedule, so that it becomes a part of your routine. You also want your market to look forward to your new posts.

2. Commit to specific days of the week.

It's not enough to say: I'm going to blog twice a week, without fail! A general statement like that is an invitation to failure. What it takes to succeed in blogging is to make a commitment like one of the following:

> **I am going to post once a week, on every Thursday.**
> **I am going to post twice a week, on Tuesdays and Fridays.**
> **I am going to post every weekday.**

Making a commitment to post new blog content on specific days adds the *power of intention*. The commitment to post on specific days converts a goal into a specific, measurable task. It also provides a deadline. If you have committed to adding blog content on Tuesdays and Thursdays, for example, you know that you have to work on your blog posts Monday and Wednesday. (Working on your blog posts a day ahead of time ensures that they will appear on schedule.)

Knowing that you have blogging deadlines on Mondays and Wednesdays encourages you to assign time each Monday and Wednesday to preparing the next blog post. You add the time to prepare your blog posts to Monday and Wednesday schedules; you can add the time commitments as repeating events to your desktop or online calendars. Soon, you'll get to the point where creating your scheduled posts becomes second nature to you!

3. Identify specific blog topics.

The final step to success is to identify the recurring topics, or themes, you're going to post about each week. For example, here's the formula I use for posting to my *Published & Profitable* blog (blog.publishedandprofitable.com):

◆ **Mondays,** I post about a planning topic.

- **Tuesdays**, my blog posts are devoted to writing topics, such as shortcuts, techniques, and tips.
- **Wednesdays**, I feature a promoting tip useful for authors or internet marketing professionals.
- **Thursdays**, I blog about a profit tip, such as ideas for recycling and reusing information, or creating new information products.
- **Fridays**, I devote to announcements about upcoming events.

Your schedule doesn't have to be as aggressive. You can choose to commit to adding new blog posts one, two, three, or four times a week. But, the important thing is that you make a commitment to post about specific topics on specific days of the week. Knowing what you're going to be blogging about on specific days of the week not only creates the time to prepare the posts, but engages your subconscious brain. As a result, while you are doing other work, driving, or sleeping, your brain is subconsciously processing ideas and looking out for possible topics for upcoming posts.

Once you create and start your baseline blogging schedule, you can add posts when you have time, or when something occurs that deserves immediate attention. You can prepare additional posts when there's a relevant event in the news, a new product or book appears, or you discover an online resource you want to share with your market.

Following the above formula saves you time, provides a structure for creating each post, and ensures that your blog will be consistently updated. The three-step formula helps you create a platform that paves the way for your occasional news post, or promoting your upcoming events, new products, and new services.

Social Media

Unless you have been living in a cave for the past couple of years, you've no doubt at least heard of social networking, the practice of connecting online with friends, colleagues, and customers online using special websites and tools created for that purpose. These social networking sites include MySpace, Facebook, LinkedIn, Twitter, and many others. It isn't a fad. It isn't an excuse to get out of work. Social networking is how people do business now. It's for real and it's here to stay.

Just how important is social media? According to Susan McKenna, vice president of e-commerce for AlternativeHealthJournal.com, in an interview in the June 2008 issue of *Response*, "people need to jump the chasm of 'talking to' and go 'talking with.' You're in a dialogue with them, and that's how we move from sales to commerce. That's what social media is going to do for marketers in the future." Carrie Mathews, a program director for the CIO Executive Council, defined social networking in a recent article as "interactive, collaborative online communities created by technology."

> **It isn't a fad. It isn't an excuse to get out of work. Social networking is how people do business now. It's for real and it's here to stay.**

According to an article in the September 2007 issue of *BusinessWeek SmallBiz*, two of the best known social networking tools, webcasts and blogs, are currently in use by more than 400,000 small and medium-sized businesses. About 260,000 other companies are podcasting. Social networking websites like MySpace and Facebook are growing tremendously in popularity. According to a survey by Universal McCann of 17,000 internet users in 29 countries, about 57 percent of respondents have joined at least one social network, and 43 percent of people in the U.S. have done so.

Recognizing the importance of social media as a business communications tool, IBM has provided its employees with in-house versions of Twitter (Blue Twit), Facebook (Beehive), and Del.icio.us (Dogear). In 2006, YouTube was purchased by search engine giant Google for over $165 billion in a stock-for-stock transaction. The 3D virtual world Second Life is "home" to over 7.5 million residents, and everyone, from small business owners to government agencies, large corporations, and even whole countries, is setting up shop there. "It would appear that social networking is not a fad but rather an activity that is being woven into the very fabric of the global internet," according to Bob Ivins, comScore's executive vice president of international markets.

Social networking is an activity that is only going to grow more common as time passes and computers become more sophisticated. According to a study conducted by Jupiter Research, end-user-generated revenues from social networking, dating, and content delivery sites are expected to rise from $527 million in 2007 to over $5.7 billion by the year 2012—and social networking sites alone are expected to account for over half this total.

Getting Started on the Right Foot at Twitter

By Roger C. Parker

Twitter (www.twitter.com) is emerging as one of the most powerful social marketing tools available to internet marketers. It's free, easy to set up, and accessed millions of times a day by users—many of whom are your clients and prospects. Here are some considerations to think about before going online and setting up your Twitter account. As always, a little planning goes a long way. By addressing these issues ahead of time, you can ensure that they receive the proper thought.

- ◆ **Username:** Your choice of username may not be as obvious as it appears at first glance. How do you want to be known to other users? Your username should provide instant recognition. Do you want to use your full name, which may not describe what you do, or should you create a nickname that describes what you do or the benefit you offer? Your registration will proceed quicker if you've already addressed this issue before you start the sign-up process.
- ◆ **Blog or website URL:** This, too, may not be as obvious as it appears. You probably have one, or more, websites, plus a blog. Your profile only allows you to link to one URL. It often makes sense to link to your blog; you probably update your blog more frequently

than your website, and your profile, links, and other sidebar information probably contain more comprehensive information about you. Another option, of course, is to link to a special landing page created especially to introduce yourself to visitors from Twitter.com. You could offer a special "get acquainted" incentive on this landing page, which would help you track the effectiveness of your Twitter presence.

◆ **Biography:** Twitter.com offers you a total of 160 characters (including spaces between words) to describe your background. That's pretty limiting Prepare your bio information ahead of time, using Microsoft Word. This gives you the time to fine-tune it before posting it. (You can always change your bio, of course, by selecting Twitter's "Settings" link.) The advantage of working with Microsoft Word is that, under the Tools menu, there is a handy Word Count feature that also counts characters and characters including spaces.

I found it useful to start by making a list of the ways I want people to think of me, then organizing the list in order of importance. If it's important for my market to think of me as an author before a father (or a stay-at-home working mother, for example), I reorganize the list. With just 160 characters to work with, you have to ask yourself: "What's more important, what I have done in the past (as qualifications) or what I am doing in the present (as a sales pitch)?"

I also found that it helps to first concentrate on the message I want to deliver, then edit the message down to the 160 character limit. Tips include replacing numbers with figures (i.e., "twenty" with "20"), eliminating adjectives and adverbs, and occasionally omitting punctuation or transition phrases that you'd normally use.

◆ **Themes:** Finally, I recommend identifying, in advance, the types of daily activities you want to be associated with. Again, create a brief bulleted list of six to ten everyday activities, tasks, or categories that describe what you do. Having a "core" list of ideas to refer to each time you post will jumpstart your post.

In my case, for example, client coaching is important. So, when I log into Twitter and review my list, it helps me see the obvious: that I am preparing for an upcoming online coaching session with a new client from Ireland. Suddenly, I've written my post. Likewise, if I'm writing a book on effective copywriting and posting sample chapters on my blog as I complete them, I can describe my progress on my current chapter at Twitter.

You can frequently repeat themes on Twitter.com. For example, you can (a) describe the current case study, or topic, of the chapter you're working on, (b) announce the chapter's availability when you post it on your blog, and (c) describe the comments, questions, and suggestions generated by your blog post.

Conclusion: As always, having an idea of what you want to accomplish, and doing as much work in advance as possible, will contribute to the success of your Twitter.com marketing.

Chapter 9

PUT YOUR MEASUREMENTS IN PLACE

Now that you've decided which tactics you'll use initially to employ your strategy, you need to put measurements in place that will tell you how well the tactics are working. **Table 9.1** summarizes the major offline marketing tactics you may need to track and measure.

Building in measurements is the difference between a plan that's a nice read and one that's a true gauge for staying on track with your goals. But what exactly will you measure? That depends on the things that really tell you whether your particular business is succeeding. You need to identify the key indicators of how well you are performing. These key indicators should always align with your goals, be important measures of success, and be measurable.

You can use a template similar to **Table 9-1** to track and compare the relative effectiveness and utility of the marketing communications methods in your plan. The first column at the left lists all the media you are using. In the columns to the right, you rank each communications method on a scale of one to five. In the table, we give an example of a CAST (comparative analysis of sales tools) analysis done for an

Table 9-1. CAST—Comparative analysis of offline sales tools

	Impact or Impression	Size of Audience	Cost Per Contact	Sales Leads	Message Control	Flexibility	Timing Control	Repetitive Contact	Reaction Speed	Credibility	Closing the Sale
Sales Engineer	5	2	1	3	4	5	5	2	5	5	5
Media Advertising	4	5	4	4	5	1	3	5	2	4	2
Reference Publications	2	4	4	3	5	1	3	3	1	2	1
Public Relations/ Publicity	3	5	5	5	2	1	1	4	2	5	1
Exhibitions/ Trade Shows	5	2	2	2	4	5	1	2	5	5	5
Catalogs/ Literature	3	3	3	2	5	2	2	3	2	4	3
Direct Mail	4	4	3	4	5	3	3	4	3	3	3
Telemarketing	2	3	2	3	4	5	5	2	5	3	2

industrial manufacturer some years ago (pre-internet). As you can see, the criteria they measured marketing tools against included ability to generate sales leads, the cost per contact made, and whether the tool resulted in leads that closed.

Decide which data will tell you how well you're doing. Then, decide what outcomes you're looking for with each. For example, if cost per sales lead is critical, which of the tools in your CAST rank a 5 or a 4 in lead-generating effectiveness? If the best tool you have generates inquiries at a cost of $50 per lead, does your business model allow you to make a profit at that cost? If not, you must continue to test lead-generating methods that generate leads at a cost that lets you make money.

What Metrics Should You Measure?

Measure your outcomes. Choose data that tells you whether you're succeeding with each aspect of your strategy. Common measurements include:

- Revenue
- Number of inquiries
- Number of orders
- Average order size
- Expenses
- Break-even sales
- Cash flow
- Receivables (funds you have billed for and expect to come in)
- Payables (funds you have promised for merchandise or services and must pay)
- Average collection days (tells how long it takes to get paid)
- New clients
- Client retention rate
- Sales revenue growth
- Cost of acquiring a client or making a sale
- Lifetime value of a client
- Promotional costs
- Conversion rate
- Website traffic
- Page views
- Click-through rates
- List growth
- Changing value of your assets
- Liabilities
- Debt-to-asset ratio
- Net annual revenues
- Gross annual revenues
- Profit margin
- Market share
- Client feedback and ratings of your service

Analyze your goals, and then decide what you need to measure to know whether you're on track.

For example, Chiropractic Marketing Plans' strategy is to dominate its field within a 10-mile radius of its office by becoming the recognized expert in their area. How will CMP know whether they're dominating the field? How will it know it is the recognized expert on marketing plans for chiropractors in its area? Perez must decide what data will give her these answers. Data she might track includes:

- Requests for information from sources she targeted through direct mail, speaking, or articles
- Referrals
- New clients
- Increase in current clients requesting annual or midyear plan reviews
- New joint ventures with practice-building coaches
- Increase in revenues
- Increase in lifetime value of clients

Calculating Marketing RDI

At least once a week I get an e-mail from someone asking me, "What's considered a good response rate for direct mail?" (I also get asked the same question for response rates to radio commercials, print ads, and online advertising.) In some ways, it's a meaningless, even absurd, question. Why? Because the only logical—and honest—answer can be "It depends." What does it depend on? The product, the marketing, the mailing list, the offer, the price, the economy, the terms, the guarantee, the cost of the mailer—even what happens on the evening news the day your piece is mailed.

My usual response is to ask my e-mail correspondent, "Well, what is your marketing goal?" By that I mean, "Are you hoping your direct mail will make a profit—that is, generate $1,000 or $2,000 or $3,000 in sales for every $500 spent on the mailing?" Many small business owners want that kind of return or better. They want direct mail to generate an ROI that's some multiple of its cost. On the other hand, traditional direct marketers, especially large ones, are often content to have a mailing bring in new customers at cost.

By bringing in new customers, we mean getting strangers whose names appear on the mailing lists we rent to place their first orders with the company. By at cost, we mean the company makes no profit on the initial order, e.g., a mailing that costs $10,000 generates $10,000 in sales.

Experienced direct marketers are often content to bring in new customers at cost because they know that once they acquire a customer, they can make money on the back end—selling additional products to that same customer. In fact, in most traditional direct marketing businesses, the bulk of the profits are made on the back end, not on the initial order, known as the front end. At least one major direct marketer told me they are actually content to bring in new customers at a slight loss, because their back end is so profitable.

> **Experienced direct marketers are often content to bring in new customers at cost.**

So whether your goal is to acquire new customers at cost, double your money on the mailing, or whatever else, you need to know the percentage response required to *break even*. For instance, if your gross profit is $70 per unit sold and mailing 1,000 pieces costs you $700, you need 10 orders to break even—a 1 percent response.

The gross profit on your product is the selling price minus the cost of goods. If your product sells for $80, and it costs you $10 to make or buy, your gross profit is $70 per unit. Yes, there is the cost of shipping and handling, but for our purposes, I will assume that you charge your customers for shipping and handling and the extra charge just covers the cost.

The cost of the mailing is calculated by adding the cost of its four components: mailing list rental, postage, printing, and letter shop—the cost to assemble the components of the direct mailing and bring it to the post office. These four expenses—are *recurring costs*, which means you incur them every time you mail.

"What about the fee I paid my copywriter and graphic artist?" I am often asked. These are one-time charges and are typically not incorporated in the break-even calculation. Rather than go through the calculations here, let me send you to a free online tool that can perform this break-even calculation for you: dmresponsecalculator.com

By the way, a lot of people also ask me: "I've heard that the average direct mail response rate is 2 percent. Is that true?" It was never really true, and is less so now. The 2 percent figure was, at one time, the average response rate to direct mail packages selling magazine subscriptions. The response rates for other products and offers were different. For instance, seminar promoters often got response rates from 0.25 percent to 0.5 percent, and sometimes as low as 0.1 percent. And response rates overall today are declining. One fundraising consultant told me that response rates for direct mail in the nonprofit field used to average 3 percent, but today, they are closer to 1 percent.

The reason for the decline: consumers are bombarded by so much mail and so many other competing advertising messages that it's more difficult to grab their attention.

Calculating and Measuring ROTI

Do you need a lot of money to conduct a marketing campaign? It depends on the media you select. Blogging and social networking cost almost no money. Television advertising and direct mail, by comparison, are rather expensive.

Virtually all effective marketing channels require either time or money. You do not need both. If you have little time but a lot of money, you can buy the advertising exposure you need. On the other hand, if you are on a beer budget but are willing to put in a lot of time and effort, you can market your products and services on a shoestring.

With marketing media that cost little money, there is still an investment to implement the tactic, and that investment is your time. That is no small investment. One can argue that time is even more valuable than money, being the one resource you cannot replace: you can always make more money, but once an hour is gone, you can never get it back.

For social media, blogging, public speaking, networking, and other time-intensive marketing methods, I measure a metric called ROTI, or *return on time invested*. To measure the cost of the time invested, you multiply the hours spent on the activity times your hourly rate. You then compare that with the revenues generated from the marketing activity. If the dollar value of the time spent is less than the value of the sales generated, the ROTI is negative and the activity is a drain on your resources. On the other hand, if the value of the clients, contracts, and orders you get from the marketing activity is many times greater than the dollar value of your time invested, it has a positive ROTI and should likely be continued or even ramped up.

For instance, a colleague told me she spent 10 hours writing a major think piece for her blog. She said it was a success because of the buzz it created and the large number of people going to her blog to read the article.

But so far, none of those people has hired her or bought anything from her. If her time is worth $150 an hour, the time invested in this blog marketing effort is worth $1,500, and the revenue produced is zero. That's a zero ROTI, which in my book means the whole effort was of questionable value and the time could have been better spent on more profitable activities.

> **If the dollar value of the time spent is less than the value of the sales generated, the ROTI is negative and the activity is a drain on your resources.**

She would argue that there are other benefits to her blogging not taken into account by the ROTI. These include gaining visibility for her ideas, establishing herself as a thought leader in her field, and increasing the number of subscribers to her blog as well as adding many followers on Twitter.

Those kinds of results are "soft metrics." A soft metric is one that generates a return other than orders, sales, and revenues. I do not dismiss the value of soft metrics. They can be beneficial. I have sought them many times in my marketing. But at the same time, if the ROTI of a time-intensive marketing activity is low, you do need to question whether it is worth your time and effort to conduct it.

Doubling Hour and Doubling Day

In the good old days of direct mail, a useful metric for helping us forecast whether our DM campaigns would be successes or failures was *doubling day*.

Doubling day was the day on which you would have received half of the responses your mailing was going to produce.

Therefore, by multiplying the number of orders received by doubling day by 2, you could reliably forecast the total number of responses and orders the mailing was going to produce.

Doubling day typically was 2 weeks or so—not from the date you dropped the mailing, but from the date you got your first response.

In e-mail marketing, we get our responses and orders much faster than with snail mail. So there is no "doubling day"—but there is a "doubling hour."

Doubling hour is the hour by which the orders received, multiplied by 2, is an accurate forecaster of the total number of orders your e-mail marketing message is going to produce.

Figure 9-1 below represents sales of a $39 e-book on internet marketing we were selling to my subscriber list. The graph shows total number of units sold as a function of time.

If you look at the graph, you can see that I sent an e-mail marketing message to my subscriber list on September 8, 2009 at 10 a.m. EST. The total number of orders produced by this e-mail was 160 units sold in 11 days.

But half that total—80 orders—was generated by 4 p.m. EST on September 8, 2009. I've found this rate of response fairly consistent in my e-mail marketing.

Therefore, "doubling hour" in my internet marketing business is the seventh hour after distributing the e-mail marketing message to my list.

I normally send my e-mail marketing messages to my list twice weekly, one on Tuesday and a second on Thursday. We may add a third message on Friday or Saturday if we have a special promotion to do for an affiliate.

The doubling hour lets me know that at 5 p.m. on the same day I distributed the message to my list, I will have received half the total orders I am going to get from that e-mail.

Look at the graph and you see that is steepest at the very beginning. That's because you get a flood of early orders right away.

In this example, we got 40 orders—a quarter of the total—within the first two hours.

This pattern of getting a quarter of the orders within two hours also holds on a consistent basis.

Therefore, after two hours, I can multiply the number of orders received by four and, with pretty good accuracy, predict the total orders the e-mail will generate—though it is not quite as reliable as the doubling hour.

All internet marketers, whether novice or experienced, know this to be true: if you don't get a bunch of orders early after you distribute your e-mail, the campaign is going to bomb.

I am often asked by internet newbies, "What kind of results can I expect in terms of sales?"

In my business, we have a primary list of around 50,000 online subscribers who get all of the offers.

(We have a second list of around 30,000 subscribers, but we'll ignore them for this discussion.)

The primary list is regularly sent e-mails selling information products ranging in price from $29 to $100.

For an e-book or other electronic information product in the $29 to $59 price range, here's how we evaluate the success of our campaigns:

25 orders is a dud—a bomb.

50 orders is a decent response.

100 orders is a very good response.

150 orders is an excellent response.

200 orders is a home run.

Notice that the decent response of 50 orders is a 0.1 percent response rate for orders.

Outsiders are surprised that the numbers are so small.

"How do you make any money this way?" they ask.

They forget what the late Gary Halbert said: the internet is the least effective marketing medium but the most efficient.

What he meant was that e-mail marketing is not very powerful, so the response rates are much lower than direct mail, which generates (when it works) 1 to 2 percent, and not a tenth of a percent.

Figure 9-1

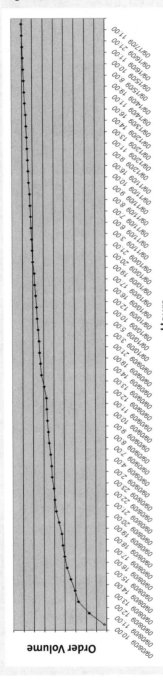

But direct mail is very expensive, costing at least $500 per thousand prospects receiving the mailer, or at minimum, 50 cents each.

E-mail marketing, by comparison, costs less than a tenth of a penny per prospect when sent to your own opt-in subscriber list (you still have to pay a small charge to your e-mail distribution service or software provider).

If I sell 100 units of a $39 e-book, my gross for that e-mail marketing blast is $3,900.

Do that twice a week, and you are making $7,800 in sales every week.

And for an internet marketer selling e-books and other electronic products, there is no manufacturing, inventory, fulfillment, or shipping cost—and the profit margin is close to 100 percent. Also, the e-mail messages go only to my own list, so my marketing costs are also close to zero.

Measuring Web Metrics

Lord Kelvin, inventor of the Kelvin temperature scale, said: "When you can measure something and can express it in numbers, you know something about it." Web metrics are the numbers that let you know something about your website's performance and ROI, and web analytics are the software that lets you measure those numbers.

In the early days of the internet, websites were the online equivalent of sales brochures or general advertising: pages posted online to disseminate product information, establish an online presence, and help position the company in the marketplace.

Today's most successful websites are the online equivalent of direct response marketing. They have specific marketing objectives and business goals, and their performance and sales can be precisely measured.

Measuring web metrics is a critical step in determining whether a website is producing a positive ROI and serving users in the manner intended. Web analytics is the study of user interaction with a website by collecting information about what the visitor does. This data is tabulated and refined into reports and visual presentations to help analysts understand whether a website is achieving a set of desired results.

The web has created a whole new array of metrics, ranging from simple to complex, for measuring web marketing performance. Some of the web metrics measured include click density analysis, visitor primary purpose, task completion rates, segmented visitor trends, and multichannel impact analysis. Other techniques used inweb metrics include web traffic data, web transactional data, and web server performance data. Each one in turn served a purpose for web masters as they sought ways to keep tabs on traffic to their websites.

Click Density Analysis: Click density analysis is used with site overlay of the web analytics tool. This tool helps you see if your visitors are clicking on what you want or clicking on something else. It is powerful because it allows you to look at your web pages and see what various segments of your customers are doing. In other words, if you segment your traffic, you know what each segment is doing when they get to your Web pages. You may find that traffic that comes from Google is different or takes different actions than traffic that comes from Yahoo!

Visitor Primary Purpose: Most web masters look at page views to show them how many visitors come to their web pages. The page views tell how many times the web page or pages were loaded, but not why the visitor showed up to begin with. Why did they come to your website? By asking them, you can find the reason for their visit. You can do this by simply placing a survey on your main web page where people enter the most, and ask them why they came and what about your website they liked or didn't like.

> The web has created a whole new array of metrics, ranging from simple to complex, for measuring web marketing performance.

Asking for this information can help you plan to sell products or provide information that will suit the majority of your visitors. The more you know about your visitors and why they show up, the better you can gear your website toward them. The drawback is that if you are trying to sell something on your site, the more questions you ask visitors, the fewer orders you get. Even asking one or two simple questions can cause many visitors to leave without taking the desired action.

Task Completion Rates: Page views were common for purposes of data collection, to determine which pages were being seen and which weren't. But web masters wanted more. They wanted to know if their visitors actually performed some action to complete a task found on a web page—for example, if someone went to the FAQ page and clicked on a link to see an article. This shows a task as being completed. This helped the web master know if the content placed on each web page actually worked. Of particular importance is shopping cart abandonment rate: how many people who start to use the shopping cart abandon it before the order is placed.

Segmented Visitor Trends: In the beginning, when key web metrics were gathered, there really was no way of separating the data. Sometimes certain data needed to be separated to be analyzed more thoroughly. Now, there are vendors such as ClickTracks (clicktracks.com) and Visual Sciences (websidestory.com) that provide segmentation of data, so the information we want to know can be separated into a readable format.

Multichannel Impact Analysis: In the past, you may have used other channels to help promote your website, including television, radio, or print ads. Unfortunately, there really was no clear-cut way to measure these channels. With multichannel impact analysis as part of the web metrics tools, you can measure the traffic generated by channels. This way, you can properly monitor where your traffic is coming from and judge which channel sources are the most productive.

Web Traffic Data: Of all the web metrics tools used, Web traffic data may be the most useful and most popular. web traffic data started out as web server logs, then became JavaScript tags. Traffic data became a goldmine for web masters, as it contained a lot of valuable information, such as number of visitors to a website, the number of bytes sent and received, the page the visitor came from, what pages were seen, the IP address of the visitor, the authenticated user name of the requester, the date and time of the request, and more.

> **When talking about Web metrics, we can't leave out such tools at Web logs, Web beacons, JavaScript tags, and packet sniffing.**

Web Transactional Data: Any time a transaction occurs on a web page, especially if the web page is set up for e-commerce, this data is recorded, then becomes available and viewable as part of the web metrics tools. This data contains the number of customers, number of orders processed, average size of the order, and total daily revenues.

Web Server Performance Data: Since the internet has become so widely used, with millions of people logging in every day (internetworldstats.com/stats.htm), there are many people doing business online. This has its advantages and disadvantages. The advantages are that more people are able to get information they need, shop, and conduct business online. On the other hand, the disadvantage is that this creates a lot of traffic and places a heavy load on web servers. This is why web performance data is critical to web masters or system administrators, who can view these data logs, see what is happening regarding traffic, and determine the course of action to take to ensure that the web server keeps operating and their clients' websites do not go down. Web server performance data also includes information about what parts of a website are viewed, what files are downloaded, and what scripts run.

When talking about web metrics, we can't leave out such tools at web logs, web beacons, JavaScript tags, and packet sniffing.

Web Logs: The original source of data collection at the dawn of the web was web logs. In the beginning, web logs were primarily used to capture errors generated by web servers. Over time, they were upgraded to capture more data, including server usage trends and browser types. When this occurred, they switched from being technically based to being marketing-based. Web logs work like this:

1. A customer types your URL into the browser.
2. Your web server receives the request.
3. Your web server accepts the request and creates an entry in the web log for the request, including the page name, the IP address and browser the customer used, and the date and time of access.
4. The web server sends the requested web page back to the customer.

The reason web logs are popular is because they are the most easily accessible source of data. Mechanisms are in place that collect the data and create web logs. Web logs are also the only data capture mechanism that captures and stores the visits and behavior of robots (software applications that run automated tasks over the internet) that are sent from search engines. Furthermore, when using Web logs, you own the data. Other web analytic tools use vendors to collect the data.

Web Beacons: Web beacons are 1x1 pixel transparent images placed in web pages, used in combination with cookies to help web masters understand the behavior of their customers. A web beacon allows the site to record every action taken by visitors when they open the page. The beacon is part of the web page, but because it is transparent, it is invisible to the eye. web beacons came about at the time banner ads were popular on the web. This was the prime way that people caught the attention of consumers when they visited certain sites. When the visitor saw the ad, they would click on it and arrive at the predestined website, where a tool was used to measure or keep count of that click.

Cookies are used to authenticate, track, and maintain specific information about users.

Other bits of information that may get recorded include the IP address of the visited Web page, the time the page was viewed, the type of browser used to retrieve the image, and any cookies (parcels of text sent by a server to a web browser) used. Cookies are used to authenticate, track, and maintain specific information about users, such as site preferences or the contents of their electronic shopping carts. Web beacons work like this:

1. A customer types your URL into the browser.
2. Your web server receives the request.
3. The Web server sends back the requested page along with whatever the "get" request included. The get request itself is a command sent by the web server, which the user initiates in the browser. This get request is sent to a third-party server for the 1x1-pixel image.
4. As the page loads on the requester's browser, it executes the call for the 1x1-pixel image, which sends the data about the page view back to the third-party server.
5. The third-party server sends the image back to the requester's browser along with code that can read cookies and capture anonymous visitor information, including the page viewed, the IP address, the time the page was viewed, the cookies that were set, and a lot more.

You may find web beacons used in e-mails, including e-newsletters or promotional e-mails, as a way to track open and response rates. One advantage to using web beacons is that they are easy to implement: they consist of only a couple of lines of code wrapped around an IMG

SRC HTML tag. web beacons can be optimized to collect only the data you want, and can collect data from multiple websites at the same time.

JavaScript Tags: JavaScript tagging happens to be a favorite for web masters. Many vendors and Web analytics rely on JavaScript tagging to collect the data they want. JavaScript allows more data to be collected, which helps lessen the load on the web server.

With JavaScript tagging, each web page requested can be sent out with no need to worry about capturing data. The data is captured on other servers, processed, and made available to webmasters for use. Here's how JavaScript tagging works:

1. A customer types your URL into the browser.
2. Your web server receives the request.
3. The web server sends back the requested page along with a snippet of JavaScript code appended to the page.
4. As the page loads, it executes the JavaScript code. This in turn captures the page view, visitor session, and cookies, and sends it back to the server collecting the data.

JavaScript tags are easy to implement because they involve only a line of code placed in a web page. If you don't have your own web server, a third-party vendor can provide the code for you. With JavaScript tagging, you have control of what data you want to capture.

Packet Sniffing: From a technical perspective, packet sniffing is one of the most sophisticated tools for data collection. Examples of data it collects include server errors, bandwidth usage, all technical as well as page-related business data, passwords, names, addresses, and credit card numbers. In a nutshell, it collects every possible bit of data that can be recorded, which creates security risks.

Packet sniffing has been around for quite some time, but despite its longevity, not too many people use it, considering IT would have to install additional software on their already-taxed web servers. The biggest vendor to supply packet sniffing technology is Clickstream Technologies (clickstream.com/). Packet sniffing uses six steps to collect data:

1. A customer types your URL into the browser.
2. The customer's request is sent to the web server for action. Before it gets to the server, it passes through a packet sniffer that collects attributes of the request, which are sent back to the packet sniffer.
3. The packet sniffer sends the request to the web server.
4. When the web server receives the request, the requested web page is sent back to the customer by way of the packet sniffer.
5. The packet sniffer takes the requested web page, captures necessary information about the web page, and stores the data.
6. The packet sniffer sends the page on to the customer.

A packet sniffer can be software installed on a web server, or a piece of hardware installed in the data center, which reroutes all traffic to the web server.

There are dozens of ways to measure website performance by tracking metrics. Here are a few of the key metrics marketers and webmasters routinely measure using analytics tools:

◆ **Unique Visits:** How many people visit the website per month, and not the total number of hits or clicks.

◆ **Page Views:** A measure of what pages on a site were seen the most. A large number of views indicates that the content on a page is of greater interest to visitors than content in other parts of the site.

◆ **Pages:** Tells us which pages cause visitors to abandon the site. A high exit rate indicates the content on the page was of little interest to visitors.

◆ **Bounce rate:** How many people driven to the site from an external traffic source (organic search, pay-per-click, banner ads) viewed just one page of the site and then left—an indication of poor search optimization and lack of compelling content.

◆ **Stickiness:** How long people stay on a particular page or website when they arrive. The longer they stay, the greater your chance of making a brand impression or sale.

◆ **Site Entry Points:** Tells you how people get into your site, and the pathway they travel to reach your landing or transaction pages.

◆ **Key Words and Phrases:** Tracking the source of traffic to determine which keywords and phrases people searched to find your site.

◆ **Conversion Rate:** Percentage of visitors to a transaction page who take the indicated action, whether it's downloading a white paper or purchasing merchandise.

◆ **Click Density:** Measures the number of clicks on each area or zone of the web page (including links, images, text, and white space) to show which spots users are actively viewing and clicking, and which zones they ignore.

Marketing Performance Reporting

Ultimately, you want to quantify the outcomes of your tactics. Then, you want to compare how your actual results stack up against expected results. You don't just want to know whether you completed the proposed activities: You want to measure the results of those activities.

So, rather than only measuring whether the two articles per month she'll use as a tactic for generating leads were published, Perez needs to measure the number of qualified leads she received as a result, and then measure whether the leads led to sales. Remember, you're trying to quantify which tactics will give you bottom-line, dollars-and-cents results.

It's important to track whether your planned actions were completed. Just remember that, ultimately, you want to measure your outcomes: revenues, new clients, commission from joint ventures, lower client acquisition costs, and so on. **Figure 9-2** shows a form you can use to keep track of inquiries and sales generated by almost any type of promotion imaginable.

Figure 9-2. Inquiries and sales form

Month _____ Year _____

Ad or mailing _____ Key code _____

Product _____ Offer _____

Total Cost _____ Total Sales_____

Day	# Inquiries	Total Inquiries to date	Days sales	Total sales to date
1				
2				
3				
4				
5				
6				
7				
8				
9				
10				
11				
12				
13				
14				
15				
16				
17				
18				
19				
20				
21				
22				
23				
24				
25				
26				
27				
28				
29				
30				
31				

Create the Tracking System

To start, create a simple system. Remember, the point is to be able to tell whether you're nailing your expected results.

First, list everything you'll track. Decide when and how often it will be tracked. List the expected result for each item. List the source of the information you'll use to get the actual result.

A simple table that will let you keep score appears in **Table 9-2**. The beauty of this table is that it's easy to change, add, or delete columns as your needs change. You can create it in Excel or Word. At the end of each month, add the printout to a three-ring binder. Create tables to summarize quarterly results. If you need a system more detailed than this one, get input from your accountant or bookkeeper on how to design it.

Table 9-2. Tracking results for month/year

Tracking Results for Month/Year								
				Cost		Outcome		
Goal	Strategy	Tactic	Data	Expected	Actual	Expected	Actual	Source Used
	Strategy 1	Tactic 1						
	Strategy 2	Tactic 2						
		Tactic 3						

Determine How Often to Review the Data

Decide what makes sense for your business. At the very least, every week, you should track your progress in meeting your monthly goals. For some businesses, it makes sense to tabulate everything daily. This may become especially important when cash flow is tight and bills are due.

The software that runs my internet marketing business tracks my key metrics—including orders, units sold, and gross revenues—in real time. You could look at it every five minutes, but you'd never get anything else done. What I do is look at the week's gross revenue to date at the end of each day. That way, I know whether I am on track to meet my revenue goal. If not, I can take actions to increase sales activity. At the end of each week, I look at a detailed report with all my metrics, including click-through rates, conversion rates, open rates, opt-outs, and new names added, and plan for the next week accordingly. The point is, you should set a regular period for entering and reviewing your results. It will soon become apparent whether you need to adjust your tactics. You can find out about the integrated e-commerce software I use in my online business at automateyouronlinebusinessnow.com.

Action...

Write What and How You'll Measure

- ◆ What data will you measure to track your results?
- ◆ How will you measure each metric?
- ◆ What system will you use?

_____

_____

_____

_____

_____

_____

_____

_____

Predicting the Probable Success or Failure of a New Product or Marketing Idea

At least once a week, someone comes to me with a business idea—typically a new product or service—and asks, "Will this work?"

Perhaps you, too, have an idea for a new product or service, but would like to know whether it has a realistic chance of success before you invest your time and hard-earned money in it.

I will give you the same piece of advice I give everyone else: Look around to see whether anyone else is doing what you propose.

If you find at least one other person doing it successfully (i.e., making money at it), then it could work for you, too—if you are smart and lucky. On the other hand, if no one else is doing it, there's no reason to think you can, and I'd probably look for something else.

This may be somewhat counterintuitive. Then again, a lot of business success principles are.

"Isn't it great that no one else is doing my idea?" someone asked me the last time I said this. "That means I thought of it first and there's no competition!"

Actually, it's almost certain that many others thought of it before you. What should trouble you is that these individuals—some of whom may be as smart or even smarter than you—evaluated the idea, and after careful consideration, decided not to proceed. In other words, the reason no one else is doing your idea is because it won't work.

Conversely, you might think that if others are doing your idea, there's already too much competition. That may or may not be the case.

But if others are doing the same idea, and making money at it, then that idea has been proven beyond a shadow of a doubt to work in the real world. And if they are making good money at it, there's a good chance you can, too. After all, you are probably as smart—or smarter—than many of those people.

Many of the people you probably think of as innovators were actually not. Bill Gates, for instance, is thought of as the creator of the first personal computer operating system, MS-DOS. But actually, another programmer created MS-DOS. Bill Gates bought it from him for $50,000 cash, made some modifications, and sold it to IBM for royalties that made him the wealthiest man in the world.

In fact, MS-DOS was not even the first PC operating system. An earlier one was CPM, a rival operating system. IBM was interested in this, but the owners of CPM couldn't find the time to meet with IBM, and the rest is history.

One other counterintuitive piece of advice: If you decide to market a new product or service, and your test campaign fails miserably, don't keep pushing to make it incrementally better in the hopes that you can turn it into a winner. It is better to cut your losses and abandon the idea—before you pour good money after bad.

For example: An individual came to me asking if I could save her business by writing a direct mail package. I asked what her first mailing, which seemed competent to me (though not first rate), brought in. Did it break even? Cover half its mailing cost? Turns out it pulled only a few orders with thousands ofpieces mailed.

I reminder her, "Even a great package might pull only double or triple a package that failed, and even if we triple the response, you won't even be close to breaking even. So this just isn't going to work." Needless to say, I did not write the package for her, though I am convinced I saved her from wasting many thousands of dollars on another test doomed to fail.

Chapter 10
WRITE YOUR PLAN

At this point, you've collected most of the information you need to write your action plan. What remains is to sit down and write it.

In addition to providing you with a roadmap for your marketing efforts for the next 12 months, the plan can save you time communicating your business vision and objectives with others. You may want to share the plan (or sections of it)—on a confidential basis, of course—with some or all of the following folks:

- Bankers
- Venture capitalists
- Private investors
- Business partners
- Affiliates
- Ad agencies
- Marketing consultants
- SEO specialists
- Other vendors
- Employees
- Freelancers
- Media reps
- Mastermind circle
- Trusted friends and advisors.

Write It Down to Get It Done

A written plan is far more likely to be implemented than a plan you have in your head. That alone increases your chances for succeeding in your business. Once you write down everything, you'll have a handy guide to refer to on a daily basis. Your written plan will provide a time-table for getting things done. This will help you stay on track to meet your goals for the year. Also, when something doesn't work, it will be easier to make small adjustments to fine tune your plan if the initial plan is in black and white.

Gather all your responses to the Action items from the previous chapters. You can find blank forms in Appendix B. If you've completed the Actions in each step, you'll soon see that you've already written most of your plan.

First, remind yourself of what you're trying to do here: plan how you're going to sell your products or services. For most businesses, that's a multistage process. Use the form shown in **Table 10-1** (there's a blank form in **Appendix B**) to identify the tactic(s) you'll use at each stage of your own selling process. If a stage doesn't apply to your sell-ing process, skip it.

Table 10-1. Stages in CMP's selling process

How will I generate as many leads as I want?	Direct mail, articles, speaking, referrals, joint ventures.
How will I qualify leads?	Call after mailing or getting leads from marketing efforts; find out the business's chief growth challenge and how committed they are to marketing; explain how I work and find out if they're interested in proceeding.
How will I get appointments to meet or present (if applicable)?	Call and qualify the lead. If there's a strong win-win potential, ask for the appointment.
What offer will I make to close the sale?	Not sure yet.
How will I follow up with qualified leads until they purchase?	Create a "touches" system to ensure ongoing, monthly contact. Make sure the methods build in value for the prospect.
How will I follow up with new clients after the sale to continue serving and selling to them?	Maintenance plan, referral plan, touches system for clients, joint ventures, surveys.

Use a Swipe File to Write Promotions Better and Faster

A "swipe" file is a collection of promotions you have collected from other marketers.

"A good swipe file is better than a college education," says master copywriter Milt Pierce.

The swipe file provides inspiration and ideas from successful marketing campaigns you may be able to use in your promotion.

By doing so, it can help overcome writer's block. With ideas from a swipe file, you can write copy better and faster.

Some marketers, however, question whether using a swipe file is legal or even ethical.

"Isn't it plagiarizing?" they wonder.

I'm not a lawyer, so I really can't answer that from a legal standpoint.

Most copywriters I know avoid plagiarizing. They do not lift headlines and body copy directly from other ads. Instead, they use them as sources of ideas for their own copy. Though sometimes the "inspired" ad may be too close to the original for some people's comfort.

For instance, did you know that David Ogilvy has been accused of stealing the headline for his most famous ad from another copywriter?

The headline for Ogilvy's classic ad for Rolls Royce was:

"At 60 miles an hour the loudest noise in this new Rolls-Royce comes from the electric clock."

It was always believed that Ogilvy came up with this brilliant way of communicating Rolls Royce quality on his own—perhaps by driving his own Rolls.

I have also heard that he found the fact about the Rolls Royce clock in an article published in an automotive trade journal.

But now others are saying he took it from another car ad, for Pierce-Arrows.

And their headline, which was published years before Ogilvy's Rolls ad, indeed is remarkably similar: "The only sound one can hear in the new Pierce-Arrows is the ticking of the electric clock."

I don't know whether Ogilvy had a swipe file and deliberately swiped the idea from Pierce-Arrows.

Today their ad is forgotten but his is one of the classic ads of all time.

Why?

I think the addition of "at 60 mph" makes the Rolls ad much stronger.

Back then, big cars were noisier than they are today, and a car that quiet at high-speed was a much more credible demonstration of quality than a car that was quiet when parked.

Lots of copywriters today keep swipe files of promotions in their industry, particularly health and financial writers.

But my old teacher, Milt Pierce, preferred to get his inspiration and ideas from promotions for products different than the one he was writing about.

When a client who is selling insurance asked Milt to create a direct mail package, he would avoid looking in his insurance swipe file.

Instead, he looked in his swipe files for totally unrelated products. Why?

The reason is simple. If you create an insurance package that looks like every other insurance package, you're just being a copycat," said Milt.

"However, if you check through other types of packages, you're more likely to come up with an original approach to the insurance package."

A good example is a recent print ad I saw for the Stauer Titanium watch. The ad shows a large photo of the watch. The headline above it reads: "We Apologize that It Loses 1 Second Every 20 Million Years."

The style and approach seem, to me anyway, to be inspired by the Ogilvy Rolls Royce ad. If it were a car ad, it would seem derivative of the Ogilvy ad—not very original. But Stauer has created a compelling ad by adapting Ogilvy's straightforward, fact-based copy approach to a watch.

It's an approach not typically used in this category, so it supports Milt's claim that applying ideas used in one industry to another can result in an interesting and effective promotion.

Create a One-Year Plan

Now that you know what you need to do to be successful at each stage of the selling process, make sure you include the tactics you identified in your action plan. A lot can change in three years, so start with a one-year plan. You already set a goal for what you want to accomplish during the next year, created strategies to succeed in achieving that goal, and identified the top three to five tactics you'll employ to implement the strategies. Now, it's time to detail the actions you'll take.

Figure 10-1. Steps in creating a one-year plan

Identify Your To-Dos

Table 10-2 lays out the action plan for implementing one of CMP's strategies:

- ◆ **Column 1:** The goal
- ◆ **Column 2:** The strategies identified to achieve the goal
- ◆ **Column 3:** The tactics to implement each strategy
- ◆ **Column 4:** The to-dos to implement each tactic
- ◆ **Column 5:** The timeline for completing the series of steps
- ◆ **Column 6** (not pictured): Who is responsible for carrying out the actions

Table 10-2. Action plan for CMP

Goal:	Strategy	Tactic	To Do	Due
Increase sales from $150K to $200K by Dec. 31	Become well known for writing marketing plans for chiropractors because no one else in CMP's coverage area is doing this.	Direct mail campaign to CMP's list four times during the year to build and nurture relationship.	Identify four hot buttons for these practices. Focus on one in each of the four mailings. Identify a way to add value to each of the mailings so recipients have a reason to both read and keep the mailing. Decide what action we want chiropractors to take after reading the mailing. Decide what kind of offer to include. Decide who will write the letter. Decide who will put the mailing together.	Jan. 15 April 15 (mail after tax deadline) July 15 Sept. 15
		Article marketing campaign	Write articles for both online and offline magazines. Get four articles published in offline magazines targeting chiropractors. Use the articles in mailings to CMP's list and on their website. Write five articles initially by Jan. 31 to send to online article directories, then add one new article each month. Add all articles to the CMP website. Decide whether to hire a ghostwriter. Begin researching and interviewing ghostwriters.	April 1 May 1 June 1 Oct. 1 Jan. 31 End of each month
		Speak to chiropractic groups	Identify networking groups that local chiropractors belong to or attend. Create four or five presentations that will appeal to our ideal client. Hire a virtual assistant. Have VA assemble speaker's kit and begin contacting organizations to get speaking gigs. Speak once a month.	Jan. 31 Mar. 1 Mar. 31 April 1
		Institute a strong referral program	Determine what the referral program should do for CMP. Decide how the program should benefit those who make referrals. Decide benefits for those who schedule appointments through referrals. Create the referral program. Add it to website and all direct mail. Look for other opportunities to promote the program.	Jan. 31

See Chiropractic Marketing Plans, Inc.'s full one-year plan in **Appendix C.**

Budget

The annual marketing budget is often determined as a percentage of the total annual sales revenues. The table below shows these percentages for a variety of businesses. These are rough guidelines only and not precise. They also ignore the stage the business is in: for startups, which have limited current revenues and desperately need to make sales and add customers, marketing budgets can be many multiples of the percentages below.

Table 10-3. Advertising budget percentages by industry

Industry	Advertising Budget as a Percentage of Sales
Advertising agencies	0.1%
Agricultural production, crops	2.9%
Air courier services	2.1%
Air transportation, certified	1.8%
Aircraft and parts	0.5%
Auto dealers, gas stations	0.5%
Auto rental and leasing	2.9%
Auto repair services and garages	4.0%
Bakery products	1.9%
Book publishers	3.8%
Business services	5.3%
Catalog showrooms	3.7%
Chemicals (wholesale)	3.5%
Coating and engraving services	2.6%
Computer program and software services	3.5%
Communications and signaling devices	4.1%
Commercial printing	1.2%
Computer equipment	1.9%
Computer stores	1.0%
Computers, micro	5.1%
Connectors	1.2%
Construction, special trade	9.8%
Dairy products	4.9%
Data processing services	1.2%
Detective and protective services	0.2%
Drugs	4.4%
Educational services	5.0%
Electric appliances, wholesale	0.8%
Electric lighting	1.1%
Electronic components	2.3%
Engines and turbines	1.8%
Engineering, architect, survey services	0.8%

Table 10-3. Continued

Farm machinery and equipment	1.6%
Financial services	0.7%
Food	7.3%
Freight forwarding	3.6%
Hardware, wholesale	6.4%
Health services	3.3%
Hospitals	5.8%
Hotels	0.4%
Industrial controls	1.7%
Industrial machinery and equipment, wholesale	2.0%
Insurance agents and brokers	0.6%
Lumber, wholesale	2.2%
Machine tools	2.0%
Material handling equipment	1.0%
Medical laboratories	0.9%
Metalworking equipment	5.4%
Management consulting	1.8%
Motor vehicle parts and accessories	1.6%
Motors and generators	1.0%
Musical instruments	3.3%
Newspapers	3.9%
Office automation systems	2.3%
Office furniture	1.4%
Optical instruments and lenses	1.5%
Outpatient care facilities	1.1%
Paint, varnish, and lacquer	3.1%
Paper and paper products	3.8%
Personal services	3.7%
PR services	1.8%
Office supplies	5.2%
Photofinishing laboratories	1.8%
Photographic equipment and supplies	3.2%
Plastics, resins, elastomers	1.6%
Pollution control machinery	0.8%
Prefabricated metal buildings	0.7%
Pumps	1.2%
Real estate agencies	2.8%
Savings and loan associations	0.7%
Securities and commodities brokers	3.8%
Semiconductors	1.2%
Ship and boat building and repair	2.3%
Soaps and detergents	7.6%
Telephone communications (wire, radio)	1.9%
Textile mill products	1.1%
Tires and inner tubes	3.1%
Training equipment and simulators	1.6%
Valves	1.0%

Budget Allocation

Once you have a marketing budget, you have to allocate it by month or season and by marketing medium. Use the worksheet shown in **Table 10-4** can be used to do this.

Table 10-4. Advertising budget allocation worksheet

Advertising Expenditures by Month and by Medium

	Jan $	Feb $	Mar $	Apr $	May $	Jun $	Jul $	Aug $	Sep $	Oct $	Nov $	Dec $
Media Print Newspaper 1. 2. 3.												
Consumer Magazine 1. 2. 3.												
Trade Publications 1. 2. 3.												
Radio AM 1. 2. 3.												
Radio FM 1. 2. 3.												
Television 1. 2. 3.												

Table 10-4. Continued

Specialty 1. 2. 3.													
Direct Mail 1. 2. 3.													
Point-of- Purchase 1. 2. 3.													
Co-op 1. 2. 3.													
Other 1. 2. 3.													

Plot Major Campaigns First

Major campaigns require more resources and time to get things done than the typical marketing actions you'll take. So plan for those first.

As you saw in the action plan above, CMP has decided to do four major direct mail campaigns to all the family wellness chiropractic practices on their target list. The mailings will go out in January, April, July, and October.

Use a major campaigns calendar like this one to help you think through the resources you'll need to complete your actions (a blank form is in **Appendix A**). That way, you won't be delayed because you failed to anticipate something you need until the last minute.

Table 10-5. CMP's major campaigns for 2008

	Campaign	Expected Cost	Actual Cost	Resources	Expected Results	Actual Results
Jan	Direct mail (referral & new client letters)	$500	$	List, sales letter, offer	1 new client	
Feb	Touch 1	$200	$	Article	3 new clients	
Mar	Touch 2	$200	$	Postcards	2 new clients	
Apr	Direct mail	$500	$	List, sales letter, offer	3 new clients	
May	Workshop; Touch 3 (calls)	$600	$	Location, handouts	5 new clients	
Jun	Touch 4	$200	$	Case study	3 new clients	
Jul	Direct mail	$500	$	List, sales letter, offer	3 new clients	
Aug	Touch 5	$200	$	Special report	3 new clients	
Sep	Touch 6	$200	$	Article	3 new clients	
Oct	Direct mail	$500	$	List, sales letter, offer	4 new clients	
Nov	Touch 7 (calls); seminar	$1100	$	Location, manuals	6 new clients	
Dec	Touch 8 (Happy Holidays)	$300	$	Cards	1 new client	
Comments:		Campaigns to repeat:			Campaigns to drop:	

Break It Down

Now that you have a plan, it might at first glance look like a lot to take on. The best way to tackle your plan is to break it down into manageable segments. This is why we began by plotting the big stuff, the major campaigns, first. It gives us time to think about what each campaign will require: the actions to complete it, the resources needed, when it has to begin to be ready on time, and a tracking system to evaluate whether it did what it was supposed to do.

Here's an easy way to approach this challenge:

- Remember, you set a one-year goal and created strategies to achieve that goal. It makes sense to ask yourself what you need to accomplish by the halfway mark to stay on track to complete the annual goal. So begin with your six-month goals.

- The halfway mark between six months and one year is nine months. Ask yourself what you'll need to complete by nine months to meet the one-year goal.

- Now, the halfway mark between your starting date and six months is three months. Ask yourself what you'll need to complete during the first three months of your plan to stay on track to meet your six-month goal.

- Three months will come and go quickly without progress unless you take regular action toward your goals. It's easy to wrap your mind around completing specific actions within the next month. So ask yourself what you must accomplish during the next month to stay on track to meet your three-month goals. Near the end of that month, do the same for the following month—knowing that you now have only two months left to hit your three-month markers.

Marketing activity and expenditures are usually not constant throughout the year. Your business may have busy seasons and slow seasons. Accounting and tax preparation firms, for example, are enormously busy from January 1 through April 15. Your marketing and media activities and budget can be used in any of the patterns shown in **Figure 10-2**. A business that has constant work all year, such as an electrical contractor, might use the steady pattern and spread its marketing efforts equally over the months. A business that is hit with periodic slowdowns could use the fighting or pulsing pattern to combat these turndowns.

Figure 10-2. Media scheduling

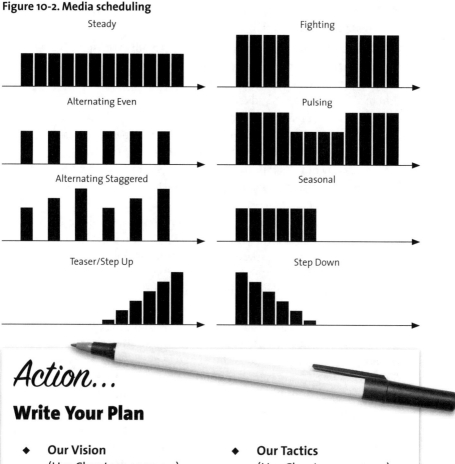

Action...

Write Your Plan

- ◆ **Our Vision**
  (Use Chapter 1 answers)
- ◆ **Our Niche**
  (Use Chapter 2 answers)
- ◆ **Our Ideal Client**
  (Use Chapter 3 answers)
- ◆ **Our Competition**
  (Use Chapter 4 answers)
- ◆ **Our Strategy**
  (Use Chapter 5 answers)

- ◆ **Our Tactics**
  (Use Chapter 7 answers)
- ◆ **Our Measurement Stick**
  (Use Chapter 9 answers)
- ◆ **Our Action Plan**
- ◆ **Our 30-day goals**
- ◆ **Our 3-month goals**
- ◆ **Our 6-month goals**
- ◆ **Our 9-month goals**
- ◆ **Our 12-month goals**

10 Ways to Stretch Your Marketing Budget

Most small businesses have modest marketing budgets, which means you have to make every dollar count. Here are 10 ways to get big results from a small budget:

1. First, use your ads for more than just space advertising. Ads are expensive to produce and expensive to run. But there are ways to get your advertising message in your prospect's hands at a fraction of the cost of space advertising.

The least expensive is to order an ample supply of reprints and distribute them to customers and prospects every chance you get. When you send literature in response to an inquiry, include a copy of the ad in the package. This reminds a prospect of the reason he responded in the first place and reinforces the original message.

Distribute ads internally to other departments—engineering, production, sales, customer service, and R&D—to keep them up to date on your latest marketing and promotional efforts. Make sure your salespeople receive an extra supply of reprints and are encouraged to include a reprint when they write to or visit their customers.

Turn the ad into a product data sheet by adding technical specifications and additional product information to the back of the ad reprint. This eliminates the expense of creating a new layout from scratch. And it makes good advertising sense, because the reader gets double exposure to your advertising message.

Ad reprints can be used as inexpensive direct mail pieces. You can mail the reprints along with a reply card and a sales letter. Unlike the ad, which is "cast in concrete," the letter is easily and inexpensively tailored to specific markets and customer groups.

If you've created a series of ads on the same product or product line, publish bound reprints of the ads as a product brochure. This tactic increases prospect exposure to the series and is less expensive than producing a brand new brochure.

If your ads provide valuable information of a general nature, you can offer reprints as free educational material to companies in your industry. Or, if the ad presents a striking visual, you can offer reprints suitable for framing.

Use your ads again and again. You will save money—and increase frequency—in the process.

2. If something works, stick with it. Too many marketers scrap their old promotions and create new ones because they're bored with their current campaign. That's a waste. You shouldn't create new ads or promotions if your existing ones are still accurate and effective. You should run your ads for as long as your customers read and react to them.

How long can ads continue to get results? The Ludlow Corp. ran an ad for its erosion-preventing Soil Saver mesh 41 times in the same journal. After 11 years it pulled more inquiries per issue than when it was first published in 1966.

If a concept still has selling power but the promotion contains dated information, update the existing copy—don't throw it out and start from scratch. This approach isn't fun for the ad manager or the agency, but it does save money.

3. Don't over present yourself. A strange thing happens to some entrepreneurs when they get a little extra money in the ad budget: they see fancy four-color brochures, gold embossed mailers, and fat annual reports produced by Fortune 500 firms. Then they say, "This stuff sure looks great—why don't we do some brochures like this?"

That's a mistake. The look, tone, and image of your promotions should be dictated by your product and your market—not by what other companies in other businesses put out.

Producing literature that's too fancy for its purpose and its audience is a waste of money. And it can even *hurt* sales—your prospects will look at your overdone literature and wonder whether you really understand your market and its needs.

4. Use "modular" product literature. One common advertising problem is how to promote a single product to many small, diverse markets. Each market has different needs and will buy the product for different reasons. But on your budget, you can't afford to create a separate brochure for each of these tiny market segments.

The solution is *modular literature*. This means creating a basic brochure layout that has sections capable of being tailored to meet specific market needs. After all, most sections of the brochure—technical specifications, service, company background, product operation, product features—will be the same regardless of the audience. Only a few sections, such as benefits of the product to the user and typical applications, need to be tailored to specific readers.

In a modular layout, standard sections remain the same, but new copy can be typeset and stripped in for each market-specific section of the brochure. This way, you can create different market-specific pieces of literature on the same product using the same basic layout, mechanicals, artwork, and plates. Significant savings in time and money will result.

5. Use article reprints as supplementary sales literature. Marketing managers are constantly bombarded by requests for "incidental" pieces of product literature. Engineers want data sheets explaining some minor technical feature in great detail.

Reps selling to small, specialized markets want special literature geared to their particular audience. And each company salesperson wants support literature that fits his or her individual sales pitch. But the ad budget can only handle the major pieces of product literature. Not enough time or money exists to satisfy everybody's requests for custom literature.

The solution is to use article reprints as supplementary sales literature. Rather than spend a bundle producing highly technical or application-specific pieces, have your sales and technical staff write articles on these special topics. Then, place the articles with the appropriate journals.

Article reprints can be used as inexpensive literature and carry more credibility than self-produced promotional pieces. You don't pay for layout or printing of the article. Best of all, the article is free advertising for your firm.

6. Explore inexpensive alternatives for lead generation, such as banner advertising, organic search, and PR. Many smaller firms judge marketing effectiveness solely by the number of leads generated. They are not concerned with building image or recognition; they simply count bingo-card inquiries.

New-product press releases lead the list as the most economical method of generating leads. Once, for less than $100, I wrote, printed, and distributed a new-product release to 100 trade journals. Within six months, the release had been picked up by 35 magazines and generated 2,500 bingo-card inquiries.

Post all your press releases in a media or press section of your website. Optimize your press releases with key word phrases to draw more organic search traffic.

7. Do not overpay for outside creative talent. Hire freelancers and consultants whose credentials—and fees—fit the job and the budget.

Top advertising photographers, for example, get $1,000 a day or more. This may be worth the fee for a corporate ad running in *Forbes* or *Business Week*. But it's overkill for the employee newsletter or a publicity shot. Many competent photographers can shoot a good black-and-white publicity photo for $200 to $250.

When you hire consultants, writers, artists, or photographers, you should look for someone whose level of expertise and cost fits the task at hand.

8. Do it yourself. Tasks such as distributing press releases or creating simple squeeze pages can usually be done cheaper in-house than outside. Save the expensive agency or consultant for tasks that really require their expertise.

If you do not have a marketing manager or assistant, consider hiring a full-time or part-time administrative assistant to handle the detail work involved in managing your company's marketing. This is a more economical solution than farming administrative work out to the agency or doing it yourself.

9. Get maximum mileage out of existing content (text and images). Photos, illustrations, layouts, and even copy created for one promotion can often be lifted and reused in other pieces to significantly reduce creative costs. For example, copy created for a corporate image ad can be used as the introduction to the annual report.

Also, you can save rough layouts, thumbnail sketches, headlines, and concepts rejected for one project and use them in future ads, mailings, and promotions.

10. Pay your vendors on time. Why? You'll save money by taking advantage of discounts and avoiding late charges when you pay vendor invoices on time. And, you'll gain goodwill that can result in better service and fairer prices on future projects.

Chapter 11

WORK IT!—
IMPLEMENTATION

You now have a plan for how you're going to create the business you envisioned. But a plan that just sits on the shelf—as so many marketing plans written by high-priced consultants do—is worthless. Remember, the marketing plan is not the end. It's a means to an end.

That end is more leads, customers, orders, and sales—and a profitable small business that generates the income required to live the lifestyle you seek. So the time for reading, thinking, planning, and writing your plan is over, at least for now. The next step is the most important of all: action.

It's time to hit the ground running. How? Lay out the actions you'll take for the next 30 days. Decide the first thing you need to do. Then, do it. Decide the next action you need to take. Then, take it. And so on. And so on. And so on. Keep taking the next step and completing the next action, and before you know it, your dream will no longer be just a dream. Begin.

What Stage Is Your Business In?

When it comes to starting and running a small business, it's useful to step back and evaluate your progress every now and then. So let me ask: where are you with your business?

The answer depends partially on you and partially on the type of business you are in. For example, today the hottest area of opportunity for small business is the internet. And in my view, internet businesses fall into one of the following six levels:

- **Level 1:** "getting ready to start" phase. This is where you are spending an inordinate amount of time and money buying and studying internet marketing courses, but you aren't actually selling anything online yet.
- **Level 2:** Dip your toe in the water. You take some actions that let you generate a few sales online. The volume and dollar amount of these sales are small—just a few extra dollars in your pocket each week.
- **Level 3:** Start making a modest number of sales on a steady basis, and your online revenues are a thousand dollars a month. You're not getting rich at this level. But to most of us, an extra twelve grand a year isn't chickenfeed. In essence, you have a highly profitable hobby. You are having fun and making money in your spare time.
- **Level 4:** Your business builds until you reach $1,000 a week or more. That translates into around $50,000 a year, a significant, though not life-changing, amount of money for most Americans. At level 4, you can earn, working an hour or two a day, more than the average American makes in a year at a full-time job.
- **Level 5:** Go from $1,000 a week to $1,000 a day. At level 5, your internet business is making you well over $300,000 a year in passive income—in the ballpark of what the President of the United States makes. And you have reached the enviable position of being able to quit your job if you so desire ... because you make enough money on the internet to support your family in a comfortable lifestyle.
- **Level 6:** Your internet marketing business grosses $1 million a year or more. With the incredibly high profit margins that can be earned with online businesses, $1 million-a-year internet

business can provide a handsome lifestyle for you and your family. At level 6, you are starting to become rich, not just "comfortable" or well off.

A few more comments about some of the levels: The most common reason I see for people not making money on the internet is staying "stuck" at level 1 for way too long. They buy every internet marketing course they see advertised—and spend much of their spare time absorbing the material.

The danger is that you become the type of person who'd rather be *reading* about starting a home business than actually *doing* it.

> **The most common reason I see for people not making money on the internet is staying "stuck" at level 1 for way too long.**

To overcome inertia and break through to the next level, you need to stop reading and studying ... and actually do something.

Take action now. Start with something small—reserving a domain name. Then set a deadline for creating your first info product. Start writing your landing page copy. You get the idea.

Do something every day and within two to three months you'll have your first product. As soon as your landing page is up, you'll start getting a few orders—mostly from organic search if you haven't done any other marketing yet.

It's not a small thing. At level 2, making money on the internet becomes a reality for you, not an abstract concept. Once you get those first orders in your shopping cart, you'll taste blood. You'll be hooked. You'll be a real internet marketer, not just a wanna be.

Once you reach level 5—$1,000 of online income a day—you can enjoy a degree of financial security and freedom most folks can only dream about.

You won't be super-rich. But you'll have the money to buy most of the things you want—and quit your day job if that was your goal.

If you are at level 5, you have to decide whether you want to take the next step—and grow to level 6; you might not. Reason: most internet entrepreneurs who reach level 6 find themselves having to make the transition from small one-person business to a "real" company.

They get office and warehouse space ... set up a studio for video production ... hire salaried employees ... get health care plans for them ... have company picnics ... in short, become a manager.

But for me, the best part of being an internet marketer at level 5 is the serenity it brings me: no meetings, no whining employees, no red tape, no office politics, and no management hierarchy.

Level 5 permits you to lead a simple, quiet life earning a handsome six-figure annual income working at home—without a boss. For me, at least, that completes the dream. I am content. I would not give up the internet marketing lifestyle—not even for a million dollars. It's just like being retired—steady money coming in from an annuity, while you are free to spend your days as you please.

Copy: The Foundation of Implementation

A radio program for a vocabulary source notes, "People judge you by the words you use." Nowhere is this truer than in marketing. To implement your marketing campaign, you have to know the fundamentals of good copy, whether you write your own copy or hire an ad agency to do it for you. Copy is dependent on you using the right words, and testing proves that something as simple as word choice can have a huge impact on result.

> **Copy is dependent on you using the right words, and testing proves that something as simple as word choice can have a huge impact on result.**

Semantics can sell more of your product or service. A number of years ago, when Clinton was still in office, I was driving in the DC area, where I almost always get lost. As I desperately tried to find K Street, I heard a radio commercial for *American Spectator*, the conservative magazine. The commercial said that if you called a toll-free number to subscribe, you would get a free premium—a "special report" titled "Inside the Clinton White House." Although I didn't call, I am pretty sure that *American Spectator*, as is typical of magazines, put together this special report by assembling reprints of a few articles they'd done on Clinton during the year into a booklet. But the phrase "special report" sounds important and exclusive, like something you'd want to have, and the title, "Inside the Clinton White House," sounds juicy. What if the radio commercial had closed with, "So call toll-free today to subscribe, and we'll give you a bunch of past articles ripped out of old issues of the magazine and stapled together"? I can't imagine the phone ringing off the hook for that one.

Another example of the power of words in marketing is the old comic book ad with the headline, "Enter the wonderful world of amazing live Sea Monkeys ... open a bowl full of happiness—instant pets!" The ad pictured a happy underwater family of cute, friendly creatures—a mom, dad, and kids— living outside the family castle, presum-

> **Words have power, and the words you choose decide a lot about what people think of you, your company, your product, and your offer.**

ably in a fish bowl, as the human youngster and his human parents who purchased the Sea Monkeys looked down in delight. Well, if you ever took the bait and mailed the coupon with your money, what you got was a plastic vial full of dried brine shrimp eggs with instructions to hatch them in warm, salty water. When mine hatched, they looked nothing like the handsome Sea Monkey family pictured in the ad. They were basically little dots moving around in a bowl of water.

Yes, words have power, and the words you choose decide a lot about what people think of you, your company, your product, and your offer—especially whether they want to buy or try it. No one wants brine shrimp eggs. But "instant pets" and "amazing live Sea Monkeys"? I'm in!

One last example: My colleague Gary Hennerberg was called on by a company in Texas that sold mail-order fruitcakes. Their fruit-cakes weren't selling like hotcakes (big surprise), and they needed to boost orders. Gary asked the bakery what ingredients were used, and to his surprise, he found that these fruitcakes contained pecans. Not only that, but they were grown locally in Texas, on the banks of a river, where the moisture made them particularly flavorful. Gary told the company to test a mailing calling the product "native Texas pecan cakes" instead of "fruitcakes." They followed his advice—and fruitcake sales soared by 60 percent. Semantics, I guess. Go figure.

Write the Way Prospects Talk

Almost universally, the great writing teachers tell us to avoid jargon, and to use small words instead of big words. "We are a society strangling in unnecessary words, circular constructions, pompous frills and meaningless jargon," writes William Zinsser in *On Writing Well* (Harper & Row, 1991, p. 127). And in *The Art of Readable Writing*, 25th Edition (Quill, 2001, p. 7). Rudolph Flesch warns, "Keep away from fancy words because you never can tell what they mean."

But in copywriting, there are certainly exceptions to this rule — times when a bigger or fancier word, or a piece of jargon, can command readers' attention and persuade them more effectively than everyday prose.

The first exception is the use of big words to create a perception of enhanced value. For example, Mont Blanc doesn't call its products "pens" in its catalog. They sell "writing instruments." Reason: People will pay $150 for a writing instrument, while they can buy a perfectly functional pen at CVS for a dollar. In a similar vein, almost no one sells used cars any more. Today a used car is called a "certified pre-owned vehicle." "Vehicle" sounds more impressive than "car." "Pre-owned" removes the stigma of "used." And who certified your pre-owned BMW or Lexus? BMW and Lexus, of course.

> **Another reason to use jargon is to create a sense of affinity between the writer and the reader.**

Another reason to use jargon is to create a sense of affinity between the writer and the reader. You want prospects to feel that you are part of their group, or at least that you know and understand them and their kind. But don't use insider jargon when writing to non-specialists.

Sociologist Susan Brownmiller defines jargon as "language more complex than the word it serves to communicate." Similarly, when editing the massive *Oxford English Dictionary*, James Murray's rule was that a definition could not contain a word more complex than the word being defined. For example, a pilot may tell flight attendants to instruct passengers to "deplane," but when the flight attendants pass this infor-mation on to the passengers, they should just say, "get off the plane."

The third application of jargon is in writing about technical topics, and a huge number of business-to-business marketers sell techni-cal products to technical audiences. Is it safe—even advisable—to use jargon in these situations?

"Have you ever listened to two computer programmers talk to each other? Or two engineers? Or two doctors?" asks copy-writer Bob McCarthy. "They all have their own language—or so it seems. Their conver-sations are peppered with technical terms, abbreviations, codes, and acronyms that make sense for the people involved." These jargon-filled conversations are not for show, either, says McCarthy. They are for expediency. They provide useful shortcuts that move the conversations along more quickly and more efficiently. "In short, it's the way they talk," concludes McCarthy, "and it's the way we need to write if we are writing on their behalf."

> **When writing about technical products or marketing to a technical audience, it's important to note the difference between technical terms and jargon.**

When writing about technical products or marketing to a technical audience, it's important to note the difference between technical terms and jargon. Technical terms are words that precisely describe the technology, process, or idea we want to convey. "Operating system" is a technical term, as is "broadband network." We should use them. They are familiar to our readers, and to avoid them would require substi-tuting lengthy and unnecessary descriptions. Technical terms were invented to concisely and clearly communicate technical information to audiences with varying degrees of education and experience.

Jargon, on the other hand, is language that is unnecessarily com-plex—more so than the idea it is meant to convey. The advantage of us-ing jargon is that with some audiences (e.g., IT professionals), it creates an affinity with the reader. The disadvantage of jargon is that, aside from sounding pompous, it is not as clear or direct as simpler substi-tutes, and therefore, your reader may wonder what you really mean.

Years ago, in a brochure describing a material handling system, I wrote that the equipment dumped the material from a storage silo into a bin. The product manager crossed out "dumped" and changed it to "gravimetrically conveyed." When his boss read this, he asked, puzzled, "What's a gravimetric conveyor?"

A health-care ad agency showed their client, a manufacturer of dental products, a web page for a new splint. The splint was a metal band attached to the back of the teeth so that the strong, healthy teeth in the mouth helped keep the loose ones from moving. The agency had written that the splint "keeps loose teeth in place." The client changed this to say that the splint "stabilizes mobile dentition." Self-important jargon, or appropriate use of a legitimate technical term? You tell me.

What about acronyms, an insidious subcategory of jargon particularly rampant in certain industries, such as telecommunications? The rule is to write out the term in the first use, with its acronym following in parentheses; e.g., short messaging service (SMS), electronic data interchange (EDI). However, this rule is typically not applied when using acronyms so commonplace that the initials communicate your idea more quickly and clearly than the term spelled out. Examples include DNA (deoxyribonucleic acid), EST (eastern standard time), scuba (self-contained underwater breathing apparatus), laser (light amplification through stimulated emission of radiation), cop (constable on patrol), and tip (to insure promptness). You can minimize confusion when using acronyms by being consistent in your usage. Don't randomly jump from USA to US to U.S.A. to US of A; pick one and stick with it throughout your document.

Even when using legitimate technical terms and acronyms, don't overdo it. A sentence packed with too many acronyms and technical terms seems cold, inhuman, and almost unreadable. The optimal ratio is no more than one technical term for every 10 words in the sentence.

Spell checkers valiantly attempt to keep up with ever-changing industry jargon, and fail miserably. Therefore, when writing business-to-business copy, keep a dictionary covering your industry close at hand. For telecommunications, the standard is *Newton's Telecom Dictionary*; for medical copywriting, it's *Dorland's Illustrated Medical Dictionary*.

Business-to-business marketers in particular worry about the level of technical language in their copy as follows: If the copy is too technical, some readers won't be able to understand it; but if the copy is too simple, some readers will feel we are talking down to them, and we will insult them. This may be accurate, but here's another rule of thumb to guide you: If you have to make a choice between making your copy too simple or too sophisticated, err on the side of making it too simple. Reason: In my nearly 30 years of writing business-to-business copy aimed at engineers, scientists, programmers, and other techies, I have never once head a prospect complain, "This brochure is too easy to read."

Writing Great Headlines

The headline is the most important part of your copy. David Ogilvy estimated that 80 percent of the selling power of an ad is in the headline. Therefore, it pays to spend extra time developing strong headlines.

The best way to get ideas for headlines when you are stuck is to keep a swipe file of successful headlines and consult it for inspiration when you sit down to write a new ad or mailing.

As a shortcut, here's a partial collection of such headlines from my vast swipe file, organized by category so as to make clear the approach being used:

- **Ask a question in the headline.**
  What Do Japanese Managers Have That American Managers Sometimes Lack?
- **Tie in to current events.**
  Stay One Step Ahead of the Stock Market Just Like Martha Stewart—But Without Her Legal Liability!
- **Create a new terminology.**
  New 'Polarized Oil' Magnetically Adheres to Wear Parts in Machine Tools, Making Them Last Up to 6 Times Longer
- **Give news using the words new, introduction, or announcing.**
  Announcing a Painless Cut in Defense Spending
- **Give readers a command—tell them to do something.**
  Try Burning This Coupon

- **Use numbers and statistics.**
  Who Ever Heard of 17,000 Blooms from a Single Plant?

- **Promise readers useful information.**
  How to Avoid the Biggest Mistake You Can Make in Building or Buying a Home.

- **Highlight your offer.**
  You Can Now Subscribe to the Best New Books—Just as You Do to a Magazine

- **Tell a story.**
  They Laughed When I Sat Down at the Piano ... But Then I Started to Play

- **Make a recommendation.**
  The 5 Tech Stocks You Must Own NOW

- **State a benefit.**
  Managing UNIX Data Centers—Once Difficult, Now Easy

- **Make a comparison.**
  How to Solve Your Emissions Problems—At Half the Energy Cost of Conventional Venturi Scrubbers

- **Use words that help readers visualize.**
  Why Some Foods 'Explode' In Your Stomach

- **Use a testimonial.**
  After Over Half a Million Miles in the Air Using AVBLEND, We've Had No Premature Camshaft Failures

- **Offer a free special report, catalog, or booklet.**
  New FREE Special Report Reveals Little-Known Strategy Millionaires Use to Keep Wealth in Their Hands—and Out of Uncle Sam's

- **State the selling proposition directly and plainly.**
  "Surgical Tables Rebuilt—Free Loaners Available."

- **Arouse reader curiosity.**
  The One Internet Stock You MUST Own Now. Hint: It's NOT What You Think!

- **Promise to reveal a secret.**
  Unlock Wall Street's Secret Logic

- **Be specific.**
  At 60 Miles an Hour, the Loudest Noise in This New Rolls-Royce Comes from the Electric Clock

- **Target a particular type of reader.**
  We're Looking for People to Write Children's Books
- **Add a time element.**
  Instant Incorporation While U-Wait
- **Stress cost savings, discounts, or value.**
  Now You Can Get $2,177 Worth of Expensive Stock Market Newsletters for the Incredibly Low Price of Just $69!
- **Give the reader good news.**
  You're Never Too Old to Hear Better
- **Offer an alternative to other products and services.**
  No Time for Yale—Took College At Home
- **Issue a challenge.**
  Will Your Scalp Stand the Fingernail Test?
- **Stress your guarantee.**
  Develop Software Applications Up to 6 Times Faster or Your Money Back
- **State the price.**
  Link 8 PCs to Your Mainframe—Only $2,395
- **Set up a seeming contradiction.**
  Profit from 'Insider Trading'—100% Legal!
- **Offer an exclusive readers can't get elsewhere.**
  Earn 500+% Gains With Little-Known 'Trader's Secret Weapon'
- **Address readers' concerns.**
  Why Most Small Businesses Fail—and What You Can Do About It
- **"As crazy as it sounds…"**
  Crazy as it Sounds, Shares of This Tiny R&D Company, Selling for $2 Today, Could Be Worth as Much as $100 in the Not-Too-Distant Future
- **Make a big promise.**
  Slice 20 Years Off Your Age!
- **Show ROI for purchase of your product.**
  Hiring the Wrong Person Costs You Three Times Their Annual Salary
- **Use a "reasons-why" headline.**
  7 Reasons Why Production Houses Nationwide Prefer Unilux Strobe Lighting When Shooting Important TV Commercials.
- **Answer important questions about your product or service.**
  7 Questions to Ask Before You Hire a Collection Agency … And One Good Answer to Each

- ◆ **Stress the value of your premiums.**
  Yours Free—Order Now and Receive $280 in Free Gifts With Your Paid Subscription
- ◆ **Help readers achieve a goal.**
  Now You Can Create a Breakthrough Marketing Plan Within the Next 30 Days … for FREE!
- ◆ **Make a seemingly contradictory statement or promise.**
  Cool Any Room in Your House Fast—Without Air Conditioning!

More Copy Tips

"Amateurs may talk about creativity, but professionals insist on structure," copywriter Martin Chorich recently said to me. In direct marketing, structure is key: If your copy does not follow the formula for persuasion, it won't work, no matter how creative you get.

There have been numerous formulas for writing persuasive copy throughout the years. The most famous of these is probably AIDA, which stands for attention, interest, desire, and action. In copywriting seminars, I've taught a variation on AIDA known as the Motivating Sequence.

The five steps of the Motivating Sequence are as follows:

Steps…

1. Get attention.

Before your promotion can do anything else, it has to get your prospect's attention. It must get the prospect to stop, open the envelope, and start reading the materials inside instead of tossing your mailing in the trash.

You already know many methods of getting attention, and see dozens of examples of them in action every day. In TV and magazine advertising, sex is often used to gain attention for products ranging from soft drinks and cars to diets and exercise programs. Or, you can make a bold statement, cite a startling statistic, ask a curiosity-arousing question, put a bulky object in the envelope, or use a pop-up graphic. You get the idea.

2. Identify the problem or need.

Most products fill a need or solve a problem that a group of prospects are facing. But what are the chances that the prospect is thinking about this problem when he or she gets your promotion? Probably not great. So the first thing you have to do is to focus prospects' attention on the need or problem your product addresses. Only then can you talk to them about a solution. For instance, if you are selling an economical office telephone system, instead of starting off by talking about your system, you might say, "Are you sick and tired of skyrocketing long-distance phone bills?"

3. Position your product as the solution to the problem.

Once you get the prospect to focus on the problem, the next step is to position your product or service as the solution to that problem. This can be a quick transition. Here's an example from a fundraising letter from the Red Cross: Dear Mr. Bly: Some day, you may need the Red Cross. But right now, the Red Cross needs you.

4. Proof.

As Mark Joyner points out in his book *The Irresistible Offer* (John Wiley & Sons, 2005), one of the questions on the tip of your prospect's tongue on receiving your promotion is, "Why should I believe you?" You answer that question by offering proof. That proof is of two sorts.

The first type of proof goes to credibility. It convinces the prospect that you, the seller, are a reputable firm or individual, and therefore someone to be trusted. A diploma from a prestigious medical school displayed prominently on a doctor's office wall is an example of proof of credibility. The second type of proof has to do with the product, and convinces the buyer that your product can do what you say it can do:

testimonials, case histories, reviews, performance graphs, and test results are examples of proof in this category.

5. Action.

The final step is to ask for action. Your goal is usually to generate either an inquiry or an order. To ask for action in direct marketing, we make an "offer." I define the *offer* as what readers get when they respond to your promotion, combined with what they have to do to get it. In a lead-generating direct mail package, the offer might be as simple as "Mail back the enclosed reply card for our free catalog." In a mail order online promotion, the offer might be "Click here, enter your credit card information, and purchase our product on a 30-day money back trial basis for $49.95 plus $4.95 shipping and handling."

I am willing to wager that every successful piece of copy you have ever mailed or e-mailed follows the steps in the motivating sequence to some extent, even if you've never heard of it before. That's because you have an instinct for how to sell, and that instinct leads you to organize your selling arguments according to the motivating sequence.

So, if you can sell instinctively, then what use is knowing AIDA, the Motivating Sequence, or other persuasion formulas? The answer is this: when you have the steps written out in front of you, you can more consciously make sure that you've handled all five steps fully and in correct sequence, and make sure no step is shortchanged or left out, increasing your odds of writing a winner.

Make Liberal Use of Free Offers

The word free is the most powerful word in direct marketing. Always has been. Still is today. Will still be 10 years from now, in my opinion.

"I saw someone use 'free' effectively on eBay recently," copywriter Charlie Byrne told me several months ago. "Rocker Jimmy Buffett was coming to town. His fans love to party—especially with Corona beer, the one you squeeze limes into." There were many tickets for the concert on sale on eBay. If you looked at the listings, you'd see "Buffett Tickets for sale!" "Jimmy Buffett—Good seats," "Buffett Tix for sale," ad infinitum. But one clever person wrote, "Buffett Tickets + Free Corona and Limes!" If you bought the tickets, he would throw in a $10 gift certificate for the local Florida supermarket chain. Charlie said, "I noticed his ad got many more hits than all the others—another demonstration of the power of a free offer."

In his book *How to Turn Words into Money*, millionaire entrepreneur and master direct marketer Ted Nicholas devotes quite a bit of space to discussing the power of free offers. "I've never sold anything that didn't sell better after offering free bonuses and gifts," says Ted. "'Free' is the most powerful word in the English language. If you're not using gifts and bonuses in your marketing operations now, your sales in many cases will go up two, three, and four times.

> **The word free is the most powerful word in direct marketing. Always has been. Still is today. Will still be ten years from now, in my opinion.**

One of my friends worked in a medical ad agency. The clients were large pharmaceutical manufacturers targeting doctors with promotions about new drugs. The agency used direct mail to invite doctors to free seminars (called symposia)—educational programs about the diseases their drugs treated, designed to get the doctors to prescribe the drugs as treatment for the diseases. They split-tested a straightforward invitation versus a version that offered a free gift—a pocket day planner—as an incentive to attend the events. The wholesale cost of the pocket calendar, including imprint of the client's logo, was about $1 each. The invitations offering doctors the free $1 pocket calendar generated six times the response from doctors (all of whom back then were making handsome six-figure annual incomes) than the invitations that didn't offer the free gift. That's six times the results just because of the offer of a little free gift—something the doctor might very well toss in the trash if it arrived unsolicited in the mail.

I get asked at least once a week, "Bob, hasn't 'free' lost its power?" The people asking the question are concerned that, because of overuse and the increasing sophistication of readers, "free" is not effective any more. My answer is always this: using the word free in and of itself is not enough today to make a promotion profitable. In the early days of direct marketing, perhaps it was. Today, there are so many people advertising free offers that simply saying a thing is free does not make you stand out. You need something more, like a powerful benefit, a unique selling proposition, or a masterfully written promotion—but once you have those things, combine them with a free offer. Even today, saying "free" still increases response significantly over the same copy without a free offer.

> **As all direct marketers know, offers are essential for generating advertising response, and free offers are usually the most attractive.**

Bottom line: Free still works.
Use free for yourself and see!

Experian is a financial information marketer specializing in consumer credit. They sell a credit monitoring service that alerts you whenever there is an important change in your credit report. The offer that draws prospects in is a simple one: "free credit report." When you sign up for a risk-free 7-day trial of the credit monitoring service, you get your credit report and credit score sent to you free.

A low-priced offer can be just as effective as free. Ken Roberts sold an options trading service that included access to online price charts for $29.95. It did rather well. But sales soared when the company began offering a "14-day trial" for $1.

The reason to charge a dollar instead of offer the trial free was to capture the prospect's credit card information in the online shopping cart (if it's free, they have no reason to enter their credit card). If the prospect does not cancel after 14 days, the company begins billing the credit card.

Since it's not worth charging a credit card for a dollar, no billing is made during the first two weeks. So the copy tells you, "If you cancel within 14 days, we'll even give you your dollar back!" In that way, the trial is actually free.

Free offers work equally well offline and online. Edith Roman Associates, a mailing list company, uses e-mail marketing to promote its mailing list services. When they offered a "Free Direct Mail Encyclopedia," click-through rates increased 25 percent, despite the fact that spam filters are triggered by the word "free." What happened? "Free" is so attractive that the increase in response far outweighed the negative effect of the spam filters.

What kind of offer can you make your prospects that could attract more business and sales? Here's a quick checklist to get you started:

- Stress your guarantee (Satisfaction guaranteed or your money back).
- Let your prospects use the product for a month without risk—meaning if they don't like it, they can return the merchandise for a full refund (Send for your free 30-day home trial).
- Give them a discount, with a reason for the discount if possible (Save 40% during our 25th anniversary sale).
- Be like Oreck and Gevalia: give them a free bonus gift with their order (Reply now and get this valuable free bonus gift).
- Or, have a two for one sale (Buy one, get one free). This works well for products the prospect wants more than one of, such as cleaning fluids or plastic storage containers for the kitchen.
- Offer to pay return shipping charges if your customers decide to return the product for a refund (If you're not 100% satisfied, we'll come to your door, pick it up, and take it away—entirely at our expense).
- Make a logical connection between the product and the offer—e.g., the Sovereign Society, a financial newsletter on offshore investing, offered a free Swiss bank account to new subscribers.

Although I have spent the last 25 years in direct marketing, the first few years were spent working in general marketing (for a couple of large corporations selling big-ticket products to business and government buyers). Our ads (this was way before the World Wide Web) always told the prospect about the product and its many benefits. But there was never an offer. We almost never told the prospect, "Respond to this ad today, and you will get these specific materials, services, and benefits."

Then in one ad, we offered a "free engineering design guide"—and response rates soared.

The conclusion: offers are vital to generating a healthy response to your marketing.

> **One more tip: If you can't think of a reason to justify why you are making a special offer, get creative.**

An account executive at a health care ad agency used direct mail to invite doctors to free medical lectures. The lectures were ostensibly about disease conditions, but the purpose was to promote a pharmaceutical company's drug for treating the disease.

One day the agency executive changed the letter, adding a P.S. that offered a free pocket diary to doctors who attended the event. He told me that response rates increased six times when the pocket diary was offered. Keep in mind that the diary cost the drug company about a dollar each, and the mailings went to M.D.s all earning six figures. Lesson: even a small free offer can significantly increase response rates.

If you have a product with multiple components, consider positioning one of the components as a free premium. Weka Publishing marketed loose-leaf services for IT professionals: large three-ring reference binders on technical topics. Included in the binder as part of the product was a sealed envelope with a CD containing a few software programs.

The company tested a mailing in which the CD was positioned not as part of the product but as a free bonus. The headline on the envelope said something like "Inside: 5 free programs to help you manage your network better and more efficiently."

Result? Positioning the software programs as a free bonus doubled response to the control mailing. Even technical professionals respond to offers where they can get something free.

In direct mail, the free gift can also be enclosed with the mailing piece rather than offered as an incentive to respond. Fundraising mailings, for instance, frequently include address labels personalized with the recipient's name and address.

Why does this work? It plays on guilt and your sense of obligation. You open the envelope, and the nonprofit has given you something of value for free. It may not be enough to get you to donate, but it certainly creates some sense of obligation to reciprocate in enough people to make it worthwhile.

Promote Yourself by Writing Articles

Recently DD, a top copywriter, e-mailed me for some advice about using articles as a marketing tool. "*An editor has contacted me about doing an article,*" wrote DD. "*Seems like a good opportunity to generate some publicity for my product—and some nice credentials for myself. Do you have any advice or precautions, like how to maximize this opportunity—things I might not know to consider when writing a magazine article to promote myself and my business?*"

Here's what I told DD: To begin with, just because an editor wants you to write an article doesn't mean you should. If you're writing articles for free as a promotional vehicle, only write for two types of publications. The first is publications whose readers are the target market for your product or service. The second is publications so prestigious that your prospects will be impressed that you were published in their pages (e.g., *Harvard Business Review*).

Now, even though you're writing the article to promote yourself, don't promote yourself in the article. The only way your article is going to build your reputation and get people interested in doing business with you is with solid content, not self-promotional blather.

Focus on the reader and the topic, not on yourself. For instance, if you're a consultant, you can include little vignettes in your article about how businesspeople applied smart management principles to solve problems, but don't take the credit. Say, "Ned, a manager at XYZ company," and describe what he did. Don't say, "When Ned called me in, here is what I did," even if you were responsible. Give credit to others, and play down your own role in the stories your articles contain. This way, you come off as modest—not as a blatant self-promoter, which quickly turns people off.

Give your readers useful hints and tips about your topic: short, practical, pithy advice on how to do their jobs or run their lives better. When they read your sage advice, they will nod their heads in recognition of your wisdom, and begin to think of you as their "guru" on this topic.

The only promotion or "advertising" in your article should appear in the "about the author" box that usually runs at the bottom of the first column of the article when it's published in the magazine. Your "about the author" copy should say who you are, what you do, and how to contact you. That means including an e-mail address or website, or both.

As for length, ask the editor. He or she will usually tell you how many words are desired. Stick to that word count. Once the article is published, the contact information in your "about the author" box will generate some response for you.

But don't leave it at that. Make your article do double or triple duty as a promotional tool. You can:

- Make reprints of your article.
- Include copies of your article in the inquiry fulfill-ment kits you mail to potential customers.
- Hand out article reprints at trade shows.
- Do a mailing of your article reprint to your clients and prospects.
- Post the articles on your website. Having lots of con-tent on your site makes visitors stay longer, and also raises your rankings with search engines.

If the response is good and your article seems to have reached the right people (your target market), immediately send an e-mail to your editor suggesting a follow-up article with infor-mation you didn't have room to include in the first article. If you like to write and have the time, or can hire a ghostwriter, why not suggest a monthly column in the magazine instead of just an article? The worst the editor can do is say no. If he or she says yes, you'll get your name in front of your potential customers 12 times a year instead of once—and you'll accelerate your recognition as a top expert in your field. Those are great results from one of the easiest and lowest-cost self-promotions you can do: writing articles.

Schedule Your Action Steps for the Next 30 Days

Knowing what you must accomplish within the next month will add a steadying sense of urgency to your work. It will propel you to follow through on the things you said you would get done today. Create a marketing calendar detailing your actions for the next 30 days. Be sure your 30-day schedule takes into account what you said you'd accomplish within the next three months in your action plan.

Figure 11-1. 30-day marketing calendar

Action Plan January 2008						
	Goals	Daily Actions				
		Mon	Tue	Wed	Thu	Fri
Week 1						
Week 2						
Week 3						
Week 4						
Comments/Results						

This format lets you see your goal for each week and what you need to do each day to achieve it.

Follow These Keys to Success

Once you fill out your calendar, use it. Follow a few keys to success:

Begin each day by reading your goals and the list of actions for that day that will take you closer to your goals. Knowing you have only 30 days to complete the actions will keep you focused.

Review your full plan regularly. Visualize the completed goal and your rewards. See your new home; smell the leather seats in your new car; hear the sounds of excited children creating their own dreams in your new youth center; enjoy the new employees you've been able to hire as your business has grown; savor the moment of your hole-in-one. Then, each night, right before you go to bed, repeat the process. This process will start both your subconscious and conscious mind working toward the goal. This will also begin to replace any of the negative self-talk you may have and replace it with positive self-talk.

Visualize your goal as a done deal. Zig Ziglar says we must "see the reaching, before we reach the reaching."

Every time you need to make a decision during the day, ask yourself, "Will this take me closer to or farther from my goal?" If the answer is "closer to," then do it. If the answer is "farther from," well, you know what to do.

The program will give you a constant reality check. You can see if it's working.

Review every day for the first 30 days. This will keep you focused and energized. You'll also quickly get a sense of what's working.

Near the end of the 30 days, assess your results. Look at what remains to be done to meet your three-month goals. See what's working and what's not. With this additional knowledge, schedule your next 30 days.

Chapter 12

REVIEW AND TROUBLESHOOT YOUR PLAN

No plan is perfect. No matter how solid your assumptions are and how thorough you are in putting together your plan, expect to make adjustments as you learn more. Reviewing your action plan on a regular basis is so critical to your success that you should schedule review dates.

Decide what you'll review, how you'll approach troubleshooting, and what you'll do when things don't quite go according to plan. Once you make any needed adjustments, it's time to do it all again: work your plan.

How often should you stop and review your plan's progress? The frequency with which I evaluate my progress and make corrections in my sales and marketing depends on the business. In my copywriting business, my jobs are typically two to four weeks in duration. So my cash flow may be uneven. Therefore, I look at my month-to-date and year-to-date gross sales at the end of every month to see whether I am on track. I also check on a weekly basis the number of active jobs and pending jobs, for which I keep two separate lists.

In my internet marketing business, where I sell products instead of services, each sale is made in a minute online. So I look at a one-week sales report that tells me, among other things my revenues for the week. I look at this twice a week: once at the end of the week to see how well I did, and once in the middle to see whether I am on track to make my weekly sales goal. I also check my sales revenues daily, to see if each day I have earned the average dollar amount needed to achieve my weekly and annual revenue goal.

How Good a Marketer Are You?

During my nearly a quarter century as a copywriter and marketing consultant, I have observed that business owners and managers fall into one of four categories as far as their competence and skill in marketing are concerned.

By recognizing which category you are in and taking the action steps recommended below, you can move up to the next level and significantly increase the ROI from your marketing dollars.

1. The lowest level of marketing competence is *unconscious incompetence*. You don't know what you are doing, and worse, you don't know that you don't know. You may even think you are a pretty sharp marketer, even though to others, that is clearly not the case. Egotistical small business owners who appear in their own TV commercials and "creative" ad agencies can fall into this category.

Do you think you are an OK marketer, and blame the lack of results generated by your marketing always on external factors, such as bad timing, bad lists, or bad luck? You are probably in the unconscious incompetence stage.

Recognize that you don't know what you're doing and it is hurting your business. Get help. Hire a professional or take a marketing course such as AWAI's Six-Figure Copywriting Course (awaionline.com/copywriting) or ETR's Million Dollar Bootcamp (etrbootcamp.com).

2. The next stage up the ladder is *conscious incompetence*. You've recognized that the reason your marketing isn't working is that you don't know what you're doing. Again, take the steps listed above.

3. Moving higher up the ladder of marketing competence you reach the stage of *conscious competence*. You've read the books, taken the courses, and understand what works. But your experience at putting it into practice is limited.

That means whenever you want to create a promotion, you have to slow down and think about what you are doing. It doesn't come naturally.

In the *conscious competence* stage, you should keep checklists, formulas, and swipe files (examples of successful promotions you admire) close at hand. Model your own efforts after the winners of others.

Don't try to reinvent the wheel. Observe what works and adapt it to your own product and market. Do this enough times, and you will slowly begin to become a true master of marketing. You will reach the highest level of marketing competence, *unconscious competence*.

4. At the unconscious competence stage, coming up with great offers, promotional ideas, headlines, and copy is second nature to you. You do it naturally, without having to consult your checklists or reference files. The quality of your work is better, and it comes faster and easier.

Marketing consultant Michael Masterson says it takes at 1,000 hours of practice to become really competent at copywriting, marketing, or anything else. If you have expert guidance, you may be able to cut that to 500 hours.

But ultimately, you learn by doing—and doing a lot. If you are at this stage, keep doing more and more marketing. When you put in 5,000 hours, you will become great, not just good, and your results will be even better.

Action step: Rank yourself using the four levels of marketing competence as described here, and follow the recommendations for whatever stage you are in.

What You Should Review

You review to stay on top of how much progress you're making. So, of course, you'll review your actual results vs. those you expected. Is there a variance? If so, why? Ask yourself, "Why were we wrong in our expectations? Did we do something wrong?" Did we stick to our plan? Think this through, looking at your actions and your numbers. Then, adjust your tactics, actions, or expectations as needed.

Look at your costs. Are you on track or in danger of going over budget? In general, what do your data tell you about how well your tactics are working? If things are better than expected, what did you do really well? Focus on duplicating that as long as the conditions surrounding it are much the same.

Major changes in your business or the marketplace may mean you need to update your plan. These changes can include:

- ◆ You add a new niche or service.
- ◆ A major company enters the niche and changes the costs of doing business—consider hardware stores when Home Depot moves in.
- ◆ New technology has rendered the way you do things antiquated and inefficient.
- ◆ You take on a partner.
- ◆ You have competition from overseas (e.g., your customers are outsourcing to cheap labor in India).
- ◆ Your sales or profits dive.
- ◆ There is a recession or economic downturn causing your customers to cut back on their spending.
- ◆ You have many more competitors than you did a few years ago.
- ◆ Demand for the product or service you offer is declining.

A Sales Tactic for Overcoming Price Resistance

One of the negative effects of the recession on small business owners is that it creates a buyer's market rather than a seller's market. In a buyer's market, consumers feel more empowered, and are more likely to exhibit price resistance. An article in *Time* magazine (8/10/09) reports that 72 percent of consumers surveyed in May 2009 said they had recently tried to negotiate with retail outlets other than auto dealerships, and of those, 80 percent were successful in getting the merchant to lower the price. So as a business owner, you must be prepared for prospects who want to haggle over price and know in advance how you will handle price objections.

In the movie *Tin Men*, starring Richard Dreyfus and Danny DeVito, an aluminum siding salesman goes into a car dealership to buy a new Cadillac. "How much is it?" he asks the car salesman about the car he wants to buy. "How much do you want to pay?" the car salesman asks back. Disgusted by what is an obvious sales tactic, the would-be buyer replies sarcastically, "A dollar ... I want to pay a dollar."

> **As a business owner, you must be prepared for prospects who want to haggle over price and know in advance how you will handle price objections.**

Many of us won't ask the prospect how much he or she wants to pay because we feel that it is somehow sleazy, and that doing so will create an uncomfortable situation. But if you did know how much your buyers wanted to spend, your sales closing ratio would shoot through the roof—because you'd be quoting prices you knew they could afford and were willing and prepared to spend. How do you ascertain what the buyer wants to spend without the awkwardness of asking outright?

When it's time to discuss price, ask the buyer, "Do you have a budget?" Note that you are not asking "What is your budget?" You are instead asking the much less threatening question, "Do you have a budget?" The buyer can only give one of two answers: yes or no, with about half of prospects saying yes and the other half saying no.

If the buyer says yes, then you ask, "Would you mind sharing with me what your budget is?" Those prospects who tell you their budget have just given you the range under which your price quotation must fall to be accepted.

But what if the buyer says, "No, we don't have a budget"? Then you ask, "Well, do you have a dollar figure in mind of what you would like it to cost?" Even if they do not have a budget worked out, many people, when asked the question in this way, will come back at you with an answer something like "I was figuring to spend around $1,000 and not more than $3,000." In effect, they really do have a budget—$1,000 to $3,000—but just never wrote it down or said it out loud before.

Good, Better, Best

A few people, however, will not share their budget no matter how you ask. "I don't want to give you my budget," they will say. "I want *you* to tell *me* what it will cost." In such cases, use the "good, better, best" method of price quotation.

Let's say you are quoting on selling the prospect a half-acre lot with a custom-built home.

Instead of just quoting your top-end home, which is $500,000, you give the prospect three options to choose from.

The first option, which you call "good," is a basic three-bedroom home with a fireplace and unfinished basement. It is $300,000—the cheapest you can offer while still giving the buyer a decent home and yourself a decent profit. The second option, which you call "better," is the same home, but with a finished basement and an added sitting room in the master bedroom suite. It is $400,000—your middle-of-the-road model. The third option, which you call "best," is the same home as in the "better" option, but with top-of-the-line landscaping, a second fire-place, and a fourth bedroom. It is $500,000—your top-of-the-line model.

You outline all options for the prospect, including the prices. Then, instead of asking whether they want a home, you ask, "Which do you want—good, better, or best?" This strategy increases the chances that your price quotation will fall within the dollar amount the prospect wants to pay.

Also, few people want the lowest-quality of three choices. So, some buyers who were looking to pay $300,000 will find a way to pay $400,000 (even if it means a bigger mortgage or borrowing from Uncle Joe), and more will select "better" over "good."

We find a similar pattern in marketing nutritional supplements by mail. If we offer three options—one bottle, three bottles, six bottles— the average unit of sale will be about 3½ bottles.

The Psychology of Pricing

Ask most experienced marketers, "What's the best price to charge for my product," and the answer will be "whatever the market will bear."

In marketing, we can test prices and quickly see which is the most profitable—generating the highest return on marketing dollars (ROMD).

Surprisingly, tests show that higher prices sometimes generate more orders than lower prices.

In one classic test, a publisher was offering loose-leaf service teaching presentation skills to business executives. Then they tested $197 vs. $297 in their advertising. $297 was the winner.

Most direct marketers conclude that you should test prices, and if the higher price wins, go with that.

While this is a sensible strategy in most instances, are there any reasons *not* to charge top dollar—or any situations in which charging a too-high price may come back to bite you—even if your price tests show the higher price is the winner?

I can think of several such situations. The first is when pricing professional services.

GD, a pricing expert, once told me that the ideal price level for your professional services is in the middle of the top third—and not "the most you can get."

Let's say the hourly rates for service providers in your industry range from $100 at the bottom to $400 at the top.

You don't want to be in the lower third of the price range, charging $100 to $200 an hour, because prospects equate a bargain price with an inferior quality product or service.

Pricing in the middle range, at $200 to $300 an hour, isn't bad. But it just makes you one of the herd—a commodity.

The top range is an hourly rate between $300 and $400. So by following GD's advice, we would set our hourly rate at $350, smack dab in the middle of the upper third. This is high enough that we are perceived as a top professional in our field, but not so high that we are always the most expensive supplier.

Well, if you are the highest-priced provider in your field out there, you will cause prospects to hesitate before hiring you.

"Every time you give your clients an estimate, they will strongly consider bidding the job out for competitive quotes rather than just signing your agreement," said GD. "One day soon, they will try someone else, find they get equivalent service for a lower price, and you will never hear from them again."

Another problem with charging outrageously high prices is that it creates ill will between buyer and seller.

The buyer feels ripped off, and complains loudly about things he might otherwise let pass.

Also, if you charge a premium price and you fail to deliver the results you promised, that client will never hire you again … and will badmouth you to others.

Here's another sign that your prices are too high: a spike in the refund rate.

So how do you put a logical limit on your pricing?

My friend, information marketing guru Fred Gleeck, has a simple rule: "I don't sell a product unless I truly believe that the content is worth at least 10 times the price I am charging," he says.

Then there is the ethical question: given our free market society, is it OK for a drug company to charge a price for a proprietary medication that only the wealthiest patients can afford—especially when doing so effectively sentences poor people with the disease to death?

Fortunately, most of us don't market products that people absolutely can't live without, though some of us price our products as if that were the case. However, no matter what your pricing is—high, low, or in between—rest assured that some folks will complain about it as being unfair.

Is there a way to prevent consumers from protesting against your high prices?

Yes, by offering them different options at different price levels, so there is an option for every budget.

Say for example you are an information marketer or consultant. You can package and price your information or knowledge as follows:

The premium consulting service … a high level of personal service rendered by you or another top specialist and priced accordingly … in the thousands of dollars.

The midrange coaching service … the customer does most

of the work, but you offer advice, support, and encouragement through weekly telephone calls, online help, or some other mechanism with a service component.

Information products ... you sell a manual, DVD, or audio learning system that teaches people how to solve the problem themselves. It's entirely packaged, reasonably priced (in the hundreds of dollars), and involves little or no personal service or support on your part.

A book ... a how-to e-book or traditionally published book giving advice on your topic ... sells for anywhere from $10 to $50.

Free content ... how-to information delivered at no cost via your blog, podcasts, free Webinars, e-newsletters, special reports, content-rich websites, or other advice you give away.

Having the low-priced options above—the inexpensive book and the free e-newsletter—makes it virtually impossible for consumers to complain that you are too expensive or unfairly priced.

You simply point out that if the prospect can't afford your high-priced products and services, they can avail themselves of your knowledge through your books or free online content.

By doing so, you avert potential criticism of you as a greedy opportunist, and can sleep nights knowing bitter people who can't afford your premium offers are not going around besmirching your reputation.

Testing Your Marketing Campaigns

I once heard on the radio that the Florida Marlins, with 23 wins and 14 losses, had the best record in Major League baseball at the time. That means the best-performing team in professional baseball loses four out of every 10 games it plays. And remember: that's the best record in baseball.

What's ironic is that businesspeople who accept this statistical truth about baseball without a second thought absolutely go bonkers when even one of their marketing programs fails. Experienced direct marketers expect a percentage of their test campaigns to under perform the control or even lose money. They accept this fact without despair, because they know that if one test mailing in every two, or every three, or even every five is a winner, they can make a lot of money.

Inexperienced direct marketers don't get this, however. As a result, countless small businesses test direct marketing once every few years, and if they don't hit a home run the first time at bat, they loudly proclaim that "direct mail doesn't work" and abandon it wholesale.

If you're a business owner or marketing professional, is there a better way to get direct marketing to work for you? Yes: simply do more testing than you do right now. For example, let's say you are planning to mail 5,000 postcards to drive people to a web page, but you can't decide which of two headlines you like: "Tastes Great" or "Less Filling." If you subjectively pick just one, your risk of selecting the wrong sales appeal—and therefore having your postcard mailing bomb—is 50%. A much better approach is to split the postcard mailing into two batches, half with the headline "Tastes Great" and the other half with "Less Filling." Each drives traffic to a different URL, so you can measure the click-through and conversion rates and then see which generates the most leads.

> **If you're a business owner or marketing professional, is there a better way to get direct marketing to work for you? Yes: simply do more testing than you do right now.**

Especially on the web, testing variations in headlines, copy, graphics, and format is relatively quick, easy, and inexpensive. Therefore, if you create a long-copy landing page to sell a product on the internet and your conversion rate is poor, don't give up on the product. Instead, test different headlines, visuals, pricing, offers, premiums, subheads, and copy leads. You'll notice that one headline pulls slightly better than another, or one price generates 40 percent more orders. Start incorporating the winners of these tests into your landing page, and in no time flat, you can take the promotion from marginally profitable to a real winner—all courtesy of testing.

I am amazed at how many marketers, both large and small, invest significant sums in developing products and promotions, both online and offline, and then just promote each product with a single promotion, doing no testing of any kind. If you are doing this, you are essentially hoping you get a hit with only once chance at bat.

In baseball, a .250 hitter who only gets one at-bat has only a one in four chance of getting on base. In reality, for product launches, the success rate is often as little as 10 percent—which means that a single promotion has only a one in 10 chance of making money. Therefore, the odds of winning with a one-shot promotion are 10 to one against. By testing different copy, offers, designs, and formats, you can significantly tip those odds in your favor. Giving your marketing multiple chances to score a winner through testing is a much more sensible way to go.

A software company was selling an integrated accounting software package for $249 by direct mail. It included general ledger, accounts payable, accounts receivable, payroll, inventory control, and a few other modules, but none of them would work on its own; they could only run if you also had the general ledger. The company sent out a mailing advertising "accounting software for a dollar." They priced all the modules—accounts payable, inventory, and the others—at one dollar each, and the general ledger at $248.

> **What's important is not what you think, like, believe, or prefer ... it's what your prospects think, like, believe, and prefer.**

In a way, it was pure semantics. The combined cost of all modules was still $249, and without the $248 general ledger, none of the others would work. So the buyer was still paying $249 for the integrated accounting software suite. But, this pricing scheme allowed the company to promote "accounting software for a dollar" on the outer envelope and in the copy. (If you really insisted, they would have sold you accounts payable for just a dollar, though no one asked for that, and it was not an option on the order form.)

The "accounting software for a dollar" mailing generated 10 times more orders than the control mailing of "integrated accounting software for $249." That's how powerful the magic of a dollar can be.

No one can predict which offer will work best, and the least effective way to make marketing decisions is through subjective judgment. Copywriter Peter Beutchel advises marketers: "Don't let personal preferences get in the way." What's important is not what you think, like, believe, or prefer ... it's what your prospects think, like, believe, and prefer.

As a marketer, you don't have to rely solely on subjective judgment. You don't have to let your personal likes and dislikes cloud your
judgment. That's because direct marketers can put almost any proposition—e.g., offer A vs. offer B, or long copy vs. short copy—to a direct
test with an A/B split.

For instance, an auto rental company that rented automobiles to
consumers by the week tested two offers. Offer A was a free upgrade
to a larger size model. Offer B was a rental discount given in exchange
for purchasing multiple weeks of rental in advance (they would get a
coupon of tickets they could redeem for each week of rental at the car
counter). To almost everyone's surprise, offer B outperformed offer A
significantly, generating nearly a tenfold increase in revenues.

So, it doesn't matter what your sister or brother-in-law does, says, or
thinks about your marketing. Their opinions don't count. What matters is that in a statistically valid A/B split test, offer A generated more
orders than offer B. As advertising legend Claude Hopkins once said:
"Almost any question can be answered, cheaply, quickly and finally, by
a test campaign."

What Price Pulls Best?

Another example: A company selling options trading education as a
home business opportunity used a subscription model, charging $29.95
a month for full access to its online training videos, other course materials, and, most important, its online commodities price charts. By
charging $29.95, they could say getting into their options trading busi-
ness cost "less than a dollar a day."

The company decided to add a 14-day trial to the order. The service
was still $29.95 a month. But when you signed up, you paid just $1
for the first 14 days, using your credit card. At the end of the 14 days,
you could cancel or continue. If you cancelled, you were not billed
further, and your dollar was even refunded (actually, the card was
never charged, since it's not worth processing an order for a dollar; the
reason to make the 14-day trial a dollar instead of free was to get the
buyer to submit his credit card information online). If you did not cancel your credit card would be billed $29.95 until you said to stop. The

$1 offer worked very well and significantly increased sales.

The reason is that when you offer any kind of installment payments, psychologically the prospect reacts primarily to the dollar amount of the first installment. He tends to discount any future payments when making his purchase decision, perhaps because he knows he has the option to cancel and avoid those payments. In the above example, the seller of the options course could literally say "get started in this great home business for just one dollar."

What price do you think is best—$49 or $156? Is this a trick question? Well, a financial publisher did an A/B split test of two prices offers for one of its investment newsletter: (a) $49 for one year vs. (b) four quarterly payments of $39 each, which equals $156 for one year. This is not a misprint; this was the actual test.

> **The technique of relying on the buyer's tendency to discount future payments also works well in internet marketing.**

The result? Offer B, four quarterly payments of $39, was the winner, even though it works out to $156 a year, which is more than three times the $49 a year cost of offer A. Why did this happen? Most likely, the prospects mentally compared a $49 payment to a $39 payment, instead of the actual price of $49 a year vs. $156—more evidence that the buyer psychologically tends to discount anything but the first payment.

Rodale has used this technique for years to sell books by mail. A typical offer might be three payments of $9.95. That means the book costs almost $30, which is not cheap for a book. But the reader doesn't hear "this book costs $30" in her head; she hears "$9.95," which seems affordable.

The technique of relying on the buyer's tendency to discount future payments also works well in internet marketing. Rich Scheffren of Strategic Profits sells high-end educational programs on monthly payment plans. In the third month, he offers an upsell—an additional product or an upgrade to the deluxe version of the product the customer already has.

But the customer does not have to pay for the upsell when he buys it, though it is shipped immediately upon ordering. Instead, half a dozen additional monthly payments are added at the end of the customer's payment schedule. Why does Scheffren wait to do the upsell until the third month instead of right up front? Rich says that if the monthly buyer has not cancelled after the third month, the likelihood that he will cancel drops astronomically, and so it is safe to sell him something more for additional payments.

How to Troubleshoot Your Plan

How should you approach troubleshooting your plan? Begin with the data you set up as benchmarks. If you see significant variances, dig deeper and ask yourself a few basic questions:

- Is the recession affecting your business?
- Are you getting fewer leads and new business opportunities than normal?
- Are your sales up, down, or flat?
- Has the dollar value of your average order declined?
- Do sales take longer to close?
- Are customers seeking concessions on prices and terms?
- Which marketing activities seem to be working well?
- Which marketing activities have seen results fall off lately?
- Can I trace new clients or increases in sales to specific sources or actions?
- Are my actions generating the expected revenues? Are they costing more than they're bringing in?
- Which actions have been most fruitful?
- Which have been least productive in terms of generating sales and clients?
- Has anything been a disaster?
- Are there any tactics or actions that have completely fallen flat?
- Are there significant changes in my industry or marketplace affecting my business?
- Which of my services is generating the most revenue?
- Which is generating the least? Why?

- Should I replace it with another tactic or action now? Next year? Why?
- What do I need to do more of?
- Are my refund rates steady or increasing?

Pinpoint which elements of your strategy are not working by looking at the numbers. (Are you getting the new clients you wanted? Are you increasing your retention rate as you desired? Are you getting the referrals you anticipated? Are those converting to new sales?) Look at each piece of your strategy to try to pinpoint what's falling short of your goals. Is your competition more successful than you expected? Why? What are they doing that you can learn from?

What to Do When It's Not Working

If things are not working, don't despair. You have options. If the deviation from your expected results is minor, you probably only need to fine-tune your actions. But if you're clearly not hitting the mark, here are a few suggestions for getting back on track:

- Adjust your service to address your niche's needs more closely.
- Repackage your product and service options to create offers with lower price points.
- Make your credit policies more liberal and offer payment plans with flexible terms and low rates.
- Massage your message. Perhaps your language is not quite connecting with your ideal client, or maybe you're mistaken about what he or she values most. Find that hot button and drive home your message right into its most sticky and most painful parts.
- How's your credibility? Do you need to enhance it with some testimonials? Maybe strengthening your guarantee can help overcome reluctance to give your service a try.
- What capabilities can you develop that will give you an advantage to offer clients?
- Are your sales coming from your niche clients or another demographic group? You might need to fine-tune your niche selection to something that more closely fits what you offer.

◆ Don't get into a price war, but do make sure you're not pricing yourself out of the market. If your prices are higher than the competition's, be sure your clients perceive your services as more valuable. This is a function of positioning properly and then building your branding or image to fit that positioning.

Consistency is important when you're trying to implement a long-term plan, so resist the temptation to abandon a strategy. Give it time to work. Remember, change and growth come in stages, often in spurts. What you're looking for is significant movement toward meeting your goals. What's significant? Those are numbers you'll need to decide as you set your benchmark measurements.

> **If your marketing is not working, you should check to make sure the product or service you offer is everything you say it is.**

When does it make sense to change strategies? Consider a change if there is a fundamental change in the basic assumptions you made about your niche, the competition, or the environment you operated in when you formed your strategy.

Non-Marketing Causes of Marketing Plan Failures

The old saying that even great marketing can't sell a lousy product, service, or organization is true. Therefore, if your marketing is not working, you should make sure the product or service you offer is everything you say it is.

One of the biggest reasons why companies lose sales is poor customer service. For example, last week I went to my local drug store to pick up a prescription, and they made a common customer service mistake I've experienced many times.

I was second in line at checkout, and there was only one cashier. The woman in front of me was taking an inordinate amount of time with her purchase, because she thought she was being wrongly charged for her photos. (There was a special photo package advertised in a sales flier, but when the clerk rang up the item on the register, a different price came up than the one advertised in the flier.)

Like you, I am busy, and I value my time. So perhaps I am less tolerant than the average Joe when a store customer argues because she isn't getting a dollar discount on her photos or the store won't honor a coupon for 10 cents off a box of crackers. In fact, when exasperated by similar situations at the supermarket, I have, at times, told the customer in front of me, "Just go ahead and buy the thing without the discount, and I will pay you the difference." Then I take out my wallet to show that I mean it. (This is never appreciated, by the way.)

So I politely told the cashier: "While this nice woman is deciding whether she wants her photos or not, could you ring me up in the meantime?" "I already started to ring her up and can't clear the register," the cashier replied. "Why not open the register next to you and ring me up there?" I asked. Said the clerk, "I can only work one register at a time: store policy."

The woman was still hemming and hawing and fuming about not getting the right price on her photo package. By this time, there were four people in line behind me, almost as annoyed as I was. "Well, why not get someone else to work that register so we can make our purchases and go?" I asked the cashier politely.

> **Even if you are the store owner, when you see the sidewalk littered with trash and your stock clerk hasn't come in yet, pick up a broom and sweep it yourself.**

At this point, the manager came to the front of the store and attempted to help the cashier clear the register—unsuccessfully, I might add, so we were all still trapped in line. I repeated my suggestion, this time to the manager, that they open the second register and put someone on it to clear up the growing line. "I have no one else in the store to put there," he replied. And I thought, *Why don't YOU do it?* Apparently, the thought never occurred to him. After several more minutes, the problem was resolved, and we got out of there.

So, what's the point of this long story? The manager was obviously impressed with himself that he had risen to a management position. I am sure he thought, "I'm a big-shot manager. Managers don't make change—they manage cashiers who make change." Here is where he and so many others who are business owners or managers misunderstand their position. They think they are the bosses of the business, and therefore somehow exempt from mundane labor. But you are not the boss of your business, even if you own it. Your customers are the boss. Your business exists to please and serve them. Whenever you fail to make serving your customers your #1 priority, and you place something else above that (like your dignity or self-importance), you are telling them, "I don't value you, and I don't want your business."

Hey, even if you are the store owner, when you see the sidewalk littered with trash and your stock clerk hasn't come in yet, pick up a broom and sweep it yourself. You are not so important that you are somehow above the need to continually provide exceptional customer service—whether that means a clean sidewalk or prompt checkout at the register. The only really important person, at least as far as the customer is concerned, is the customer.

SR, a friend of mine, was one of the top freelance copywriters in direct marketing before he retired, and a brilliant writer of conversational-style sales letters. He was so successful that he had a full-time secretary to handle his grunt work, like making photocopies and going to the post office. All SR wanted to do was the high-level work: thinking, researching, and writing for his clients.

One Thursday afternoon, the marketing manager of a great potential client—a major company with tons of work and money—called him. They were eager to establish a working relationship with SR and to send big, fat checks his way. But, the marketing manager asked, could SR overnight a package with some samples of his copy first? (This was pre-internet, so there was no e-mail.) The marketing manager just had to convince a few senior executives to sign off on the purchase order, and one of them wanted to see SR's work before doing so. They were in a hurry to get started, so the marketing manager would present SR's samples to his senior executive at a meeting the next day.

Feeling full of himself (as SR related to me), he said, "Well, my secretary puts packages together, and she is out today and Friday. I can have her send them on Monday." There was dead silence. Then the marketing manager, much less friendly, came back on the line and said, "Hey, this is a major new campaign. I tell you what. Maybe, if it isn't too much trouble, *you* could put those samples in an envelope and overnight them to me yourself?"

"Of course, I was too arrogant, and wrong," says SR. "Customers want what they want when they want it. To not give it to them is to risk losing their business." Customers want what they want when they want it. To not give it to them is to risk losing their business.

Honor Your Refund Policy Pleasantly

Another aspect of customer service where businesses fall short is refund policy. Many marketers, both large and small—and I include myself among the latter—go bonkers when customers return products for a refund.

BK, an executive with one of the biggest and most famous direct marketing publishing companies, told me each refund request drives the company's owner crazy. "Our books contain great information, incredibly valuable," he says. "Why should we allow someone to read the book, benefit from all that great content, and then cheat us by sending it back for a refund?"

Offering a money-back guarantee reduces buyer reluctance and increases buyer confidence, resulting in more orders.

Perhaps you may feel similarly, or you're asking the same question. If so, let me share with you a few important facts about re-funds in your business.

First, a refund doesn't mean your prod-uct is bad or the customer doesn't like it. It may mean that, after reviewing your prod-uct carefully, they decide your product is not right for them. Example: A customer returns your $300 DVD set on investing in real estate. "It actually seems like a great program," the customer says in his refund request. "But after watching it, I've decided this isn't a business I want to get into; it just does not appeal to me." To me, this is a perfectly legitimate and reasonable position for the customer to take. Don't you agree? In this case, offering a refund is not only a legal requirement, but also eminently fair: Qhy would you want your customer to be out-of-pocket $300 for something he can't use?

Second, offering a refund doesn't cost you money. It makes you money. Novice marketers fret about offering a money-back guarantee. "If I do that," they worry, "won't some customers take advantage of me by, say, using my product and then sending it back for a refund?" (For instance, a woman buys a fancy dress from an e-commerce site offering a 30-day money-back guarantee, wears it to a wedding, and after the wedding, returns it for a refund.)

> **Longer guarantees are better than shorter guarantees. If you are currently offering a 10- or 15 day money-back guarantee, extend it to 30 days.**

Yes, some folks will do that. But here's the thing: offering a money-back guarantee reduces buyer reluctance and increases buyer confidence, resulting in more orders. In almost every instance, the greater revenues and profits from the increase you get in orders by offering a guarantee is much greater than the small amount of money you lose issuing refunds. After all, would you buy a product for $30 or $300 or more, sight unseen, without a money-back guarantee? Of course not.

Also, longer guarantees are better than shorter guarantees. If you are currently offering a 10- or 15-day money-back guarantee, extend it to 30 days. Already offering a 30-day money-back guarantee? Test a 60- or 90-day money-back guarantee. The longer guarantee term invariably increases response rates and sales, because it eliminates the concern buyers have with short guarantees—specifically, that they will forget to open and try the product, and by the time they get around to looking at it, the guarantee will have expired and they'll be stuck with it.

Amazingly, the longer guarantee actually reduces refund requests, rather than increasing them; buyers are in no hurry to evaluate and return the product, because you are allowing them to try it according to a more leisurely schedule. Result: The buyers soon forget about the guarantee and keep the product, whether they actually use it or not.

Generous and unconditional guarantees sell more product than conditional and miserly guarantees. Ever see a guarantee that says, "Money back if product is returned in saleable condition"? The prospect worries that you'll claim it arrived scratched or broken, and won't honor your guarantee because it's damaged and can't be resold.

Similarly, some sellers of information products offer a money-back guarantee, but only if you offer documented proof that you followed their system and it did not work for you. But what if I get your system, and something comes up, and I decide I don't have time to work through it? Are you telling me I'm stuck with it because I didn't use it? The more unconditional your money-back guarantee, the higher your response rates. Conditional guarantees depress orders.

Here's one interesting thing to consider: a couple of years ago, I began selling e-books online. With a physical book, the guarantee is, "If you don't like it, return the book, and we will refund your money." But you can't really return an e-book. I thought about eliminating the guarantee, but realized that was absurd. Instead, I stress the fact that they can get a refund without returning the product in my guarantee, rather than downplay it. My standard e-book guarantee reads: If you are not 100 percent satisfied for any reason—or for no reason at all—just let me know within 90 days. I'll refund your $29 payment in full. No questions asked. And you can keep the e-book FREE, with my compliments. That way, you risk nothing.

Result: my refund rate on e-books is lower than for any other information product I sell, including CDs and hard copy books. In fact, I get virtually no refund requests on e-books, though one could say my guarantee openly invites people to take advantage of me. The offer also increases orders: DP, a colleague who tested this guarantee on his own e-books, found that it increased conversion rates (sales) online by 18 percent.

Yes, there are a few con artists out there. But most people—especially when you are open and fair with them—are honest, and will be fair with you in return. So, follow my advice on refunds in your business. Then watch your sales volume and profits soar. I guarantee it—or your money back!

Steps...

How to Keep Working Your Plan

1. Every day, be renewed by your vision.

Your mind can be your greatest asset or your most tiring obstacle. So begin your day by renewing your mind with the clarifying power of your vision. When W. Clement Stone wrote, "Whatever the mind of man can conceive and believe, it can achieve," he knew these were far more than simple words on a page. There simply is no substitute for the power of belief. When you believe, obstacles that would throw your entire day into chaos suddenly become bleeps that you just intuitively know how to solve without expending valuable time or energy. Don't laugh this off as touchy-feely. This is one of the most inexpensive and profitable investments you'll ever make in yourself. Just do it.

2. Focus on your niche.

Become the expert in all things involving your niche. Don't limit your knowledge to the services you offer. The more you know about your niche's priorities and challenges, the more valuable a resource you can become to them. Become familiar with other professionals who can assist your niche with challenges outside of your expertise. When you're tempted to work with clients outside your niche, make sure the time and payoff will be worth it and won't draw you away from your commitment.

3. Stay close to your ideal client.

Networking, surveys, online community forums, trade magazines, and associations are all great ways to keep sharp about the things that matter to your ideal client. Also, stay on top of the news, and ask yourself how your client's needs will be affected by changes in the business and world environment.

4. Keep your eyes on your competition.

If your clients stop thinking that you offer a competitive advantage in addressing their needs, you lose; the competition wins. Enough said. Don't be the last to know what your competition is doing.

5. Make sure you're positioned to win.

If you're doing the first four steps, you'll know when it's time to change your tune, tweak your message, and speak a new language that's more in tune with what your ideal client needs. Ask yourself, "Is my unique selling proposition still unique? Does anyone do it better? What one thing can I do to serve my clients better?" That's how you stay unique.

6. Take action every day.

Stick close to your plan. Follow your schedule. Complete the actions you say you will complete in your daily schedule. At the end of the week, give yourself a grade for effort. Then, give yourself another one for accomplishment. If you're getting As for effort and Cs for accomplishment, troubleshoot.

7. Focus on one project at a time.

One of the greatest mistakes people make in setting goals is trying to work on too many things at one time. There is tremendous power in giving focused attention to just one idea, one project, or one objective at a time.

8. Ask yourself good questions.

As you think about your goals, instead of wishing for them to come true, ask yourself *how* and *what you can do* to make them come true. The subconscious mind will respond to your questions far more effectively than just making statements or wishes.

9. Congratulate yourself.

You're halfway home. You've done something that less than 3 percent of the population has done—set goals and create a plan for achieving them. Every study on the subject tells us you're far more likely than most to succeed with your plans if you will only do one thing: *Take action!*

Be that external force. Plan your work, then work your plan, and you'll have an unstoppable money-making system that can grow your business beyond even your most amazing vision.

Don't Waste Your Customer's Time

Decades ago, my mentor, Milt Pierce, wrote what became a long-running control mailing for *Good Housekeeping*. The envelope teaser: "31 Ways Good Housekeeping Can Save You Time and Money." Why did this direct mail package remain unbeaten in the mail for over a quarter of a century?

Back then, saving time and money were two big appeals. And they remain so today. In fact, in the 21st century, saving your customer time is more important than ever. Why? Because your customers, like the Egyptian mummies, are "pressed for time." We all have too much to do ... and not enough time to do it.

One reason people are so busy is more working women: When both spouses work, there's no one at home to take care of all the household business ... and so a working person has to do it. What does this mean for you as a marketer? Simply this: In your sales and marketing efforts, if you can show the customer how you can save him time or serve him faster, your sales will skyrocket. Conversely, wasting the customer's time is one of the surest ways to turn prospects off.

For example: in my little copywriting business I have a "virtual office"—my assistants work in their own homes many miles away from my office in northern New Jersey. Because of this, I work in complete isolation. So, some days, I break up the isolation by going out for a quick lunch to a local coffee shop.

While I was eating lunch a few weeks ago, at the busiest peak of the lunch hour, two young women walked in. I immediately identified them as salespeople by the way they carried themselves, their manner, and their corporate attire.

Sure enough, instead of asking for a menu, they asked Peg, the waitress, if they could speak with the owner—who also happens to be the short-order cook. Peg walked over to the grill and relayed the message to him. His irritation was immediate, visible, and audible. In other words, he was pissed.

Peg came back and told the women, "I'm sorry, but it is the middle of lunch hour, and he is busy with orders." Crestfallen, the two salespeople thanked Peg and left. Peg then turned to me, and said, "How stupid can they be—to call on a restaurant owner during lunch hour?"

Of course, she is right: by making a sales call during the height of lunch hour, these sales amateurs showed an utter disregard for the prospect's time. He returned the favor by refusing to see them or buy what they were selling.

In contrast, here's an example of a company that won a big sale by making an extra effort to respect the customer's busy schedule and save him time: Years ago, I did some work for a company—let's call them ABC Software—that was a software distributor to the corporate market.

A salesperson for ABC once told me the following story: She had been trying to get a big corporate account—let's call it XYZ Corporation—to buy its software from ABC. One of the advantages ABC offered was that it did not require a separate purchase order (PO) for each purchase. The customer only had to issue a blanket PO one time to ABC to cover all purchases. This saved purchasing departments a lot of time.

But even though ABC did not require a separate PO for each software package purchased, XYZ's accounting department did. "My hands are tied," said XYZ's purchasing manager to ABC's salesperson. "I'd like to use you, but I just don't have time to fill out all those POs."

"Not a problem," replied ABC Software's persistent salesperson. "Just give me a stack of blank POs. Whenever you want to buy a software package, just let me know. I will fill out the PO for you, and then fax it to you for your signature." By offering to lift the paperwork burden from the customer onto her shoulders, the salesperson saved that customer a lot of time ... and as a result, won a major national account.

Appendix A
GLOSSARY

A

A/V Audiovisual.

Account executive An advertising agency employee who serves as the liaison between the agency and the client.

Advertisement A paid message in which the sponsor is identified.

Account An advertising agency's client.

Ad click rate Sometimes referred to as *click-through*, this is the percentage of ad views that resulted in an ad click.

Ad clicks Number of times users click on an ad banner.

Ad views (impressions) Number of times an ad banner is downloaded and presumably seen by visitors.

Address A unique identifier for a computer or site online, usually a URL for a website or marked with an @ for an e-mail address.

Advertising manager A professional employed by an advertiser to coordinate and manage the company's advertising program.

Affiliate marketing A system of advertising in which site A agrees to feature buttons from site B, and site A gets a percentage of any sales generated for site B.

Affiliate program An arrangement in which a company pays you a percentage of the sale for every online customer they get through a link from your website to theirs.

Affinity marketing Marketing efforts, including e-mail promotions, banners, or offline media, aimed at consumers on the basis of established buying patterns.

Agora Model Online business model in which you build a large opt-in e-list, and then drive sales by sending e-mails with product offers to your list.

Agora Publishing A publisher of consumer newsletters credited with inventing the Agora Model.

Anchor A word, phrase, or graphic image; in hypertext, it is the object that is highlighted, underlined, or "clickable" that links to another site.

Applet An application program written in Java that allows viewing of simple animation on web pages.

Art director An ad agency employee responsible for designing and producing the artwork and layout for advertisements.

Art A photograph or illustration used in an advertisement.

ASP (application service provider) Third-party vendor that develops and hosts internet and intranet applications for consumers.

Audiovisual presentation A presentation involving both pictures and spoken words. TV commercials, slide shows, videotapes, and films are all audiovisual presentations.

Avatar A digital representation of a user in a virtual reality site.

B

B&W Black and white.

Bandwidth How much information (text, images, video, or sound) can be sent through a connection.

Banner ad A small boxed message that appears atop commercial websites (usually the home page) or on the first page of an e-zine and is usually hot-linked to the advertiser's site.

BBS (bulletin board system) Software that enables users to log into e-mail, Usenet, and chat groups via modem.

Billings The fees an ad agency charges its clients.

Bleed An illustration that goes to the edge of the page. Bleed artwork has no borders or margins.

Blue chip A highly profitable company or product.

Boilerplate Standard copy used because of legal requirements or company policy.

Book See *portfolio*.

Bookmark A bookmark is an easy way to find your way back to a website just like a bookmark helps you keep your place in a book you are reading.

Bounce What happens when e-mail returns as undeliverable.

Bounceback Second mailing sent to a prospective customer who responded to an ad. Bouncebacks are designed to increase response to the initial mailing of product information.

Brand manager A manager employed by an advertiser to take charge of the marketing and advertising of a brand.

Brand The label by which a product is identified.

Branding A school of advertising that says, "If the consumer has heard of us, we've done our job."

Broadband A data-transmission scheme in which multiple signals share the bandwidth.

Broadside A one-page promotional flyer folded for mailing.

Brochure A booklet promoting a product or service.

Browser An application used to view information from the internet.

Budget The amount of money the advertiser plans to spend on advertising.

Bulk mailing The mailing of a large number of identical pieces of third-class mail at a reduced rate.

Bullet A heavy dot used to separate lines or paragraphs of copy.

Buried ad An ad surrounded by other ads.

Business-to-business (B2B) advertising Advertising of products and services sold by a business to other businesses.

Buttons Objects that, when clicked once, cause something to happen.

C

Cache A storage area for frequently accessed information.

Campaign A coordinated program of advertising and promotion.

CGI (common gateway interface) An interface-creation scripting program that allows web pages to be made on the fly based on information from buttons, checkboxes, text input, and so on.

Chat room An area online where you can chat with other members in real time.

Click The opportunity for a visitor to be transferred to a location by clicking on an ad, as recorded by the server.

Click-through rate The percentage of users who click on a hyperlink (usually in an online ad or e-mail) to reach the web page to which the link is attached.

Client A company that uses the services of advertising professionals.

Clios Advertising industry awards given for the year's best television commercials.

Collateral Printed product information such as brochures, fliers, catalogs, and direct mail.

Considered purchase A purchase made after careful evaluation of the product.

Consumer advertising Advertising of products sold to the general public.

Consumer products Goods sold to individuals rather than to business or industry.

Consumer One who buys or uses products and services.

Contest Sales promotion in which the consumer uses his skill to try and win a prize. Some contests require proof of purchase.

Conversion Getting an online user to take a specific action, typically registering online in exchange for free content or purchasing a product from a website.

Cookie A file on your computer that records information such as where you have been on the World Wide Web. The browser stores this information, which allows a site to remember the browser in future transactions or requests.

Copy The text of an ad, commercial, or promotion.

Copy/Contact An ad agency copywriter who works directly with the client instead of through an account executive.

Copywriter A person who writes copy.

CPC Cost per click.

CPL Cost per lead.

CPM Cost per 1,000 for a particular site. A website that charges $15,000 per banner and guarantees 600,000 impressions has a CPM of $25 ($15,000 divided by 600).

CPT Cost per transaction.

CPTM Cost per targeted 1,000 impressions.

Creative director Ad agency employee responsible for supervising the work of copywriters, art directors, and others who produce advertising.

Creative Describes activities directly related to the creation of advertising. These include copywriting, photography, illustration, and design.

D

Demographic overlay Adding demographic data to a prospect or customer list by running it through the computer and matching it against other lists that already contain the data.

Demographics Statistics describing the characteristics of a segment of the population including age, sex, income, religion, and race.

Direct mail Unsolicited advertising material delivered by mail.

Direct response The school of advertising that says, The internet is an interactive medium. If the consumer interacts with our marketing efforts, we've done our job.

Direct response Advertising that seeks to get orders or leads directly and immediately rather than build an image or awareness over a period of time.

Domain part of the DNS (domain naming system) Name that specifies details about the host. A domain is the main subdivision of internet addresses, the last three letters after the final dot, and it tells you what kind of organization you are dealing with. There are six top-level domains widely used in the U.S.: .com (commercial), .edu (educational), .net (network operations), .gov (U.S. government), .mil (U.S. military), and .org (organization).

Downscale Consumers on the low end of the social scale in terms of income, education, and status.

Drill down Used to express what a surfer does as he or she goes further into a website, deeper into the back pages, deeper into data.

E

E-commerce Using electronic information technologies on the internet to allow direct selling and automatic processing of purchases between parties.

E-list A direct mail list containing internet addresses and used to distribute promotional messages over the internet.

E-mail Abbreviation for electronic mail, a network service that allows users to send and receive messages via computer.

E-zine A part promotional, part informational newsletter or magazine distributed on the internet.

Editorial Those portions of a magazine's or newspaper's reading matter that are not ads—articles, news briefs, fillers, and other material produced by the publication's editors and writers.

Emoticons The online means of facial expression and gestures. The most used are **:)** (happy), **:L** (sad), **:o** (surprised) or **:J** (innocent).

F

FAQ A commonly used abbreviation for frequently asked questions.

Farm out Assign work to an outside vendor rather than handle it in-house.

Feature story A full-length magazine article.

Fee The charge made by an agency or advertising professional to the client for services performed.

Firewall A security barrier placed between an organization's internal computer network—either its IS system or intranet—and the internet.

Flame An intentionally crude or abusive e-mail message.

Floater Similar to a pop-up or pop-under, except it is not blocked by pop-up blockers because it is part of the web page or landing page HTML code. The floater captures the visitor's e-mail address, usually by offering free content.

Forms The pages in most browsers that accept information in text-entry fields.

Four As American Association of Advertising Agencies, an industry trade association.

Four color Artwork reproduced in full color.

Fractional ad An ad that takes less than a full page in a magazine or newspaper.

Freelance A self-employed copywriter, photographer, artist, media buyer, or other advertising professional.

Frequency The number of times an ad is delivered to the same browser in a single session or time period. A site needs to use cookies to manage ad frequency.

FTP (File transfer protocol) A protocol that allows the transfer of files from one computer to another. FTP can also be used as a verb.

Full-service agency An ad agency that offers its clients a full range of advertising services including creative services, media buying, planning, marketing, and research.

G

General advertising Advertising that seeks to instill a preference for the product in the consumer's mind to promote the future sale of the product at a retail outlet or through a distributor or agent. This is the opposite of direct response advertising.

GIF (graphic interchange format) A common compression format used for transferring graphics files between computers.

H

Hit When a page request is made, all elements or files that comprise the page are recorded as hits on a server's log file.

Home page The page designated as the main point of entry of a website or the starting point when a browser first connects to the internet.

Host A server connected to the internet (with a unique IP address).

House organ A company-published newsletter or magazine.

HTML A coding language used to make hypertext documents for use on the web.

HTTP (hypertext transfer protocol) A standard method of publishing information as hypertext in HTML format on the internet.

HTTPS-SSL HTTP with SSL (secure socket layer) encryption for security.

Hyperlink The clickable link in text graphics on a Web page that takes you to another place on the same page, another page, or a whole other site.

Hypertext Electronic documents that present information that can be read by following many directions through links, rather than just read linearly like printed text.

I

Image The public's perception of a firm or product.

Impulse buy A purchase motivated by chance rather than by plan.

In-house Anything done internally within a company.

Industrial advertising Advertising of industrial products and services.

Inquiry fulfillment package Product literature sent in response to an inquiry.

Inquiry A request for information made by a potential customer responding to an ad or promotion.

Internet A collection of approximately 60,000 independent, interconnected networks providing reliable and redundant connectivity between disparate computers and systems by using common transport and data protocols.

Internet domain name The unique name that identifies an internet entity.

Interstitial An interstitial ad is an intrusive ad unit spontaneously delivered without specifically being requested by a user.

IP address (internet protocol address) Every system connected to the internet has a unique IP address, which consists of a number in the format, A, B, C, or D, where each of the four sections is a decimal number from 0 to 255.

ISP (internet service provider) A business that provides access to the internet.

J

Java An object-oriented programming language created by Sun Microsystems that supports enhanced features such as animation or real-time updating of information.

Jingle Music and lyrics used in a commercial.

JPEG (joint photographic experts group) A newer graphics format that displays photographs and graphic images with millions of colors, compresses well, and is easy to download.

K

Keyword A word or phrase used to focus on online research.

L

Landing page Any web page designed to generate conversion or other direct action, as opposed to a page that just provides content or links to more content.

Layout A drawing used to get a rough idea of how a finished ad, poster, or brochure will look.

Lead See *sales lead*.

Letter shop A firm that reproduces sales letters and other advertising literature.

Lift letter A second letter included in a direct-mail package designed to increase response to the mailing. Also known as a *publisher's letter* because it is primarily used in mailings that solicit magazine subscriptions.

Link An electronic connection between two websites.

List broker A person who rents mailing lists.

Listserver A program that automatically sends e-mail to a list of subscribers. It is the mechanism used to keep new groups informed.

Load Usually used with *upload* or *download*, it means to transfer files or software—to load—from one computer or server to another computer or server.

Log or log files File that keeps track of network connections.

Login The identification or name used to access—log into—a computer, network, or site.

Logo The name of a company set in specially designed lettering.

Lottery Winners are chosen by chance and must make a purchase to enter.

M

Madison Avenue The mainstream of the New York City advertising community. Refers to agencies located in the heart of midtown Manhattan.

Mailing list An automatically distributed e-mail message on a particular topic going to certain individuals.

Market A portion of the population representing potential and current customers for a product or service.

Marketing communications Communications used in marketing a product or service. Marketing communications includes advertising, public relations, and sales promotion.

Marketing The activities companies perform to produce, distribute, promote, and sell products and services to their customers.

Mass advertising Advertising aimed at the general public.

Mechanical Type and artwork pasted up on a board for reproduction by the printer.

Media Any method of communication that brings information, entertainment, and advertising to the public or the business community.

Merchandising Activities designed to promote retail sales. On speculation, work that the client will pay for only if he likes it and uses it.

Metatags Used to identify the creator of a web page, what HTML specs the page follows, and the keywords and description of the page. Model of selling information products online.

Modem A contraction for modulation/demodulation, it is the device that converts a digital bit stream into an analog signal and back again so computers can communicate across phone lines.

N

Name squeeze page A landing page, usually brief, designed to capture the user's e-mail address, either in exchange for an offer of free content or as a condition of allowing the reader access to copy on a landing page or other web page. Also known as a *squeeze page*.

Netiquette (internet etiquette) The rules of how to behave on the internet.

Netizen An active internet user.

Newbie A term to describe anyone new to an area, whether it be a particular forum online or the internet.

Newsgroup A discussion group on Usenet devoted to talking about a specific topic.

O

One-time offer (OTO) A product offer usually made to those who have subscribed to your e-zine or joined your e-list, that they will see once and not again.

Opt in To agree to receive promotional e-mails when registering on a particular website from the site owner and other companies.

Opt out To request that an e-list owner take your name off the list or at least make sure you are not sent promotional e-mails.

Order page When you click the Order Now button on a landing page, you are taken to an order page describing the offer and allowing you to place your order online.

P

Page All websites are a collection of electronic pages formatted in HTML.

Page views Number of times users request a page.

Pay-per-click An advertising pricing model in which advertisers pay agencies based on how many consumers clicked on a promotion.

PDF files Adobe's portable document format (pdf) is a translation format used primarily for distributing files across a network or on a website. Files with a .pdf extension have been created in another application and then translated into .pdf files so they can be viewed by anyone, regardless of platform.

Per diem Fees charged by the day.

PI Per-inquiry advertising. Advertising for which the publisher or broadcast station is paid according to the number of inquiries produced by the ad or commercial.

Pop-over A page that pops up on the screen when you visit a website or landing page, the purpose of which is to capture the e-mail address of the visitor, usually by offering free content.

Pop-under A page that pops up on the screen when you attempt to leave a landing page or website without placing an order, the purpose of which is to capture the e-mail address of the visitor, usually by offering free content.

Portfolio A presentation folder containing samples of your work. Shown to prospective employers when you are interviewing for a job.

Premium Gift offered to potential customers as motivation for buying a product.

Press release Written news information mailed to the press.

Product manager A manager employed by an advertiser to supervise the marketing and advertising of a product or product line.

Promotion Activities other than advertising used to encourage the purchase of a product or service.

Prospect A person with the money, authority, and desire to buy a product or service; a potential customer.

Psychographics Statistics relating to the personalities, attitudes, and lifestyles of groups of people.

Pub-set Ads designed and typeset by the publication in which they will appear.

Public relations The activity of influencing the press so that they print (and broadcast) stories that promote a favorable image of a company and its products.

Publisher's letter See *lift letter*.

Puffery Exaggerated product claims made by an advertiser.

Pull The response generated by an advertisement.

R

Red Book Refers to both *The Standard Directory of Advertising Agencies* and *The Standard Directory of Advertisers*.

Reel A strip of film or videotape containing sample commercials written by the copywriter.

Reply card A self-addressed postcard sent with advertising material to encourage the prospect to respond.

Research Surveys, interviews, and studies designed to show an advertiser how the public perceives his product and company or how they react to the advertiser's ads and commercials.

S

Sales lead An inquiry from a qualified prospect.

Sales promotion A temporary marketing effort designed to generate short-term interest in the purchase of a product; for example, coupons, sales, discounts, premiums, sweepstakes, and contests are all examples of sales promotion.

Space The portion of a magazine or newspaper devoted to ads.

Special report Free content offered as an incentive for the visitor to take action, typically either placing an order or giving you her e-mail address.

Split run test Two versions of an ad run in different copies of a publication to test the effectiveness of one version against the other.

Squeeze Pages See *name squeeze pages*.

Storyboard Rough series of illustrations showing what a finished TV commercial will look like.

Sweepstakes A sales promotion in which prizes are awarded by chance and the consumer does not have to make a purchase to enter.

T

Teaser Copy printed on the outside envelope of a direct-mail package.

Trade advertising Ads aimed at wholesalers, distributors, sales reps, agents, and retailers.

Transaction page An order page.

Two color An ad or sales brochure printed in two colors, usually black and a second color such as blue, red, or yellow.

Type Text set in lettering that can be reproduced by a printer.

U

Universe The total number of people who are prospects for your product.

Upscale Prospects at the upper end of the social scale in terms of income, education, and status.

V

Vertical publication Magazine intended for a narrow group of special-interests.

Step 1...

Write Your Vision Statement

It's time to create your own vision statement. Don't worry about trying to make it perfect. What's important at this point is to begin the conversation with yourself about the business you're trying to create. Begin with a clean sheet of paper. Imagine your business three to five years in the future, and answer the following questions.

- ◆ What service(s) do you perform?
- ◆ For whom? (What types of clients? If you have specific clients in mind, list them.)
- ◆ Where is your business located? Do you work at home or in an office? Describe everything.
- ◆ You've just met yourself on the job. What do you do in the business? Are you an owner or a hands-on employee? What is your life like? What about your life makes you happy?
- ◆ How much do you and the business earn? (The amounts won't be the same.)
- ◆ Do you have employees? If so, how many? What do they do? What value do they add to the business? What skills and training do they have? Be as specific as possible.
- ◆ What does this business look like when you sell it or turn it over to relatives?
- ◆ What does this business do better than any other? What are you known for?
- ◆ How do you feel about this business? What inspires you about this business?
- ◆ What are the four or five keywords you use when describing

your business to others? What are the words your clients use when describing to others what you do for them?

Write your vision statement.

_____

_____

_____

_____

_____

_____

Step 2...

Describe Your Niche

Write a description of your niche. The following formula can help:

I (We) _____ ,
    (describe the service you perform)

for _____ ,
    (describe the group you perform your services for)

so they _____ .
    (describe the results they can expect)

Describe:

_____

_____

_____

_____

_____

_____

_____

_____

Step 3...

Identify Your Ideal Client

Monthly Client Report

Tracking who buys what every month is a great way to learn more about your clients and to identify the potential lifetime value of your average client. You can create a form similar to the one below in Excel, Access, or even Word.

Client Report (Month/Year)								
	Services Purchased	Problem Solved	Date	Amount	YTD $	Last Purchase Date	Client Since (m/d/y)	Lifetime Value to Date
Client 1								
Client 2								
Client 3								
Totals				$	$			$
Comments:								

Client Profiles

Create a client profile for each of your clients, and add to it whenever you have contact with that client. A sample profile you might build in Access or another database follows. Remember, knowing and understanding your clients' wants and needs better than your competitors do is one of the keys to successful niche marketing.

Client Profile	
CONTACT INFORMATION	
Client name	
Title	
Company	
Phone number	
Fax number	
Address, city, state, zip	
PURCHASING HISTORY	
Client since	
Services purchased (dates and amounts)	
Biggest challenges	
Perceived value of solving their challenges	
Client's competitors	
Their main clients	
Year-to-date purchases	
Referrals given	
Lifetime value	

CLIENT PREFERENCES	
Preferred method of contact	
Frequency	
Birthday	
Anniversaries	
Favorite restaurant(s)	
Spouse	
Children	
Hobbies	
Likes/dislikes	
WORLD NEWS	
Issues affecting them	
MARKETING EFFORTS	
Type/dates/results	
Next action (schedule it)	

Profile Your Ideal Client

Write a description of your ideal client. Add as much detail as you need to be clear about who this client is. What is your client's most pressing problem? What aspirations does he or she have that might drive buying habits? What influences your ideal client's purchasing decisions?

_____

_____

_____

_____

_____

_____

_____

Describe your current clients.

_____

_____

_____

_____

_____

How closely do your actual and ideal clients match? Describe what they have in common. Describe how they differ. If there is a disparity, describe the changes you intend to make to bring them closer together.

_____

_____

_____

_____

_____

_____

What does your ideal client want to experience when doing business with you? Is it the same as what your current clients want?

_____

_____

_____

_____

_____

_____

_____

_____

_____

What do you need to do to find more of your ideal clients?

_____

_____

_____

_____

_____

_____

_____

_____

_____

Step 4...

Describe the Competition

Use the table to identify your competitors' strengths and weaknesses. Think back to the things you identified as important to your ideal client. How well are competitors addressing those issues? Do you see any gaps? Opportunities?

Feature	Your Business	Competitor 1	Competitor 2	Competitor 3	Competitor 4	Competitor 5
What service(s) do they offer?						
Primary focus						
Perceived advantage						
Message						
How do they position themselves?						
What do they do well?						
Strengths (other)						

Segments of your niche they ignore						
Things they don't do well						
Reason clients like them						
Reason former clients don't like them						
Things you can learn from them						
Things you do better than they do						
Things you do they can't copy or improve						

Things they do that can take business away from you	How do they price their services?	How do they package their service? (with special offers, bonuses, guarantees, payment plans, longer service hours, more service providers, etc.?)	Weaknesses	Opportunities for you

Write a summary of what you found in analyzing your competitors. Where are the opportunities for you?

_____

_____

_____

_____

_____

_____

_____

_____

Step 5...

Strategize

Positioning Statement & Goal Setting

A general format for writing a positioning statement includes the following:

[Your service type]
FOR *[Your ideal client type]*
THAT NEED/WANT TO *[The problem you solve*
and why your solution is different]

Remember, your positioning statement should focus on what you do, whom you do it for, and the unique benefit for your clients. Focus on only one promise. Write your positioning statement.

_____

_____

_____

_____

_____

_____

_____

Write your goals for your business for the next year. Focus on no more than three to five major goals. (You don't want to be overwhelmed.)

_____

_____

_____

_____

_____

_____

_____

_____

_____

_____

_____

_____

Write your strategy for meeting your one-year goals.

_____

_____

_____

_____

_____

_____

_____

_____

_____

_____

_____

_____

_____

Step 6...

Identify the Tactics You'll Use

Identify the three to five tactics you'll begin with and why you think they're your best choice given your goals and strategies.

_____

_____

_____

_____

_____

_____

_____

_____

_____

_____

_____

_____

_____

_____

_____

_____

_____

Step 7...

Put Your Measurements in Place

What data will you measure to track your results?

How will you measure each metric?

What system will you use?

Step 8...

Write Your Plan

Stages in the Selling Process

At every stage of the sales process, there's a dance going on between you and your prospect. Selling requires getting and staying in step with your client. Think through what you need to do at each stage of the selling process to get to the next stage. Then, fill in the following table. Keep this in mind as you develop client profiles and tactics for getting your clients' attention.

Stages in the Selling Process	
How will I generate as many leads as I want?	
How will I qualify leads?	
How will I get appointments to meet or present (if applicable)?	
What offer will I make to close the sale?	
How will I follow up with qualified leads until they purchase?	
How will I follow up with new clients after the sale to continue serving and selling to them?	

List your major campaigns.

	Campaign	Expected Cost	Actual Cost	Resources	Expected Results	Actual Results
Jan		$	$			
Feb		$	$			
Mar		$	$			
Apr		$	$			
May		$	$			
Jun		$	$			
Jul		$	$			
Aug		$	$			
Sep		$	$			
Oct		$	$			
Nov		$	$			
Dec		$	$			
Comments:		Campaigns to repeat:			Campaigns to drop:	

Advertising Budget Worksheet

Advertising Budget								
	Total	Magazines	Web	TV	Radio	Direct Mail	PR	
Jan								
Feb								
Mar								
Apr								
May								
Jun								
Jul								
Aug								
Sep								
Oct								
Nov								
Dec								
Total								

Marketing Plan Format

Our Vision (Use Step 1 answers)

Our Niche (Use Step 2 answers)

Our Ideal Client (Use Step 3 answers)

Our Competition (Use Step 4 answers)

Our Strategy (Use Step 5 answers)

Our Tactics (Use Step 6 answers)

Our Measurement Stick (Use Step 7 answers)

Our Action Plan (Step 8 answers)

Our 30-day goals

Our 3-month goals

Our 6-month goals

Our 9-month goals

Our 12-month goals

Step 9...

Implement

Plot your to-dos for the next 30 days. Then, begin.

	Action Plan January 2008					
	Goals	**Daily Actions**				
		Mon	**Tue**	**Wed**	**Thu**	**Fri**
Week 1						
Week 2						
Week 3						
Week 4						
Comments/Results:						

MODEL MARKETING PLAN

Chiropractic Marketing Plans, Inc.'s Marketing Plan

Our Vision

To be the planning resource chiropractors in Southern California think of first when looking for tools to grow their practice, because they know we know their industry even better than they do.

Our Mission

To give chiropractors the know-how to grow a successful practice, starting with a plan that details how they will proceed.

Our Niche

We develop marketing plans for chiropractors located within a 10-mile radius of our office, so they know how to refocus their actions and resources on the clients most likely to help them achieve their vision for their business.

Our Ideal Client

Using the listed resources, we have decided to redefine CMP's ideal client as family wellness chiropractic practices that emphasize care for parents and children. This type of clinic focuses on nutrition, exercises, and massage as part of their care.

We also know the following about the chiropractors located within a 10-mile radius of our office:

- ◆ 70% are in private practice.
- ◆ 28% specialize in family practice.

- Another 1% specialize in pediatric practice.
- They see an average of 127 patients per week.
- Their average patient spends $1,200 in the first year.
- Their average patient visits 30 times per year and spends $40/visit.
- New patients make up 60% of their patient load.
- They retain 40% of old patients.
- They average 7 new patients each week.
- Their average practice billings are $350–500K per year.
- Their average practice earnings are $110K.
- The average chiropractor's age is 42.
- They are 80% male.
- **Trigger:** They want more acceptance of what they do by the public and MDs.
- They get information from the state trade association, association magazines, health magazines and journals, business magazines, and the internet.
- They sell pillows, vitamins, and massage services to complement treatments.
- **Hot buttons:** Revenues are stagnant; they need to increase their new patient average; dependence on health insurance payments is growing; they want more referrals from and joint ventures with MDs; and they feel the public still lacks understanding of how much chiropractic treatment can benefit them.

Our Competition

We have found four chiropractic coaching businesses within our niche area. However, none emphasizes marketing plans.

Analyzing Yellow Pages ads, card deck and newspaper ads, and other sources, we learned that these competitors' messages address the same desired outcomes for prospects—growing their practices. So they're indirect competitors, because, even though they don't offer the same service, prospects could view them as a solution.

Three of the coaching services are new, whereas CMP has a successful four-year track record. The coaching is done over the telephone, whereas we work one-on-one, in person, with clients to develop their plans. The in-person conversations create opportunities for more in-depth discussions and often lead to growth approaches the owner had not considered.

So clients see value in the personal meetings. The disadvantage is that they're more time-consuming than telephone consultations. Still, if the meetings result in more satisfied clients and those clients refer others, this is an advantage, and clients perceive it as one.

The main advantage the competitors offer is a promise to help chiropractors implement change. This is a more costly alternative. CMP can appeal to those who believe they can carry out their own implementations once they have a plan. Another option is to team with one of the coaches.

So, our main opportunity lies in serving those who want to do their own implementations. For those wanting full-service, practice-building assistance, we can team with one or more coaches.

Our Strategy

Positioning statement: Action plans for the family chiropractic practice that wants growth without pain, because the right alignment with the right plan should never hurt.

CMP provides action plans for family chiropractic practices. CMP offers the only growth planning for practices struggling with growth issues.

Goals for this year: Increase revenues from $150,000 to $200,000.

Currently average 29 clients per year throughout Southern California, about two to three each month; current retention rate is 35 percent who review every year.

Strategy for Achieving Goals This Year

Dominate this field within a 10-mile radius of our office. Forty-two chiropractic practices fit the profile of our target market in our coverage area. We need to close about one-third of those this year.

1. Add 15 net clients.
2. Increase retention rate to 40 percent.

3. Earn income by matching clients with implementation specialists when plan is complete.
4. Add midyear review service.

Our Tactics

After careful analysis, we believe the tactics most likely to be effective for us are:

1. Form joint ventures with coaches who specialize in building chiropractic practices.
2. Write articles for both online and offline magazines.
3. Institute a strong referral program.
4. Use direct mail.
5. Speak to chiropractic groups.

Our Measurement Stick

Because CMP's goals require increases in revenues, number of clients, and frequency of purchase by clients, we'll use the following data for measurements:

- Revenue
- Expenses
- Break-even sales
- Cash flow
- Receivables
- Payables
- Average collection days
- New clients
- Client retention rate
- Cost of acquiring a client or making a sale
- Lifetime value of a client
- Client feedback
- Major campaign costs
- Other marketing costs
- Requests for information from sources we target through major campaigns
- Increase in current clients requesting annual or midyear plan reviews
- Number of purchases
- Close ratio
- New joint ventures with practice-building coaches
- Website visitors
- Page views
- Click-through rates
- Commission
- Taxes
- Earnings (net profits)

We'll use the following type of layout to track our results.

Tracking Results for Month/Year

Goal	Strategy	Tactic	Data	Cost Expected	Cost Actual	Outcome Expected	Outcome Actual	Source Used
Increase sales by $50K	Increase referrals by 20%	Referral program	Referrals received	$100 direct mail		Subjects for 3 new case studies for articles, website, & direct mail; 3 written testimonials for website; 1 new client		Ask new clients how they heard about us; ask anyone requesting info how they heard about us; responses to direct mail requests for referrals; testimonials on file
	Become the expert	Publish one new article each month	Article published; leads; meetings; new client			1 article published; 5 qualified leads; 2 meetings; 1 client		Magazines in which the articles were published
		Speak once per month to target group	Speaking event; leads; meetings; new client			1 speech; 10 qualified leads; 4 meetings; 2 new clients		Events where the speeches were given

Our One-Year Action Plan

This identifies the major things CMP will need to do over the next year to accomplish our goals.

Goal: Increase sales from $150K to 200K by December 31			
Strategy	**Tactic**	**To Do**	**Due**
Become well known for writing marketing plans for chiropractors because no one else in CMP's coverage area is doing this	Direct mail campaign to CMP's list four times during the year to build and nurture relationship	Identify four hot buttons for these practices. Focus on one in each of the four mailings. Identify a way to add value to each of the mailings so recipients have a reason to both read and keep the mailing. Decide what action we want chiropractors to take after reading the mailing. Decide what kind of offer to include. Decide who will write the letter. Decide who will put the mailing together.	Jan. 15 April 15 (mail after tax deadline) July 15 Sept. 15
	Article marketing campaign	Write articles for both online and offline magazines. Get four articles published in offline magazines targeting chiropractors. Use the articles in mailings to CMP's list and on their website. Write five articles initially by Jan. 31 to send to online article directories. Then add one new article each month. Add all articles to the CMP website. Decide whether to hire a ghostwriter. Begin researching and interviewing ghostwriters.	April 1 May 1 June 1 Oct. 1 Jan. 31 End of each month
	Speak to chiropractic groups	Identify networking groups that local chiropractors belong to or attend. Create four or five presentations that will appeal to our ideal client. Hire virtual assistant to assemble speaker's kit and begin contacting organizations to get speaking gigs. Speak once a month.	Jan. 31 Mar. 1 Mar. 31 April 1

	Institute a strong referral program	Determine what the referral program should do for CMP. Decide how the program should benefit those who make referrals. Decide benefits for those who schedule appointments through referrals. Create the referral program. Add it to website and all direct mail. Look for other opportunities to promote the program.	Jan. 31
Dominate our field within a 10-mile radius of our office	Form joint ventures with coaches who specialize in building chiropractic practices	Determine what CMP wants from a JV with a coach. Decide how the JV would work to benefit clients. Identify the qualifications and criteria CMP wants. Contact each of the coaches in our coverage area. Interview to learn their approach, methods, and results. Discuss a joint venture if a win-win. If none of the locals is a good prospect, take the criteria developed and expand the search to a wider area in Los Angeles County. Decide how to promote the JV.	Jan. – Mar.
	Develop "touches" system to ensure list is contacted once a month	List will receive direct mail every three months. Develop contacts for the other eight months. Decide what those eight touches should be. Direct list to CMP website and try to secure opt-in to receive e-mail. Call after every direct mailing. Use the other months to send articles of interest to chiropractors, postcards, marketing tips, and other useful information.	Jan. 31 (develop touch system)
Add 15 net clients	Focus on increasing retention, increasing referrals, and adding clients from lead-generating speeches and articles	Same as under "Develop Referral Program," "Develop Maintenance Program," and DM, article, and speaking tactics. Also, conduct at least one workshop and one seminar during the year.	Jan. – Dec.

Increase our client retention rate to 40%	Develop a maintenance program	Develop list of benefits of reviewing a plan at least annually. Offer incentive for reviewing the marketing plan every year and another for every six months. Develop the offers. Include them to current clients at the time of purchase of services and in direct mail three or four times a year. Include offer for those who make referrals.	Jan. – Dec.
Earn income by matching clients with coaches	Develop a JV program	Survey clients and prospects to see if they would use both services. Find out what they would want/expect. Determine what CMP wants from a JV with a coach. Decide how the JV would work to benefit clients. Identify the qualifications and criteria CMP wants. Contact each of the coaches in our coverage area. Interview to learn their approach, methods, and results. Discuss a joint venture if a win-win. If none of the locals is a good prospect, take the criteria developed and expand the search to a wider area in Los Angeles County. Decide how to promote the JV. Work out the details for introducing the program to clients. Tie in the JV to the workshop(s) and seminar.	Jan. – Mar.
Add a midyear review service to increase the frequency of usage of our services	Create the service	Outline content of midyear review. Write the program. Price it. Develop list of benefits of a midyear review. Include in direct mail letters and discussions with current clients. Offer to current clients at the time of purchase of services and in direct mail three or four times a year. Create offer in direct mail and touches calls.	Jan. – Dec.

These are the major marketing campaigns we will launch to meet our goals:

	Campaign	Expected Cost	Actual Cost	Resources	Expected Results	Actual Results
		CMP's Major Campaigns for 2008				
Jan	Direct mail (referral & new client letters)	$500	$	List, sales letter, offer	1 new client	
Feb	Touch 1	$200	$	Article	3 new clients	
Mar	Touch 2	$200	$	Postcards	2 new clients	
Apr	Direct mail	$500	$	List, sales letter, offer	3 new clients	
May	Workshop; Touch 3 (calls)	$600	$	Location, handouts	5 new clients	
Jun	Touch 4	$200	$	Case study	3 new clients	
Jul	Direct mail	$500	$	List, sales letter, offer	3 new clients	
Aug	Touch 5	$200	$	Special report	3 new clients	
Sep	Touch 6	$200	$	Article	3 new clients	
Oct	Direct mail	$500	$	List, sales letter, offer	4 new clients	
Nov	Touch 7 (calls); seminar	$1,100	$	Location, manuals, meals	6 new clients	
Dec	Touch 8 (Happy Holidays)	$300	$	Cards	1 new client	

Breakdown of Our Goals

30-Day Goals: Add one client. Maintain retention rate of existing clients at 35 percent. Stay within $500 marketing budget.

3-Month Goals: Achieve 36 percent retention rate. Add six clients. Start marketing for the seminar in May. Stay within $900 marketing budget. Complete one successful joint venture with a coach; collect $1,000.

6-Month Goals: Achieve 37 percent retention. Complete workshop.

Add 17 new clients year-to-date. Stay within $2,200 marketing budget. Complete four successful joint ventures.

9-Month Goals: Achieve 38 percent retention. Add 26 clients year-to-date. Complete seven successful joint ventures. Start marketing for the seminar in November. Stay within $3,100 marketing budget.

12-Month Goals: Achieve our 40 percent retention of clients. Complete seminar successfully. Add 37 clients for the year, bringing our total to 49 clients for the year. Complete nine successful joint ventures with coaches with $1,000 fee. Gross $200,000. Stay within $5,000 marketing budget.

CMP's growth has been steady with no obvious seasonal impact. We expect growth to remain steady as we increase our retention rate and add the new review service.

Our Budget

Service		
Marketing Plans	$185,000	
Reviews	6,000	
Joint Venture Commission	9,000	
Total Revenues		**$200,000**
Expenses		
Marketing	$5,000	
Operating & Administrative Expenses	82,000	
Total Expenses		**$87,000**
Profit Before Taxes		**$113,000**

We will review this plan every week for the first 30 days of its implementation and then monthly thereafter.

Appendix D

MARKETING CONSULTANTS

Working With—or Becoming— an Independent Marketing Consultant

If you do not have the time or desire to write your own marketing plans, or you seek a fresh viewpoint, you can hire a marketing consultant to help you. Or perhaps you are reading this book because you already are a marketing consultant or want to become one. Becoming a marketing consultant offers many advantages as a career, because you can:

- ◆ Set your own hours because you are in control
- ◆ Get a great deal of personal satisfaction from helping businesses grow while business owners and stakeholders benefit personally for themselves and their loved ones
- ◆ Take vacation time and as much time as you plan for when and where you want
- ◆ Spend more time with your family and loved ones and more easily adapt your schedule to theirs
- ◆ Often get direct and immediate positive feedback on the impact you are having for your clients (in the world of marketing it is easy to track results including the results you are responsible for)
- ◆ Continually expand your knowledge and grow professionally by tapping into a vast array of resources including online, print, seminars, and special events
- ◆ Have as much work variety as you want depending on how you structure your consulting practice, which of the many services you wish to offer, and what types of business you want to serve (as opposed to working for a company as a marketing manager, reporting to the same boss, working at the same

desk, and working on the same types of projects)

◆ Have fun applying your creativity and analytical skills to solve marketing problems

◆ Earn a six-figure income

◆ Avoid the time-sucking and wearing task of long commutes

◆ Dress how you want including no suit and tie

◆ Adopt any work style you like—you can be a recluse who works by phone and internet never leaving his house or battling bad weather

◆ Or, work with clients on site and travel all of the world delivering your services.

The choice is completely yours! You can change your work style any time you want. Marketing consulting services:

◆ Are needed by most small to medium-sized businesses, because few have all of the marketing expertise they need in house

◆ Require almost no investment on the part of the person who wants to enter this business. There are no franchise fees, no expensive equipment to buy, no raw materials or goods to inventory, and no high-priced office that needs to be furnished and rented

◆ Offer the ability to sell and deliver multiple services providing almost limitless opportunities to gain additional revenue from existing clients

Why There Is High Demand for Marketing Consultants

There is high demand for marketing consultants for many reasons, including:

◆ Increased competition facing most businesses today resulting in a need for more effective marketing

◆ A more rapid rate of change in products, services, and technology in the business world. These new products, services, and technologies necessitate changes in marketing approaches to address what's happening in the world of business

♦ The realization by many business owners that being competent in their business niche is not enough. Marketing is increasingly becoming the differentiator in companies that just get by and companies that are highly profitable

♦ A continually expanding array of marketing communications choices requiring more expertise in picking how to communicate with prospects and customers. Consider the number of channel choices we have on television today, the number of magazines we can now subscribe to, and the millions of choices of websites to visit. Advertising and marketing channel fragmentation makes deciding where and how to promote your business more of a challenge

♦ A huge and growing demand for internet marketing assistance. As more and more companies create an internet presence, and as a continuing array of marketing choices and technologies evolve, companies needs help in deploying effective internet marketing strategies. Although the internet does lower the barriers to worldwide marketing, internet marketing requires a new and constantly changing skill set most businesses don't have or will not invest in internally

What Is Marketing Consulting?

Marketing consulting is a service provided by solo, freelance consultants or larger organizations to help companies improve their sales results in a variety of ways. Following are examples of how marketing consulting could help clients. A marketing consultant could help clients:

♦ Expand market share
♦ Enter a new market
♦ Effectively communicate messages to potential prospects
♦ Improve effectiveness of marketing activities
♦ Identify and solve marketing problems
♦ Identify and deploy new or expanded marketing methods

What Skills Are Required to Be a Successful Marketing Consultant?

The skills required to be a successful marketing consultant will vary depending on the nature of the services to be offered. Following is a list of general skills needed for any marketing consultant followed by additional skills that might be required based on the services planned to be offered:

General skills required:

- Excellent written and verbal communications skills
- Sales ability
- Natural curiosity and interest in business, regardless of the type of business
- High energy level
- Extensive knowledge of advertising and basic marketing principles
- Organizational skills
- Ability to stay focused and work independently
- Creativity
- Analytical and problem-solving ability
- Ability to work well with business-people from the owner of a company to the lowest-level employee

Other skills that might be required depending on services offered:

- Public speaking
- Copywriting
- Graphics design knowledge
- Online and offline research
- Internet marketing
- Internet search engine optimization
- Publicity and public relations
- Database marketing
- Search engine optimization
- Market research
- Unique selling proposition development

- Direct response marketing
- Broadcast advertising
- Yellow Pages advertising
- Print advertising
- Telemarketing script development
- Knowledge of computer programs such as Microsoft Word, Excel, and PowerPoint

Fees for Marketing Plan Writers

If you pay a professional marketing consultant to write your plan, expect to be charged in the range of $3,000–$10,000.

Low: $3,000

Average: $5,000

High: $8,000–$10,000

Higher fees generally reflect the writer's need to do more extensive research on your industry, target market, and clients to complete your plan. They also generally apply to larger companies with multiple products and services and markets.

When the Marketing Plan Is Part of a Business Plan

A marketing plan is only one part of a total business plan. Unless you're seeking outside funding from a bank or investors, you'll rarely need to produce an entire business plan. (However, if you really want to master the workings of your business, producing a business plan for yourself is still a good idea. Look in the Resources section for information on sources for developing a complete business plan.)

Will your marketing plan be different if it's going to be part of a business plan submitted to outside funding sources? That depends.

Funding sources want to know that you have thought through your business and have a realistic view of how you'll generate profits. They're interested in the numbers and anything that affects the numbers, because they need to see how you'll generate the return they expect. They want to see how you've assessed the business environment you operate in, your assumptions about what it will take to succeed, your competition, your strategy for succeeding, and your funding apart from what they might lend you.

So, yes, they are interested in your marketing plan, but not necessarily in all the tactical details. Remember, your plan is for you. It tells you what actions you need to take to ensure growth and create your vision. The specific actions are not necessarily of interest to your bankers.

So how would the marketing plan portion differ? It would be more concise and focused largely on assessing the market you serve, your strategy for serving that market differently from your competitors, and how you plan to apply all your resources to get the highest return on them.

Appendix E
SOURCES & RESOURCES

References

Allen, David. 2001. *Getting Things Done*. New York: Penguin.

Antion, Tom. 2005. *Electronic Marketing for Small Business*. Hoboken, NJ: John Wiley & Sons.

Crispell, Diane. 1993. *The Insider's Guide to Demographic Know-How: Everything You Need to Find, Analyze, and Use Information About Your Customers*. Ithaca, NY: American Demographics Press.

Davis, John. 2007. *Measuring Marketing: 103 Key Metrics Every Marketer Needs*. Singapore: John Wiley & Sons.

Gerber, Michael E. 1995. *The E Myth Revisited: Why Most Small Businesses Don't Work and What to Do About It*. New York: HarperCollins.

Harding, Ford. 1994. *Rain Making: The Professional's Guide to Attracting New Clients*. Avon, MA: Adams Media.

Hayden, C. J. 1999. *Get Clients Now!* New York: AMACOM.

Hines, Randall and Lauterborn, Robert. 2008. *Print Matters: How to Write Great Advertising*. Chicago: RACOM.

Johnson, Winslow. 2004. *Powerhouse Marketing Plans*. New York: AMACOM.

Joyner, Mark. 2005. *The Irresistible Offer*. Hoboken, NJ: John Wiley & Sons.

Luther, William. 2001. *The Marketing Plan*. 3rd ed. New York: AMACOM.

McDonald, Malcolm. 2004. *Marketing Plans: How to Prepare Them, How to Use Them*. 5th ed. Burlington, MA: Elsevier.

Ogden, James R. 1998. *Developing a Creative and Innovative Integrated Marketing Communication Plan: A Working Model*. Upper Saddle River, NJ: Prentice-Hall.

Porter, Michael E. 1980. *Competitive Strategy: Techniques for Analyzing Industries and Competitors*. New York: The Free Press.

Rice, Craig S. 1990. *Strategic Planning for the Small Business: Situations, Weapons, Objectives, and Tactics*. Holbrook, MA: Bob Adams.

Websites on Business Planning

SBA Small Business Planner
sba.gov/smallbusinessplanner/index.html

SCORE Template Gallery
score.org/template_gallery.html

Business Owner's Toolkit
toolkit.com/small_business_guide/sbg.aspx?nid=P02_0001

American Express Small Business Plan Resources
www133.americanexpress.com/osbn/tool/biz_plan/index.asp

BizStats
Free business statistics, benchmarks, and financial ratios, with a special section for sole proprietors. bizstats.com

Planning Software

Marketing Plan Pro

Software contains more than 100 sample editable marketing plans for businesses of all types.
mplans.com

Business Plan Pro

Software contains more than 500 sample editable business plans for businesses of all types. bplans.com

Associations, Clubs, Organizations

Direct Marketing Association, Inc.
1120 Avenue of the Americas
New York, NY 10036-6700
(212) 768-7277

Direct Marketing Club of New York
224 Seventh Street
Garden City, NY 11530
(516) 746-6700

International Association of Business Communicators (IABC)
One Hallidie Plaza, Suite 600
San Francisco, CA 94102
(415) 544-4700
iabc.com

National Mail Order Association
2807 Polk St. NE
Minneapolis, MN 55418-2954
(612) 788-1673
nmoa.org

Mailing Lists

Creative Access
3701 N. Ravenswood Ave., #207
Chicago, IL 60613
(312) 440-1140

Edith Roman Associates
One Blue Hill Plaza, 16th floor
Pearl River, NY 10956
(800) 223-2194
edithroman.com

Mailing List and Marketing Database Software

Act
1505 Pavilion Place
Norcross, GA 30093
(770) 724-4000
act.com

Telemagic
(800) 835-MAGIC
telemagic.com

Books

Bly, Robert. *The Copywriter's Handbook: A Step-by-Step Guide to Writing Copy That Sells*, 3rd ed. New York, NY: Henry Holt, 2006. How to write effective copy.

Cates, Bill. *Unlimited Referrals*. Wheaton, MD: Thunder Hill Press, 1996. How to get lots of referral leads.

Periodicals

Advertising Age
740 North Rush Street
Chicago, IL 60611
(312) 649-5200

Adweek
49 East 21st Street
New York, NY 10010
(212) 529-5500

B-to-B
740 North Rush Street
Chicago, IL 60611
(312) 649-5260

Commerce Business Daily
Government Printing Office
Washington, DC 20401
(202) 512-0132

Direct Marketing
Hoke Communications
224 Seventh Street
Garden City, NY 11530
(516) 746-6700

DM News
19 West 21st Street
New York, NY 10010
(212) 741-2095

Public Relations Journal
33 Irving Place
New York, NY 10003
(212) 998-2230

Sales and Marketing Management
633 Third Avenue
New York, NY 10017
(212) 986-4800

Target Marketing
North American Publishing Co.
401 North Broad Street
Philadelphia, PA 19108
(215) 238-5300

Marketing and Business E-Newsletters

Bencivenga's Bullets
bencivengabullets.com
Master copywriter Gary Bencivenga's
can't-miss e-newsletter based on his
decades of tested results

Early to Rise
earlytorise.com
Daily e-newsletter on business success,
wealth, and health by marketing guru
Michael Masterson

Excess Voice
nickusborne.com/excess_voice.htm
Nick Usborne's e-newsletter on online
copywriting. Informative and great fun

Marketing Minute
yudkin.com/markmin.htm
Weekly marketing tip from consultant
Marcia Yudkin

Paul Hartunian's Million-Dollar Publicity Strategies
prprofits.com
Great marketing e-newsletter focusing
on publicity

The Copywriter's Roundtable
jackforde.com
John Forde's superb e-newsletter on
copywriting

The Direct Response Letter
bly.com
My monthly e-newsletter on copywriting and direct marketing

The Success Margin
tednicholas.com
Ted Nicholas's must-read marketing
e-zine

Websites

smallbusinessadvocate.com
The Small Business Advocate
Radio show and website dedicated to
small business.

theadvertisingshow.com
"The Advertising Show" (radio show on
advertising)

Directories

Bacon's Publicity Checklist
332 South Michigan Avenue
Chicago, IL 60604
(800) 621-0561
Media lists for mailing press releases.

Directory of Major Mailers
North American Publishing Co.
401 North Broad Street
Philadelphia, PA 19108
(215) 238-5300
Directory of companies that sell via
direct marketing

Encyclopedia of Associations
Gale Research
Book Tower
Detroit, MI 48226
(313) 961-2242
Directory of major U.S. industry and professional associations.

O'Dwyer's Directory of Corporate Communications
J. R. O'Dwyer & Co., Inc.
271 Madison Avenue
New York, NY 10016
(212) 679-2471
Communications directors at large corporations and associations.

O'Dwyer's Directory of Public Relations Firms
J. R. O'Dwyer & Co., Inc.
271 Madison Avenue
New York, NY 10016
(212) 679-2471
Lists U.S. public relations firms.

Standard Rate and Data Service
1700 Higgins Road
Des Plaines, IL 60018-5605
(800) 851-7737
srds.com
Comprehensive directory of publications that accept advertising.

INDEX

A

"About the author" copy, 248
Abraham, Jay, 116
A/B split testing, 262, 263
Accounting software offer, 261
Account status updates, 163
Acquisition of customers, 114, 115–117
Acronyms, 236
Action exercises
  Describe Your Ideal Client, 72–74
  Describe Your Niche, 40
  Describe Your Strategy for Achieving
    Your Goals, 109
  Identify the Tactics You'll Use, 157
  Write What and How You'll
    Measure, 207
  Write Your Description of the
    Competition, 84
  Write Your Goals for Your Business
    for the Next Year, 108
  Write Your Plan, 223
  Write Your Vision Statement, 15–18
Action plans. *See* Marketing plans
Ad agencies, 30
Adjusting marketing plans, 265–266
Admiral Bird Society, 132
Advantages, in benefits hierarchy, 119
Advertising
  branding with, 19, 92
  budgets, 217–220
  features vs. benefits, 118–121
  in newsletters, 163
  prices, 132
  product flaws, 121–123
  role of USP, 18–21, 94–97
  saving costs, 224–225
  targeting ability, 143–144
  Yellow Pages, 106–108
Advertising Age, 128
Advertising budget allocation work-
  sheet, 219–220
Age for starting a business, 41–42
Agora Publishing, 162, 165, 178
AIDA, 240
Airplane test, 6
Alexander, Jim, 20, 122
Alternating even pattern of marketing, 223
Alternating staggered pattern of mar-
  keting, 223
Amazon.com, 14, 163
American Cancer Society telethons, 59
American Red Cross vision statement, 15
American Spectator, 232–233
Andersson, Axel, 139
Annual goals, 101–102
Annual plans, 215–223, 217–220
Apple story, 121–122
"The Apprentice," 54–55
Aqualungs, 82
Article reprints, 226
Article writing, 247–249
Attention-getting copy, 240–241
Average order amounts, 47

B

Back-end sales, 114, 191
Baker, Sam Sinclair, 17
BDF formula, 50–51
Beliefs, desires, and feelings, 50–51
Benefits
  hierarchy of, 118–121
  identifying most meaningful, 62–63
  products as, 117

in USPs, 18, 96
Bestseller lists, 36
Beutchel, Peter, 261
Bill-me orders, 129–130
Biographies (Twitter), 185
Blackmer, 20, 122
Blogging, 180–182
Blogs, negative publicity on, 76
Bob Bly's Direct Response Letter, 165
Bob Bly's Direct Response ROI Calculator, 179–180
Bock, Wally, 32
Books as products, 117
Bookstores, market research in, 35–36
Boucke, Christian, 139
Bounce rate, 203
Bowling, Inc. vision statement, 15
Branding
    with celebrity spokespersons, 92–93
    by large companies, 19, 155, 156
Break-even response rates, 191
Brine shrimp, 233
Brownmiller, Susan, 234
Budgets
    creating for marketing plans, 217–220
    of prospective customers, 45
    for prospective purchases, 255–256
    stretching, 224–227
Buffett, Jimmy, 242–243
Bundling pricing, 141
Burnett, Hank, 132
Business cards, 82
Business opportunity seekers, 158–159
Business stages, 230–232
Business Technology Advisor, 163
Business unit marketing, 155, 156
Busy doctor syndrome, 147–148
Buyer's markets, 254
Buying behavior, 62, 64
Buying motives, 123–124
Buying processes, 64
Byrne, Charlie, 242–243

C

Campaign calendars, 220–221
Canadian Cancer Society vision statement, 14
Capabilities brochures, 102–103

Career training, 135
Case study. *See* Chiropractic Marketing Plans case study
CAST analyses, 187–188
Categorizing competitors, 77
Celebrity fundraisers, 60
Celebrity spokespersons, 92–93
Charitable giving, 59–60
Chiropractic Marketing Plans case study
    action plan, 215–216
    campaign calendar, 221
    competitive research, 83
    defining ideal client, 71–72
    marketing tactics, 156–157
    strategy analysis, 110–111
    vision statement, 15
    writing goals, 102
Chorich, Martin, 240
Cialdini, Robert, 131
Claims, offering proof for, 97–101
Clancy, Kevin, 12
Click density analysis, 197–198, 204
Clickstream Technologies, 202
ClickTracks, 198
Client Profile form, 69–70
Clients. *See* Customers; Ideal clients
Clubs, 164
CMP, 163
Coca-Cola, 19
Coffee, 24
Cold calling, 147–148
Colonel Sanders, 12
Commands, in headlines, 237
Commissions, 116
Commodities, services as, 29
Communication tactics, 142
Comparison headlines, 238
Competition
    action exercise to describe, 84–86
    denial of, 75–76
    finding niches underserved by, 77–79
    information sources about, 80
    keeping track of, 273
    keyword use by, 154–155, 168
    for niche markets, 30–31
    price-based, 125
    top competitors, 76–77

Computer operating systems, 209
Computers' impact on newsletter publishing, 24–25
ComputerWorld magazine, 163
Conditionality of guarantees, 65–66, 270–271
Conscious competence in marketing, 253
Conscious incompetence in marketing, 252
Consistency of blog postings, 180–181
Consultants, 227, 315–320
Consumer Reports magazine, 107–108
Conversational copy, 9–10, 139–140, 234–237
Conversion rate, 204
Conversion series, 177
Cookies, 201
Copywriter's Roundtable, 165
Copywriting
    conversational, 9–10, 139–140, 234–237
    free offers in, 242–247
    headlines, 237–240
    reusing copy, 227
    role in plan implementation, 232–233
    to stimulate behavior, 138–139
    structure in, 240–242
    swipe files, 213–214
    for websites, 169–170
Core values, 13–14
Corporate marketing, 155, 156
CPM, 209
Creative talent, 227
Credibility
    by discussing weaknesses, 122
    as micro-niching benefit, 32
    of testimonials, 100
    of websites, 164
    writing for, 140, 241
Credit cards, government use, 56, 57, 58
Crispix, 92
Current clients, learning from, 68
Customer databases, 46–49
Customer identification
    action exercise, 72–74
    beliefs, desires, and feelings, 50–51
    buying behavior, 62, 64
    gathering personal data, 52–54, 62–63

government markets, 56–58
    information-seeking behavior, 67–68
    nonprofit, 59–60
    overview, 27–28, 43–44
    qualifying prospects, 44–46
Customer profiles, 56
Customers
    acquisition cost, 115–117
    buying motives, 123–124
    for internet information products, 86–88
    lifetime value, 60–61, 113–114
    matching marketing tactics to, 143
    potential responses from, 138
    testimonials from, 99–101, 238
Customer service problems, 266–269
Customer service tactics, 142

D

Daily actions, 273. *See also* Implementation (marketing plan)
Daily Reckoning, 162, 165
Damico, Joan, 138
Databases, customer, 46–49
Data review schedules, 206–207
Day planner promotion, 127, 243
Demand, creating, 125
Demographic data, 53
Describe Your Ideal Client exercise, 72–74
Describe Your Niche exercise, 40
Describe Your Strategy exercise, 109
Description tags, 169
Desire of prospective customers, 45
Dictionaries, 236
Differentiation
    of benefits, 120
    describing in USPs, 19, 91–93
    discovering, 19–20
    in positioning statements, 93
DiGeorgia, James, 122
Direct mail
    costs, 196
    doubling day, 194
    free gifts with, 246–247
    goals for, 190–192
    lead generation from, 146
Disclaimers, 122–123
Discounts, in headlines, 239

Division marketing, 155, 156
Dormant accounts, reactivating, 151
Doubling day, 194
Doubling hour, 194–196
"Do you know?" formula, 26–27
Dreamers, 158–159
Drop-in-the-bucket technique, 139
Dunkin' Donuts, 24

E

EABS Bank vision statement, 14
eBay offers, 242–243
eBay searches, 37
eBay vision statement, 14
E-book guarantees, 66–67, 271
Edith Roman Associates, 245
Elevator pitch, 25, 26–27
E-mail addresses, gathering, 165, 167, 172–180
E-mail alerts, 163–164
E-mail marketing
    common methods, 161–167
    doubling day, 194–196
    lead generation from, 146–147
E-mail surveys, 52
Emotional appeals in fundraising, 60
Emotion in purchasing decisions, 123–124
E-newsletters. See E-zines
Entertainment at trade shows, 81–82
Ethnographies, 52
Exclusivity, 132, 239
Exercise machines, 135–136
Experian, 244
Expertise, 33, 146, 149
E-zines
    advertising in, 163
    building opt-in e-lists with, 175, 178
    publishing, 162, 165–167

F

FAB Pyramid, 118–121
Failure, predicting, 208–209
Fax surveys, 52
FCB Grid, 123–124
Features, 92, 117, 119
FedEx, 90
Fighting pattern of marketing, 223

Financial services, 132
Finn, Kevin, 139
Fiscal years, 57
Fit of prospective customers, 45–46
Five-lives exercise, 7
Flaws, turning into selling points, 121–123
Flesch, Rudolph, 234
Focus groups, 52
Foote, Cone, & Belding, 123
Forde, John, 165
Forms
    Advertising Budget Allocation Worksheet, 219–220
    Client Profile, 69–70
    Inquiries and Sales, 205
    Literature Specifications Sheet, 103–106
    Product Definition and Description Ranking Sheet, 118
    Tracking Results for Month/Year, 206
Franchising, 11–12
Franklin Mint, 131–132
Freelancers, 227
Free offers, 127, 242–247. See also Premiums
Free-on-free name squeeze pages, 175–176
Free reports, 175–176, 232–233
Frequency of blog postings, 180
Frequency of purchase, 47
Front-end sales, 114
Fruitcakes, 233
Fundraising, 59

G

Gates, Bill, 208–209
George Foreman grills, 92–93
Gerber, Gary, 92
Get requests, 201
Giveaways. See Premiums
Gleeck, Fred, 8, 23, 33, 139, 258
Goals
    describing, 101–102
    importance to success, 1
    for marketing campaigns, 190–192
    starting with, 12–13
    strategies for achieving, 109
The Godfather, 41

"Good, better, best" method, 256
Good Housekeeping, 274
Good Keywords software, 169
Google, 164, 183
Google AdWords, 174–175
Google Alerts, 76
Google Groups, 37–38
Government information sources, 70
Government markets, 56–58
Gross profit, 191
Grumpy old men, 63
GSA Schedules, 58
Guarantees
    in headlines, 239
    improving results with, 245, 270–271
    strength, 65–67, 270–271
    to support pricing, 129–130

H
Hacker, Bob, 139
Halbert, Gary, 158
Hancock Shoe Company, 29
Hartunian, Paul, 165
Hatch, Denny, 139
Headline writing, 237–240
Hennerberg, Gary, 233
Hershey, Milton, 42
Hewlett-Packard, 178
High-priced products, selling, 131–132
Hobbies, 36, 158
Honesty, Bryan, 140
Hopkins, Claude, 20
Hotline names, 47
HTML e-zines, 166
Huff, Dianna, 76, 167
Huntsinger, Jerry, 59
Hutcheson, Susanna K., 9

I
IBM, 12–13, 183, 209
Ideal clients. *See also* Customer
    identification
    description exercise, 72–74
    gathering data about, 52–54
    importance of knowing, 43, 51
    lifetime value, 60–61
    staying close to, 272
    view of competitors, 76–77

Ideal day essays, 4–7
Identify the Tactics You'll Use exercise,
    157
Implementation (marketing plan)
    copywriting, 232–237, 240–242
    free offers, 127, 242–247
    headline writing, 237–240
    importance, 229
    stages of business, 230–232
    thirty-day action plans, 249–250
    tips for persevering, 272–274
Inbound marketing tactics, 144–149
Income, 2–3, 33
Indirect competitors, 77
Individual stories, 59–60
The Information Marketing Club, 8
Information-seeking behavior, 67–68
Information sources, 70
Inner circle of e-mail senders, 162–164
Inquiries and Sales form, 205
Installment payments, 131–132, 263
Intel, 19
Internal routing codes, 57
Internet
    keyword evaluation, 153–155
    market research using, 36–38, 52
Internet information marketers
    competition, 86–88
    customer databases, 49
    earnings and lifestyle, 3
    stages of business, 230–231
Internet marketing
    blogging, 180–182
    building opt-in e-lists, 172–180
    doubling day, 194–196
    e-mail, 161–167
    recommended vendors pages, 171–172
    search engine optimization, 154,
        167–170
    social media, 182–185
Interviews, 52
Introductory pricing, 141
Investments, market demand, 159
Involvement, in purchasing decisions,
    123–124
ITT Tech, 135
Ivins, Bob, 184

J

Jargon, 10, 234–235
JavaScript tags, 202
Joyner, Mark, 241

K

Kalan, Barnaby, 140
Karasik, Paul, 26, 27
Kaufmann, Don, 164
Kennedy, Dan, 140
Kentucky Fried Chicken, 12
Key copy drivers, 139
Keyword research tools, 88
Keywords
    evaluating, 153–155
    organic search lead quality, 145
    search engine optimization and,
        167–168, 169, 170
    tracking those used by visitors, 204
    in vision statements, 16–18
Keyword selection services, 36
Kiplinger Letter, 24–25
Koch Engineering, 80, 81
Krieg, Peter, 12

L

Landing pages, 172, 173, 176, 177, 185
Large company marketing, 155, 156
Lead generation, 144–149, 226–227
Leads, in copywriting, 140
Lewis, Jerry, 60
Library research, 35, 52
Lifestyle, 3–9, 134–136
Lifetime customer value
    acquisition cost vs., 115–117
    defined, 60–61, 113–114
    of online subscribers, 175
List-building campaigns, 174–175
Literature Specifications Sheet, 103–106
Loss leaders, 124
Lowballing, 133–134
Ludlow Corp., 225

M

M&Ms, 20, 96
MAD FU formula, 45
Magazine columns, 8
Magazines for niche markets, 36

Magazine subscription offers, 129–130
Mailing lists
    e-mail, 165, 167, 172–180
    government markets, 56
    hotline names, 47
    potential benefits, 55
Mail surveys, 51–52
Marketing campaigns, testing, 259–262
Marketing consultants, 315–320
Marketing performance reporting, 204
Marketing plans. *See also* Implementa-
    tion (marketing plan)
    benefits of writing, 211–212
    budgets, 217–220
    campaign calendars, 220–221
    purpose, 1
    reviewing, 251–252, 254
    scheduling activities, 222–223
    sharing with others, 211
    to-do lists, 215–216
    troubleshooting, 264–269
Marketing skills, 252–253
Market research
    for large companies, 50
    methodologies, 51–52
    suggestions, 34–38
Market segments, 27–28
Masterson, Michael, 253
Mathews, Carrie, 183
McCarthy, Bob, 235
McDonald's, 24
McKenna, Susan, 183
Measurement
    choosing metrics, 188–190
    comparing to goals, 190–192
    doubling hour and doubling day,
        194–196
    marketing performance reporting, 204
    overview, 187–188
    return on time invested, 192–193
    tracking systems and data review,
        206–207
    web metrics, 197–204
Media scheduling patterns, 223
Meetup.com, 37
Meta tags, 154–155, 168–169
Micro-niching, 30–33

Microsoft vision statement, 14
Military bases, 57
Million-Dollar Publicity Strategies, 165
Milwaukee Public Library vision statement, 14–15
Mission statements, 1, 34
Misspelled keywords, 168
Modular literature, 225–226
Money-back guarantees, 65–67, 129–130, 245, 270–271
Money making information products, 159
Money spent on average orders, 47
Mont Blanc pens, 10, 234
Montesdeoca, Wendy, 167
Monthly client reports, 61
Monthly columns, 248–249
Motivating Sequence, 240–242
Motivations for buying, 123–124
MS-DOS, 209
Multi-buyers, 47
Multichannel impact analysis, 199
Murray, James, 234
Muscular Dystrophy Association, 60

N

National Enquirer, 158
Needs, focusing copy on, 241
Negotiating, 148
New products, 117
News bulletins, 163
News in headlines, 237
Newsletter Publishers Association, 24, 25
Newsletter publishing industry changes, 24–25
Newsletters, online. *See* E-zines
Niche marketing
    action exercise, 40
    elements of, 28–31
    identification exercise, 40
    impact on pricing, 125–126
    for internet information products, 87–88
    maintaining focus, 272
    suggestions for identifying niches, 34–40
Nicholas, Ted, 243
Non-negotiating prices, 141
North Point Church vision statement, 14

O

Offers, writing, 242–247
Ogilvy, David, 213–214, 237
Older males, 63
One-on-one interviews, 52
1shoppingcart.com, 49
One-year plans, 215–223
Online conversion series, 177
Online criticism, 76
Online marketing. *See* Internet marketing
Online trading services, 116
Opt-in e-lists, 172–180
Options trading service offer, 244–245, 262–263
Organic search, 145
Outbound marketing tactics, 144–149
Outsourcing, 6

P

Packaging tactics, 141–142
Packet sniffing, 202–203
Pages metric, 203
Page views, 198, 203
Parker, Roger C., 180
Patterns of marketing activity, 222–223
Pavlish, Mike, 139
Pay-one prices, 141
Pay-per-click advertising, 154
Perceived value of premiums, 126, 127
Perel, David, 158
Permission to use testimonials, 101
Personal stories, 59–60
Peters, Tom, 149
Photographers, 227
Piano stabilizer bars, 97
Pierce, Milt, 47–48, 213, 214, 274
Plagiarism, 213
Pocket day planners, 127, 243
Pockmarked apples, 121–122
Podcasting, 183
Pop-under windows, 178, 179
Positioning examples, 78–79, 90
Positioning statements
    creating, 90–91
    offering proof, 97–101
    purpose, 78, 89–90
Predictability of blog postings, 180–181

Premiums
  adding value to offers with, 126–128,
    242–247
  in headlines, 240
  at trade shows, 82
  use in fundraising, 59
Press releases, 150–152
Price levels, 258–259
Price resistance, 254–256
Pricing
  adjusting, 266
  controllable factors, 124–130
  focusing on lifestyle, 134–136
  in headline copy, 239
  high-priced product approaches,
    131–132
  psychology of, 257–259
  during recessions, 151
  strategies for services, 133–134, 141,
    257–259
  testing, 257, 262–264
Primary skills, 23–24
Problems, focusing copy on, 241
Procurement offices, 57
Product Definition and Description
  Ranking Sheet, 118
Products. *See also* Pricing
  benefits hierarchy, 118–121
  creating, 117
  high-priced, 131–132
  turning flaws into selling points,
    121–123
Product/service tactics, 141
Profiles, customer, 56
Promises, in headlines, 239
Propositions, 94
Prospects, 44–46
Proving claims, 97–101, 241–242
Psychographic data, 53
Psychology of pricing, 257–259
Public relations, 147, 150–151
Puffery, 17
Pulsing pattern of marketing, 223
Pump marketing, 19–20

Q
Qualifying prospects, 44–46
Question headlines, 237, 239

Questions for troubleshooting plans,
  264–265

R
Radiology Business Managers
  Association, 143
Railroads, 24
Reality in Advertising (Reeves), 18
Recency of purchase, 46–48
"Recession-Proof Business Strategies,"
  151–152
Recommended Vendors lists, 171–172
Recurring costs, 191
Reeves, Rosser, 18, 20, 21
Refunds, 130, 269–271. *See also*
  Guarantees
Repeat orders, 114
Reports, offering, 232–233, 238
Reprints, 226
Researching niche markets, 34–38
Response rates, 192, 195
Responses, potential, 138
Return on investment
  as focus of pricing message, 128–129
  in headlines, 239
  lead generation tactics compared,
    144–147, 150
  for trade show exhibits, 81
Return on time invested, 192–193
RFM principle, 46–48
Roberts, Ken, 244
Robots, 200
Rodale, 263
Rolls Royce, 213
ROM Cross Trainer, 136
ROTI (return on time invested), 192–193
Routing codes, 57

S
Sales
  front- and back-end, 114
  overcoming price resistance, 254–256
  steps in, 52
Sanders, Harland, 11–12
SAP implementation, 35
Savings, in headlines, 239
Scheduling marketing activities, 222–223
Scheffren, Rich, 263

The Science in Science Fiction, 8
Sea Monkeys, 233
Search.com, 36
Search engine optimization, 153–155, 167–170
Searches, online, 36–37
Seasonal pattern of marketing, 223
Second Life, 183
Segmented visitor trends, 198–199
Self-storage industry marketing, 33
Selling points, turning flaws into, 121–123
Selling process, 212
Semantics, 232–233
SEO Book, 36–37
Server performance data, 199–200
Services, pricing, 133–134, 141, 257–259
Shenson, Howard, 148
Shoemaker, John, 140
Silver Rule of marketing, 149
Silver, Yanik, 125
Site entry points, 204
Skills, primary, 23–24
Slaunwhite, Steve, 140
SMART goals, 101
SmartPay cards, 56, 57, 58
Snob appeal, 132
Social networking, 146, 182–185
Soft metrics, 193
Software offers, 261
Software service notices, 163
Source codes, 154–155, 168
Sovereign Society, 128
"So what" test, 138–139
Spacky.com, 154, 168
Spam complaints, 173
Specialized Information Publishers Association, 25
Special reports, 232–233, 238
Split testing, 67, 127, 262
Stabilizer bars, 97
Stages of business, 230–232
Starbucks, 24
Starving crowd markets, 158–159
State Farm, 78, 96
Steady pattern of marketing, 223
Stelzner, Michael, 146
Step-down pattern of marketing, 223

Step-up pattern of marketing, 223
Sticker shock, 131–132
Stickiness of website, 203
Stories, in headlines, 238
Strategies, describing, 109
Stretching budgets, 224–227
Strong guarantees, 65–67
Success
    customer stories, 99–101
    differing views, 2–4
    predicting, 208–209
Sunset Playhouse vision statement, 15
Supply and demand forces, 125
Surveys, 51–52, 198
Suspects, 43–44
Swipe files, 213–214, 237

T

Tactics
    defined, 137
    inbound vs. outbound, 144–149
    in large corporations, 155, 156
    message selection, 138–140
    selecting, 141–142, 150–153
    for target markets, 143
Target markets, 92, 143. *See also* Niche marketing
Task completion rates, 198
Teaser pattern of marketing, 223
Technical terms, 10, 235, 236–237
Telephone surveys, 51
Telethons, 59
Testimonials, 99–101, 238
Testing marketing campaigns, 259–262
Testing prices, 257
Thirty-day action plans, 249–250
Tier pricing, 141
Time, saving, 274–275
Time-intensive marketing methods, 192–193
Timeliness, 140
Tin Men, 255
Title tags, 169
To-dos, in annual plans, 215–216
Top competitors, 76–77
Tracking Results for Month/Year Form, 206
Tracking studies, 52
Tracking systems, 206

Trade associations, 143
Trade shows, 80–82
Traffic data, 199
Transaction confirmations, 163
Travel, 2
Tremendous whack theory, 140
Trump, Donald, 54–55
Twitter, 184–186

U

Ultimate benefits, 119–120
Unconditional guarantees, 66, 270–271
Unconscious competence in marketing, 253
Unconscious incompetence in marketing, 252
Underserved market segments, 38–40
Unique selling propositions (USPs)
    basic requirements for, 18–19, 91–93
    offering proof, 97–101
    strengthening, 91–97
    tips for writing, 19–21
Unique visits, 203
Upselling, 263–264
Urgency of prospective customers, 46
Used cars, 234
Username selection, 184

V

Value, adding, 126–128, 141
Values, 2–4, 13–14
Vendor invoices, 227
Videos at trade shows, 82
Vigoda, Abe, 41–42
Vision
    creating business to fulfill, 27–28
    daily renewal from, 272
    need for, 1, 14, 21
    pursuing, 11–12
    starting with, 12–13
Vision board exercise, 17–18
Vision statements, 13–18
Visitor primary purpose, 198
Visual Sciences, 198

W

Watson, Thomas, 12–13

Weaknesses, turning into selling points, 121–123
Web analytics, 197–204
Web beacons, 200–202
Webcasts, 183
Web logs, 200
Web server performance data, 199–200
Websites
    capturing e-mail addresses on, 177–180
    of competitors, examining, 154–155, 168
    improving Google rankings, 164
    keyword due diligence, 153–155
    optimizing, 154, 167–170
    performance metrics, 197–204
    Recommended Vendors lists, 171–172
Web traffic data, 199
Web transactional data, 199
Weka Publishing, 246
Westinghouse, 126–127, 155
White papers, 152
Whitney, Russ, 9
Wonder Bread, 95
Wording of guarantees, 66
Wording of offers, 232–233
Wordtracker.com, 168
Write What and How You'll Measure exercise, 207
Write Your Description of the Competition exercise, 84
Write Your Goals exercise, 108
Write Your Plan exercise, 223
Write Your Vision Statement exercise, 15–18
Writing goals, 102. *See also* Copywriting

Y

Yahoo! Groups, 37–38
Yellow Pages advertising, 106–108
Young, James Webb, 121–122
Young, Valerie, 4, 6–8
YouTube, 183

Z

Ziglar, Zig, 51
Zinsser, William, 234